CW01333277

Doctor Who

The Cultural History of Television

Breaking Bad: *A Cultural History*, by Lara Stache
Cheers: *A Cultural History*, by Joseph J. Darowski and Kate Darowski
Doctor Who: *A Cultural History*, by Graham Gibson
Fierce Females on Television: A Cultural History, by Nicole Evelina
Frasier: *A Cultural History*, by Joseph J. Darowski and Kate Darowski
Friends: *A Cultural History*, by Jennifer C. Dunn
Gilmore Girls: *A Cultural History*, by Lara Stache and Rachel Davidson
The Golden Girls: *A Cultural History*, by Bernadette Giacomazzo
In Living Color: *A Cultural History*, by Bernadette Giacomazzo
Law & Order: *A Cultural History*, by Bernadette Giacomazzo
Mad Men: *A Cultural History*, by M. Keith Booker and Bob Batchelor
Mystery Science Theater 3000: *A Cultural History*, by Matt Foy and Christopher J. Olson
Northern Exposure: *A Cultural History*, by Michael Samuel
Seinfeld: *A Cultural History*, by Paul Arras
Sex and the City: *A Cultural History*, by Nicole Evelina
The Simpsons: *A Cultural History*, by Moritz Fink
Star Trek: *A Cultural History*, by M. Keith Booker
The Wire: *A Cultural History*, by Ben Lamb

Doctor Who

A Cultural History

Graham Gibson

To Lynne,

From one Doctor Who fan to another,

Graham

ROWMAN & LITTLEFIELD
Lanham • Boulder • New York • London

Rowman & Littlefield
Bloomsbury Publishing Inc, 1385 Broadway, New York, NY 10018, USA
Bloomsbury Publishing Plc, 50 Bedford Square, London, WC1B 3DP, UK
Bloomsbury Publishing Ireland, 29 Earlsfort Terrace, Dublin 2, D02 AY28, Ireland
www.rowman.com

Copyright © 2025 by Graham Gibson

All rights reserved. No part of this publication may be: i) reproduced or transmitted in any form, electronic or mechanical, including photocopying, recording or by means of any information storage or retrieval system without prior permission in writing from the publishers; or ii) used or reproduced in any way for the training, development or operation of artificial intelligence (AI) technologies, including generative AI technologies. The rights holders expressly reserve this publication from the text and data mining exception as per Article 4(3) of the Digital Single Market Directive (EU) 2019/790.

British Library Cataloguing in Publication Information Available

Library of Congress Cataloging-in-Publication Data Available

ISBN 9781538192405 (cloth)
ISBN 9781538192412 (epub)

For product safety related questions contact productsafety@bloomsbury.com

∞™ The paper used in this publication meets the minimum requirements of American National Standard for Information Sciences—Permanence of Paper for Printed Library Materials, ANSI/NISO Z39.48-1992.

Dedication

I would like to dedicate this book to my wife, Caroline, and my son, Xander, who represent Doctor Who *fans of different generations, aptly demonstrating the show's enduring appeal.*

Contents

Introduction ix

PART I: ORIGINS AND HISTORY

1. Origins and History 3
2. The Doctor 15
3. The Tardis 31
4. Controversy and Censorship 41
5. The End? 51
6. A Return 59

PART II: CHARACTERS AND SPECIES

7. The Time Lords 69
8. Companions 81
9. Recurring Characters 97
10. A Bestiary of Nemeses 109
11. The Master 121
12. His Own Worst Enemy 137

PART III: CULTURAL IMPACT AND INFLUENCE

13	Gender Identity and Awareness	145
14	Changes in Pronouns and Ethnicity	153
15	Impact on Popular Media	165
16	Spin-Offs	173
17	The Eternal Optimist	181
18	From Then, to Now, and Beyond	189

Appendix: Essential Episodes	199
Bibliography	201
Notes	205
Index	215
About the Author	221

Introduction

Nineteen sixty-three was an eventful year. British politics had been rocked by the Profumo Scandal, in which John Profumo, secretary of state for war in Harold Macmillan's conservative government, had become involved in an extramarital relationship with nineteen-year-old model and showgirl, Christine Keeler. What really set the cat among the pigeons was national security concerns. The man who had introduced Keeler to Profumo, Stephen Ward, was of interest to MI5, being a friend of Yevgeny Ivanov, the Soviet naval attaché and a man suspected of being engaged in espionage. Keeler subsequently claimed that she had also had a sexual relationship with Ivanov. Despite Profumo initially claiming that there had been no impropriety, he eventually confessed and resigned from his position.

Britain was being rocked once more, but in a very different way, as Beatlemania took hold, with the Beatles recording their debut album *Please Please Me* in the Abbey Road Studios. The band stormed the charts with hits such as "She Loves You" and "I Want to Hold Your Hand," turning them into a national sensation.

It was also the year that an audacious feat of larceny was carried out in what has become known in the United Kingdom as the Great Train Robbery, during which £2.61 million was stolen from a train heading from Glasgow to London after signal lights were tampered with, bringing it to a halt. Although no firearms were used in the heist, the train driver, Jack Mills, was beaten with a metal bar, resulting in serious head injuries.

Across the Atlantic, on November 22, John F. Kennedy, president of the United States, was assassinated as his motorcade traveled through Dealey Plaza in Dallas, Texas. The shooter, Lee Harvey Oswald, opened fire from a window in the nearby Texas School Book Depository. Kennedy was rushed to the Parkland Memorial Hospital and was pronounced dead. It was an act of violence that sent shock waves around the world.

In Britain, the very next night, a brand-new science-fiction show was shown by the British Broadcasting Corporation (BBC), starting slightly later than scheduled because of announcements regarding the events of the previous day. There is an apocryphal belief that the first episode was delayed by ten minutes because of this, but in reality, it was only delayed by eighty seconds and was repeated the following week for those who missed it.

The titles began, spilling shifting patterns of light across the screen, accompanied by low, rhythmic, thrumming, electronic music. A higher-pitched melody starts to play, rising to a crescendo as the words DOCTOR WHO appear. The titles fade out, but the music lingers a little while longer as a British policeman (colloquially known as a bobby) moves along a foggy street in London, sweeping a flashlight beam around him. He approaches a set of large wooden gates and checks to see that they are secured properly before moving on, revealing the writing on them . . .

I.M. FOREMAN
Scrap Merchants
76 Totter's Lane

. . . and so begins a television program that has left an indelible mark on popular culture ever since. While its origins may have been small, it has since achieved a Guinness World Record for the largest-ever simulcast of a television drama to ninety-four countries across six continents with the fiftieth-anniversary special shown in 2013. It also holds the title of the longest-running science-fiction television series in the world.

I am proud to say that although the show has its humble origins in the United Kingdom, it has grown to achieve cult status in many other countries, particularly America, which hosts the world's largest and longest-running *Doctor Who* fan convention called Gallifrey One, a nonprofit event founded in 1989 and run annually since 1990 (except for 2021, when the world was in the grip of the COVID-19 pandemic). It stands as a testament to the enduring nature of the show, bringing together Whovians (the adopted term for this particular branch of fandom) from all walks of life who share a common bond—their love of *Doctor Who*.

I was born six years after *Doctor Who* started, missing out entirely on the William Hartnell years, and literally being a baby during the latter part of the Patrick Troughton years, but some of my earliest memories are of a tall, white-haired man (Jon Pertwee) and a blue police box. I had learned to read before I even went to school, and I had a voracious appetite for stories, especially science-fiction. During my school years I read Arthur C. Clarke,

Isaac Asimov, and Ray Bradbury (*Fahrenheit 451* remains one of my all-time favorites, and as is as much a powerful cautionary tale today as it ever was), and while my interest—no, make that "obsession"—with science-fiction continued, and there were all manner of books, films, and television series vying for my attention, *Doctor Who* was always first and foremost.

I was not the only one. Influential science-fiction writer Harlan Ellison (1934–2018) once wrote in his foreword to the Pinnacle Books rerelease of the 1979 Terrance Dicks novelization *Doctor Who and the Revenge of the Cybermen*, "I envy you your first exposure to this amazing conceit. And I wish you the same delight I felt when Michael Moorcock, the finest fantasist in the English-speaking world, sat me down in front of his set in London, turned on the telly, and said, 'Now be quiet and just watch.'"

Furthermore, in his foreword to the Pinnacle Books rerelease of the 1977 Terrance Dicks novelization, *Doctor Who and the Talons of Weng-Chiang*, he recalled giving a talk at an American science-fiction convention, where he told the attendees, "the greatest science-fiction series of all time is *Doctor Who*! And I'll take you all on, one-by-one or all in a bunch to back it up!"

There has long been a perception that science-fiction and fantasy are looked down on as a legitimate genre. Even among science-fiction writers, there are accusations that those who write "hard" science-fiction are more elitist than those who do not. Writer Ursula K. Le Guin (1929–2018) said in an interview for *The Paris Review* in 2013, "The 'hard' science-fiction writers dismiss everything except, well, physics, astronomy, and maybe chemistry. Biology, sociology, anthropology—that's not science to them, that's soft stuff. They're not that interested in what human beings do, really. But I am. I draw on the social sciences a great deal. I get lots of ideas from them, particularly from anthropology. When I create another planet, another world, with a society on it, I try to hint at the complexity of the society I'm creating, instead of just referring to an empire or something like that."

In the same interview, when she is asked about her engagement with human complexity and psychology in her books, she says, "It's helped to make my stuff more accessible to people who don't, as they say, read science-fiction. But the prejudice against genre has been so strong until recently. It's all changing now, which is wonderful. For most of my career, getting that label—sci-fi—slapped on you was, critically, a kiss of death. It meant you got reviewed in a little box with some cute title about Martians—or tentacles."

These days science-fiction and fantasy have well and truly entered the mainstream. We need only look at the stunning cinematic adaptations of the 1965 novel *Dune* by Frank Herbert (1920–1986), brought to life by French Canadian filmmaker Denis Villeneuve (born 1967), as well as the *Lord of the Rings* Trilogy (*The Fellowship of the Ring*, 1954; *The Two Towers*, 1954; and *The Return of the King*, 1955) by J. R. R. Tolkien (1892–1973), brought to life by Peter Jackson (born 1961), to know that there is a distinct appetite for such genres.

Tales of the Doctor and his exploits have spanned a wide range of media, including books (written and audio) and video games. The people behind these may be licensed to use the intellectual property of the franchise, but there is much dispute over the canonicity of a lot of this material because they often contradict—to a greater or lesser extent—events that occur in the television series. There has never been an official stance made on what is and is not canon, such as what Disney did when they bought the rights to *Star Wars* (distinguishing stories that are regarded as non-canon under the Expanded Universe label). Many fans love and embrace such media, but for this book, I will generally be focusing on what is considered to be the only true canonical source in the "Whoniverse"—the television show itself (although to be fair, even that has contradicted itself over the years).

Doctor Who recently celebrated its sixtieth anniversary, and whether you are new to the franchise or this is the earliest days of you dipping your toe in, I heartily welcome you and hope that it will leave as profound an impression on you as it did me.

***

Author's Note: *Doctor Who* has changed in many ways over the years, and one of the biggest changes in the modern era is that it has been established that the Doctor can regenerate into a female body. Since the majority of the Doctor's regenerations—including the most recent one—have been male, when using generalizations about the character, I will use he/him pronouns, unless it is appropriate to do otherwise. I wish to assure readers that there is no intention whatsoever to marginalize anybody's gender. All views expressed in this book, unless stated otherwise, are my own.

PART I

ORIGINS AND HISTORY

Chapter 1

Origins and History

Figure 1 The First Doctor. BBC / Photofest © BBC

From a cultural perspective, *Doctor Who* may be an exceedingly British show, but it took a Canadian to bring it to our screens. Sydney Cecil Newman (1917–1997), an Ontario-born film and television producer, moved from Canada to the United Kingdom in 1958 to be a producer on *Armchair Theatre* for Associated British Corporation (ABC). Due to internal restructuring, it was not long before he found himself their new head of drama.

In 1960 he created a show called *Police Surgeon*, starring Ian Hendry (1931–1984) but this failed to gain traction with audiences and was canceled after only thirteen episodes. Looking for a new vehicle for Hendry, Newman devised *The Avengers*, a gritty spy drama that premiered in 1961. Hendry played the lead role of Doctor David Keel, a man whose life is changed when his fiancée is murdered, and he is drawn into a shady world of crime and espionage through his association with John Steed, played by Patrick Macnee (1922–2015), a hard-boiled, trenchcoat-wearing secret agent.

As *The Avengers* progressed, Steed was elevated to lead character. The show veered away from Newman's original darker vision, becoming more lighthearted in nature. Steed also saw a sartorial change—Savile Row suits, bowler hats, and a tricked-out umbrella—which, along with his newfound quirky sense of humor, helped propel him into being one of the most iconic super-suave superspies of the 1960s.

Newman's high-profile successes at ABC had not gone unnoticed by the BBC, which was keen to give their own drama department a boost to stave off competition. In 1961, Kenneth Adam (1908–1978), director of television at the BBC, offered Newman the position of BBC head of drama, which he eagerly accepted.

BBC controller Donald Baverstock (1924–1995) requested Newman develop a show for a fifty-two-week run to fill an early Saturday-evening slot between the popular sports coverage show *Grandstand* and music panel show *Juke Box Jury*, when there was a notable dip in ratings. Being a big fan of science-fiction, Newman posited that an educational science-fiction drama aimed at that slot would have family viewing appeal.

Head of serials Donald Wilson (1910–2002) had commissioned a feasibility report in early 1962, written by drama script editors Alice Frick and Donald Bull, looking into the BBC producing science-fiction television shows. A follow-up report was commissioned in mid-1962, written by Alice Frick and John Braybon. Between them, the reports concluded that the best way forward would be for the BBC to create its own original material rather than just adapting existing literary works of science-fiction. The reports highlighted four specific points that should be adhered to regarding such original material.

1. They do not include Bug-Eyed Monsters.
2. The central characters are never Tin Robots (since the audience must always subconsciously say "My goodness, there's a man in there and isn't he playing the part well").
3. They do not require large and elaborate science-fiction type settings since, in our considered opinion, the presentation of the interior of a space-ship, or the surface of another planet, gives rise to exactly the same psychological blockage as the above-mentioned robots and B.E.Ms (in our opinion, this has already resulted in a failure of the current ITV series, which has included The Yellow Pill, Dumb Martian and Little Lost Robot).
4. They do provide an opportunity for genuine characterisation and in most cases, they ask the audience to suspend belief scientifically and technologically on one fact only, after which all developments follow a logical pattern.[1]

They also concluded that two types of science-fiction plots were "reasonably outstanding," those dealing with telepaths and those dealing with time travel.

Frick and Braybon's report not only correctly identified elements of science-fiction that had become well-worn tropes, and which should quite rightly be avoided, but highlighted areas that were worthy of further exploration. Undoubtedly, this report was a critical foundation stone upon which *Doctor Who* would be built.

Wilson, along with scriptwriter Cecil Edwin "Bunny" Webber (1909–1969), and script editors Alice Frick and John Braybon, had a brainstorming meeting on March 26, 1963, to discuss what such a science-fiction show should include. Wilson championed the inclusion of a time machine, while Frick thought that a flying saucer would be more appropriate and certainly in the public consciousness, with there being a great body of literature surrounding them. Braybon suggested that the series be set in the future and revolve around a world body of scientific troubleshooters (an idea that never made it into *Doctor Who*, but which was close in concept to what Gerry Davis and Dr. Kit Pedlar created in 1970 with *Doomwatch*). Webber had the notion that great scientific minds from the past could continue in some way and be contacted to discover if there had been any further advances that they had made that could contribute to current discoveries.

Webber was tasked with creating characters that would populate the science-fiction series, and he outlined the following:

- THE HANDSOME YOUNG MAN (First character)
- THE HANDSOME WELL-DRESSED HEROINE AGED ABOUT 30 (Second character)
- THE MATURE MAN, 35–40, WITH SOME "CHARACTER" TWIST (Third character)

Webber was dismissive of there being any children involved in the series, noting "Child characters do not command the interest of children older than themselves." Working with the concept of the scientific troubleshooters, he recommended that "Each of them is a specialist in certain fields, so that each can bring a different approach to any problem. But they are all acutely conscious of the social and human implications of any case, and if the two men sometimes become pure scientist and forget, the woman always reminds them that, finally, they are dealing with human beings."[2]

Newman reviewed the group's findings and approved of incorporating a machine that could travel in space and time, but he did not like the scientific troubleshooter premise, arguing that he wanted the show to be partly educational and that the audience would struggle to learn anything from a group of scientists who already knew so much. As to Webber's notion of not including any child characters, Newman scrawled on the report, "need a kid to get into trouble and make mistakes" and suggested the inclusion of a teenage girl to fill that role.

Newman very much had his finger on the pulse of what audiences wanted, quickly ascertaining that they would derive little from a group of know-it-all experts, and understanding that the inclusion of a youth character, prone to being rash and making errors, would be a vital point of engagement for younger viewers.

Newman conceived of the mysterious central character, the Doctor, who was hundreds of years old and traveled in space and time in a machine that was larger on the inside, introducing two of the core fundamentals. Wilson began work on scheduling the as-yet-unnamed series, and outlined budgets of £2,300 per episode, with a further £500 to create the space-time machine.

The bare-bones character outlines that Webber had originally conceived of were expanded upon.

> BRIDGET (BIDDY). A with-it girl of fifteen, reaching the end of her Secondary School career, eager for life, lower-than-middle class. Avoid dialect, use neutral accent laced with latest teenage slang.

> MISS MCGOVERN (LOLA) 24. Mistress at Biddy's school. Timid but capable of sudden rabbit courage. Modest, with plenty of normal desires. Although she tends to be the one who gets into trouble, she is not to be guyed: she also is a loyalty character.

CLIFF 27 or 28. Master at the same school. Might be classed as ancient by teenagers except that he is physically perfect, strong, and courageous, a gorgeous dish. Oddly, when brains are required, he can even be brainy, in a diffident sort of way.

Webber's characters of Biddy, Lola, and Cliff evolved into Susan Foreman, Barbara Wright, and Ian Chesterton. Susan's character developed even further when James Anthony Coburn (1927–1977), the writer who worked on what would become the premier story of "An Unearthly Child," suggested that Suzanne (as he called her) was not from Earth but was from the same place that the Doctor originated from and that she was of "royal blood." It was felt that it might be seen as inappropriate for an older man to be traveling with a much younger girl, so the plotline about being of royal blood was dropped, and she became the Doctor's granddaughter instead.

His outline for the main character of "Dr. Who" is, perhaps, the most interesting of all. He wrote, "A frail old man lost in space and time. They give him this name because they don't know who he is. He seems not to remember where he has come from; he is suspicious and capable of sudden malignance; he seems to have some undefined enemy; he is searching for something as well as fleeing from something. He has a 'machine' that enables them to travel together through time, through space, and through matter."[3]

Webber added what he called his *Secret of Dr. Who*. He wrote, "In his own day, somewhere in our future, he decided to search for a time or for a society or for a physical condition which is ideal; and having found it, to stay there. He stole the machine and set forth on his quest. He is thus an extension of the scientist who has opted out, but he has opted farther than ours can do, at the moment. And having opted out, he is disintegrating. One symptom of this is his hatred of scientists, inventors, improvers. He can get into a rare paddy when faced with a cave man trying to invent a wheel. He malignantly tries to stop progress (the future) wherever he finds it, while searching for his ideal (the past). This seems to me to involve slap up-to-date moral problems, and old ones too."[4]

It is obvious that Webber's interpretation of the Doctor's background misses the mark. While he has attempted to provide motivation for the character's behavior, he has done so at the expense of eliciting sympathy from viewers. Surely nobody would condone the Doctor meddling to prevent scientific and technological progress in the selfish pursuit of a utopian society. With such an impetus, there would be little redemptive opportunity for the character.

Newman's response to this "secret background" for the Doctor was, "Don't like this at all. Dr. Who will become a kind of father figure. I don't want him to become a reactionary."[5]

Webber also created a *Second Secret of Dr. Who*, in which he wrote, "The authorities of his own (or some other future) time are not concerned merely with the theft of an obsolete machine; they are seriously concerned to prevent his monkeying with time, because his secret intention, when he finds his ideal past, is to destroy or nullify the future."

Newman's response to this second secret was a rather direct, "nuts!"[6] but it is not that far off what would become the Time Lords seeking to reprimand the Doctor, not because of the theft of the time capsule, but because of his continual interference in other species and cultures.

Taking Newman's advice on board, Webber worked on an updated character outline for Dr. Who, writing "A name given to him by his three earthly friends because neither he nor they know who he is. Dr. Who is about 650 years old. Frail looking but wirey [sic] and tough like an old turkey—is amply demorstrated [sic] whenever he is forced to run from danger. His watery blue eyes are continually looking around in bewilderment and occasionally a look of utter malevolence clouds his face as he suspects his earthly friends of being part of some conspiracy. He seems not to remember where he comes from but he has flashes of garbled memory which indicate that he was involved in a galactic war and still fears pursuit by some undefined enemy. Because he is somewhat pathetic his three friends continually try to help him find his way 'home,' but they are never sure of his motives."

Here, Webber depicts the Doctor as far more vulnerable than in his initial outline, being prone to bouts of confusion and paranoia. Having only snatches of memory from his past to rely on, and a sense of lingering threat, he is understandably reluctant to be open and trusting. As a result, audiences are far more likely to be sensitive toward his plight.

Webber had plenty of story ideas as well, writing, "Was it by means of Dr. Who's machine that Aladin's [sic] palace sailed through the air? Was Merlin Dr. Who? Was Cinderella's Godmother Dr. Who's wife chasing him through time? Jacob Marley was Dr. Who, slightly tipsy, but what other tricks did he get up to that Yuletide?" While his early scripts for the show were never actually used, some of the elements in them found their way into other stories, and the treatment documents that he drew up were used as guidelines thereafter.

John Reith (1889–1971), first director-general of the BBC, had summarized the purpose of the BBC, declaring that it was to inform, educate, and entertain, three principles that Newman's vision of *Doctor Who* was eminently tailored toward. He recruited Verity Lambert (1935–2007), whom he had previously worked with. In an article in *Doctor Who Magazine*,[7] he recounts, "I remembered Verity as being bright and, to use the phrase, full of piss and vinegar. She was gutsy and she used to fight and argue with me, even though she was not at a very high level as a production assistant." When

Verity arrived, she was assigned a more experienced associate producer, Mervyn Pinfield (1912–1966), to assist her.

One of the most important decisions that Lambert made was casting William Hartnell to play the lead role, a choice that clearly worked, but which was not without its troubles. Throughout his term on the show, Hartnell increasingly suffered from declining health and mental acuity, a result of undiagnosed arteriosclerosis. This affected his ability to learn his lines properly and to repeatedly misdeliver them even when he did. His Doctor was always supposed to be cantankerous, but this was given an unintentionally added layer due to Hartnell's own frustrations with himself concerning his lines. Lambert clashed with Hartnell over what she perceived to be his unwillingness to learn his lines, and though he was angry at the time, he was also contrite and sent her flowers by way of apology.

Newman insisted on sticking to the advice of there being no "bug-eyed monsters" on *Doctor Who*, so when the first script featuring the Daleks by Terry Nation (1930–1997) appeared, there was a clash of opinions. Script editor David Whitaker (1928–1980) and Lambert were genuinely impressed by it, but Wilson disagreed, telling her not to use it, and if she did, it would be the end of *Doctor Who*. Since they had no alternative scripts that could be used, and with the clock ticking on production, they had no choice but to run with it. When it aired to tremendous reception from the public and critics alike, Wilson conceded that Lambert obviously knew the show better than he did. Newman was livid, thinking that Lambert had defied him, but she talked him down with the reasoning behind her decision, and he latterly admitted that it was the Daleks that made *Doctor Who*.

At twenty-eight, Lambert was the youngest producer at the BBC, and the only woman in the drama department. She may have won over most of her colleagues with her determination and aptitude, but the British press was not as considerate, frequently prioritizing her attractive looks and young age over her achievements in their coverage. There were scandalous rumors spread concerning her relationship with Newman, suggesting that her appointment was the result of an affair with him rather than her being hired on the merits of her competency, something Lambert vehemently denied throughout her life. Then, the BBC was a very straitlaced, very male-oriented organization in the early 1960s, and there would have been a lot of ruffled feathers when Lambert was given such an opportunity by Newman.

Over the years, Lambert put to bed a few misconceptions that sprang up about *Doctor Who*. The show has had its detractors, many of whom reject its importance, dismissing it as nothing more than children's television. In a *Daily Mail* newspaper interview, Lambert stated, "I have strong views on the level of intelligence we should be aiming at. *Doctor Who* goes out at a time when there is a large child audience, but it is intended more as a story for the whole family." She added, "Children today are very sophisticated, and I don't allow scripts which seem to talk down to them."[8] She reaffirmed her position in an interview on BBC's *Nationwide* current affairs program in 1983, coinciding with the show's twentieth anniversary, stating, "It was a series that was designed to appeal to eight- to fourteen-year-olds, which of course it didn't, it appealed to everyone."

Waris Hussein (born in India in 1938 as Waris Habibullah) was another vital person in the group who brought *Doctor Who* to the screen. Along with Lambert, he was responsible for the choice of Hartnell to play the first Doctor, feeling that he had the qualities necessary for the role. Hussein was the first Asian BBC drama director, and the youngest at twenty-four, so he faced his own round of prejudices and gossip at the BBC, and as he wrote in a *MailOnline* article, "Nobody expected a woman, an Indian and a Canadian to succeed."[9]

Being the director of the very first *Doctor Who* story, "An Unearthly Child," Hussein was not overly impressed with the script by Anthony Coburn. In the same *MailOnline* article, he said, "At Cambridge, I had directed contemporaries such as Ian McKellan and Derek Jacobi, and when I saw the *Doctor Who* scripts with cave dwellers talking in grunts, I thought my career had taken a wrong turning." Nevertheless, Hussein quickly embraced the opportunity, realizing that things could be done on this show that he would not have the chance to do elsewhere in the drama department.

Because *Doctor Who* was an unknown quantity, and not many at the BBC had faith in it, the crew were assigned Studio D in Lime Grove Studios to film in. Lambert hated the space as it was cramped and antiquated, having been built in 1915 by Gaumont Films before being purchased by the BBC in 1949, and Hussein joked that the cameras stationed there were bigger than the Daleks. If it got too hot in the studio, as it did in the summer months, the fire suppression sprinklers would activate, drenching the set and the actors on it. It was only ever intended to be used until the building of the new BBC Television Centre was completed, but even after it officially opened in June 1960, Lime Grove Studios continued to be used. The site was finally closed down in 1991 and subsequently demolished in 1993.

Having filmed a pilot on Friday, September 27, 1963, it was viewed by Newman, who thought it was terrible and told Lambert and Hussein that by all rights he should fire them both, but he believed in them and gave them a second chance. In multiple interviews over the years, Hussein has talked about how nervous all the cast and crew were, resulting in stilted performances (all except for Carole Ann Ford, whom Newman told to tone her performance down and to not be quite so "weird").

The title of the series, *Doctor Who*, has been attributed to Rex Tucker (1913–1996), the show's caretaker producer until Lambert was brought on board, but he, in turn, said it came from Newman himself. Wilson subsequently claimed that he was responsible for the name, something that has never been disputed, not even by Newman himself.

Lambert had been listening to Les Structures Sonores, a French group who played music on glass tubes, producing an "otherworldly" sound. She contacted them to see if they might be interested in working on the title score for the show, but they were simply too busy. She then approached Desmond Briscoe (1925–2006), head of the BBC Radiophonic Workshop, to see what in-house options were available. The Radiophonic Workshop was founded in 1958 to provide audio material for radio and television using electronic and electroacoustic techniques. She was referred to Ronald "Ron" Grainer (1922–1981), a Queensland-born composer who spent most of his professional career working in the United Kingdom, and he thought it was an exciting opportunity to compose a score that would have an electronic arrangement for the show. Grainer would go on to compose some of the most memorable scores among British television shows, including *Steptoe and Son*, *The Prisoner*, and *Tales of the Unexpected.*

Once Grainer had finished his score, he then passed it on to Delia Derbyshire (1937–2001) so that she could work on its electronic realization. It would become one of the very first television themes to be created and produced entirely electronically and Grainer was amazed at what she, assisted by Dick Mills (1936–), had created. Her arrangement, albeit slightly modified over time, remained as the core *Doctor Who* theme for seventeen years, right up until 1980, when it received a brand-new arrangement by Peter Howell (born 1949), to accompany a new title sequence as part of John Nathan-Turner's complete revamp of the series when he became producer.

Grainer attempted to get Derbyshire credited as cocomposer, but the BBC wanted members of the Radiophonic Workshop to remain anonymous, and she remained uncredited for her work on-screen until the fiftieth-anniversary special.

Hussein also contacted the Radiophonic Workshop to discuss the sound effects that he needed for the show, particularly the materialization and dematerialization sounds of the Tardis (the space-time machine the Doctor and his companions traveled in) and so he met with Brian Hodgson (born 1938), a composer and sound technician. Hodgson spent time contemplating what sound the Tardis might make, and when thinking about the phrase 'the ripping or the tearing of the fabric of time and space," he decided he wanted a sound effect to reflect that. There was a piano in the Radiophonic Workshop that had most of its chassis removed, leaving the inner frame with the piano strings exposed. He took his mother's front door key and scraped it up and down one of the piano strings, giving him the base "ripping" sound he was looking for. He then altered the speed and played the sound back through feedback machines to produce a rippling, echoing effect, manipulating it so that it sounded like the effect was both heading toward and moving away from the listener. Lastly, as they had just recently acquired a white noise generator, he fed some white noise into the overall effect and the unforgettable sound of the Tardis was born.

Bernard Lodge (born 1933), a graphic designer, was approached to work on the title graphics and he used the "howlaround" effect—a process whereby a video camera is pointed directly at its own playback monitor, creating a video feedback effect—thus creating the background for the surreal title sequence. Lodge had informed Lambert that as well as overlaying the title words "DOCTOR WHO," which he felt should be in a plain typeface so as not to overcomplicate the sequence, he could also overlay Hartnell's face for dramatic effect. This was demonstrated by creating test footage where the head and shoulders of Jim Stephens, a vision mixer, was overlayed on the title sequence, but Lambert thought it was far too scary. As a consequence, Hartnell's face never appeared in the title sequence, and it was not until 1967 that the face of his successor, Patrick Troughton, first appeared as part of the title sequence, something that became a regular feature throughout the remainder of the classic series.

Three main sets were designed by Peter Brachacki (1926–1980) for use in this story. The first was the scrapyard at 76 Totter's Lane where the Tardis is located, the second was Susan's classroom and another corridor at Coal Hill School, and the third, and most important of all, was the Tardis interior, which was so large it took up almost half the space of Studio D.

The first episode of "An Unearthly Child" was reshot on Friday, October 18, 1963, integrating all the changes that Newman had requested, but that was not the last hurdle. Baverstock was yet to commit to the longevity of the series, and since there was already budgetary overspending, he concluded, "Such a costly serial is not one that I can afford for this space in the financial year. You should not therefore proceed any further with the production of more than 4 episodes."

Lambert was called into a meeting with Joanna Spicer (1906–1992). As the assistant controller of planning, she had initially backed the idea of a science-fiction series for early Saturday evenings, but budgetary concerns had now given her pause. Lambert found her "terrifying," but she persuaded Spicer that if the show was allowed to run its course, then they would make budgetary adjustments along the way to compensate for the initial overspend and still meet targets in the long run. A new budgetary agreement was drawn up, and this, in turn, persuaded Baverstock to extend *Doctor Who* to thirteen episodes.

On November 22, 1963, Baverstock committed to a further thirteen episodes, taking the total to twenty-six, and promised to decide on a further thirteen episodes in the new year. As *Doctor Who* was going from strength to strength, it would be another twenty-six years before the show was threatened with being pulled off the air.

Chapter 2

The Doctor

Figure 2 The Second, Third, and First Doctors. BBC / Photofest © BBC

Who *is* the Doctor? The very title of the show, *Doctor Who*, is a question, one that has been on the lips of viewers since the show began. So integral is it to the mythos of the series that it became part of the lore, being referred to as "the first question, the oldest question in the universe, hidden in plain sight" (2023 episode "The Time of the Doctor").

We know that the Doctor is a Time Lord, from Gallifrey (although, in the latter series, even the veracity of this is brought into doubt, but more on that later). We know that he travels in time and space in his Tardis. We know that when he is close to death, every cell in his body regenerates, giving him a new appearance and a new personality to go with it. Most importantly, we know that he helps people, the defenseless and the disenfranchised, because if there is one thing the Doctor truly hates, it is the abuse of power. So, while we have come to know certain things about the Doctor over the years, the inescapable truth is that, overall, there remain more things unknown than known.

We are not even certain about his age. We know that he is at least nine hundred years old, although in the 2013 fiftieth-anniversary special, when asked about his age, the Eleventh Doctor says, "I don't know, I lose track. Twelve hundred and something, I think, unless I'm lying. I can't remember if I'm lying about my age, that's how old I am."

To familiarize ourselves with the Doctor, as best we can, we must look at each of his, or her, regenerations. In doing so, we can examine the Doctor's individual personalities and idiosyncrasies, seeing what makes them distinctive, but all the while remaining part of the whole.

THE FIRST DOCTOR

William Hartnell, 1963–1966

Appearance: An older man with long white hair. He wears Edwardian attire, a black frock coat, light-colored waistcoat, wing-collar shirt, dark ribbon tie, checked trousers, an opera cloak, and an astrakhan wool hat. He carries a monocle attached to a length of ribbon around his neck and wears a silver ring with a large blue stone on the middle finger of his right hand (this is almost a precursor to the ubiquitous sonic screwdriver used by later Doctors as it has many properties—it is linked to the Tardis, can deflect an overabundance of electrical energy, and is even used in facilitating hypnotism).

Personality: Initially cantankerous, mistrusting, and even deceitful. He thinks little of putting himself and his companions in danger to satisfy his burning curiosity. He is quick to temper and has a very high opinion of himself, sneering at those whose ideas he thinks are inferior. While he may appear frail, he is tough and resolute and harbors a surprising ruthlessness. Over time, especially as he comes to better know and understand the human companions he abducts, he mellows and becomes less mercurial, establishing a genuine fondness toward them.

Actor: William Henry Hartnell (1908–1975) was an English actor who was initially reluctant to take on the role, but he eventually saw it as a welcome change from the gruff, military types that he was often typecast as. He likened his Doctor to a wizard and conceived of him deliberately getting the names of people and things wrong, feigning disinterest. It was his failing health that caused him to abandon the role, one that he had come to embrace with affection.

THE SECOND DOCTOR

Patrick Troughton, 1966–1969

Appearance: A shorter, scruffier man, with black hair in a style close to that of the 1960s Beatlemania "mop top" era. He wears a rumpled, oversized frock coat, shirt, braces, bow tie, and baggy checked trousers. It is a look that has often been described as "cosmic hobo." He sometimes wears a large fur coat, tied around the waist with a length of string, and he briefly wears a battered, stovepipe hat. His features are lined and expressive, switching from a furrowed brow to an impish smile in the blink of an eye.

Personality: Outwardly lighthearted, mischievous, and bumbling, he likes to lure his enemies into underestimating him. He has a remarkable aptitude for scheming, and while he is very protective of his companions, he is not beyond manipulating even them to achieve his goals. He owns a recorder (the musical instrument) which he plays small ditties on, partly for his amusement, but mostly because it helps him think. Most notably, he is the first regeneration to possess and use a sonic screwdriver.

Actor: Patrick George Troughton (1920–1987) was an English actor who thoroughly enjoyed the challenge of playing the Doctor, although he was not nearly as much of a fan of the attention that the role generated. A very private man in his personal life, he believed that for an actor to be effective, people should not associate them too strongly with any particular role. That, and his finding the scheduling increasingly grueling, led to him giving up the part.

THE THIRD DOCTOR

Jon Pertwee, 1970–1974

Appearance: Tall, statuesque, and sporting a head of curly, white hair. His more refined look includes velvet smoking jackets of various colors (black, green, and red), black Inverness capes (lined in either red or purple), ruffle shirts, a bow tie or a cravat, black trousers, and black dress shoes. He frequently wears black leather gloves and has a brief flirtation with a trilby hat, which he wears at a rakish angle.

Personality: Far more action-oriented than his predecessors, he likes to drive a lot while he is exiled on Earth, either in his modified vintage yellow motorcar that he nicknames "Bessie," or in his futuristic hover car (dubbed the "Whomobile"). He is proficient in Venusian aikido, regularly using its techniques to disarm and/or stun adversaries. He will assume that in any given situation he is the smartest person in the room—which is especially annoying because it is usually true. He loves using high-tech jargon.

Actor: Jon Devon Roland Pertwee (1919–1996) was an English actor who had been born into a theatrical family. During World War II he served in the Navy before moving into Naval Intelligence, where he worked alongside James Bond author Ian Fleming. A self-confessed lover of gadgets, he taught commandos how to use things like compasses hidden in brass buttons and smoking pipes that fired bullets. All this clearly influenced his Bond-like interpretation of the Doctor. He left that role to return to theater, although he admits he did not want to become typecast.

THE FOURTH DOCTOR

Tom Baker, 1974–1981

Appearance: A more casual, bohemian sense of style, he is tall, has a shock of brown curly hair, bulging eyes, and an enormous, toothy grin. His wardrobe tends to be a little more diverse than that of his earlier regenerations. He swaps between a short reddish-brown jacket with patches on the elbows and three full-length coats (one dark brown, one light brown, and one light gray). He wears a white shirt (initially with a tie or a cravat but settling on it being open-collared), a checked waistcoat, tweed trousers, and brown shoes or boots. Two of the most memorable items among his apparel are his battered brown fedora and his immensely long multicolored scarf (which he claims was knitted for him by Madame Nostradamus). Toward the end of his tenure, his attire takes on two significant changes. The first is that the browns and grays of yesteryear give way to varying hues of burgundy and maroon, and the second is that, in a staggeringly self-referential move, red question mark motifs appear on either side of his shirt collar. His is, by far, the most iconic outfit of classic-era *Doctor Who*.

Personality: This Doctor can be bombastic in both his physicality and his verbosity, even babbling at captors, which only serves to antagonize them. He likes to rile his enemies, winding them up to the point of making mistakes. He enjoys being the center of attention, relishing the admiration of others, even if he tries to brush it off with faux humility. He can very quickly become dismissive of the opinions of those around him, cutting them off mid-sentence. He never allows himself to get too attached to his companions, so when they eventually part from him, he is likely to mutter a brief goodbye and leave without a single backward glance. He carries a small paper bag of Jelly Babies (sweets) with him, offering one to allies and enemies alike, often to their bewilderment.

Actor: Thomas Stewart Baker (1934–) is an English actor. Raised as a devout Catholic, when he was a teenager, he became a novice brother in a Catholic monastery but left after six years when he realized that he had lost his faith and wanted to break each of the Ten Commandments. Baker secured the role of the Doctor while he was working as a laborer on a building site, a job he undertook while he was looking for acting parts. He wanted his Doctor to appear more alien and aloof. Baker left the role after finding himself disagreeing more and more with new series producer John Nathan-Turner.

THE FIFTH DOCTOR

Peter Davison, 1982–1984

Appearance: Tall and youthful looking with longish blond hair. He wears the attire of an Edwardian cricketer, a cream-colored frock coat with red piping, a white shirt (continuing the red question mark motifs on the collar), a white cricketer's jumper, striped trousers, and white plimsolls. This Doctor favors a cream-colored Optimo-style panama hat with a red band around it, which he rolls up and keeps in his coat pocket when not wearing it. He keeps a stalk of celery affixed to the left lapel of his coat and which he claims would turn purple if he is in the presence of certain gases that he is allergic to (although such an allergy seems to be limited to this regeneration alone). He sometimes wears half-moon spectacles, usually when examining something, and he likes to carry a cricket ball around with him. This is the first outfit the Doctor wears that is consistent throughout his time, so it has much more of a costume feel about it.

Personality: Sensitive and honorable with an air of indecisiveness. This Doctor gets off to a rough start as he is the first to have a troublesome regeneration, leaving him with some confusion, switching back and forth between mannerisms and phrases that his predecessors used. Fearing that his regeneration is going to fail, he seeks a period of respite to help him heal. Once he restores his equilibrium, he becomes one of the more empathic versions of the Doctor, promoting honesty, trying to look on the bright side of things, and giving those he is unsure about the benefit of the doubt.

Actor: Peter Malcolm Gordon Moffett (1951–), known professionally as Peter Davison, is an English actor. Davison found a love of acting and became a household name in Britain in the late 1970s for his role as Tristan Farnon in the BBC adaptation of James Herriot's *All Creatures Great and Small*. At twenty-nine, Davison was the youngest person so far to take on the role of the Doctor, which accounts for the character's vigor. Taking Patrick Troughton's advice on how to avoid being typecast, he left *Doctor Who* after three years. His daughter Georgia Moffett (1984–) is married to David Tennant, who plays both the Tenth and Fourteenth Doctors.

THE SIXTH DOCTOR

Colin Baker, 1984–1986

Appearance: Tall and with a head full of blond curly hair and rounder facial features. He wears a multicolored, multi-patterned, patchwork frock coat in bright, garish colors, but it fails to hit the avant-garde, landing instead somewhere between carnival showman and clown. He dons neckties in red, blue, or green with white polka dots, and a gaudy waistcoat adorned with a mint-green watch chain. His outfit is completed with yellow striped trousers and green leather lace-up boots, partly covered by red spats, and the now standard red question marks that decorate his shirt collar. He also wears a variety of cat brooches on the left lapel of his coat, which he occasionally touches for luck. While the prior outfits had been thematic in terms of era or style, series producer John Nathan-Turner wanted this Doctor to have a tasteless costume to reflect his "alienness."

Personality: Like his predecessor, this Doctor's regeneration is an unstable one, leaving him arrogant and aggressive. While the worst of his belligerent impulses diminish as he adjusts to his new self, his persistent conceitedness and patronizing nature serve to make him one of the least likable Doctors. There was an intention for him to mellow over time, but as Colin Baker was fired from the role, this never came to pass.

Actor: Colin Baker (1943–) is an English actor. Despite studying law and training to become a solicitor, Baker was drawn to acting, joining the London Academy of Music and Dramatic Art. He found fame portraying Paul Merroney in the popular BBC series *The Brothers* in the mid-1970s. He even found a part in another BBC sci-fi classic, Terry Nation's *Blake's 7*, in 1981. Baker admits that he would have liked to play the part for many years, had he not been fired, something that became a condition of BBC1 controller Michael Grade agreeing to commission another series.

THE SEVENTH DOCTOR

Sylvester McCoy, 1987–1989

Appearance: Shorter than previous Doctors, with brown wavy hair, and soulful eyes, he sees a return to a modular-style outfit, with subtle variations on a nonconformist theme. He switches between light and dark baggy jackets, festooned with pockets. Under these is a knitted yellow tank top with green trim and horizontal zigzag lines, featuring a repeating pattern of red question marks. The familiar question mark motifs are still present on his shirt collar, but John Nathan-Turner decided to emphasize this part of his "branding," which many felt was going too far. This was taken even further with the Doctor carrying a black umbrella (colloquially known as a "brolly" in the United Kingdom) that has a bold red question mark incorporated into the design of the handle. Accessories are the order of the day with this Doctor, and he has an intricately pattered handkerchief in reds, golds, and greens, used as a makeshift band around his panama hat, and a silk paisley scarf which embellishes his jacket, neatly tucked under the collar and lapels. The top half is complemented by baggy checked trousers and two-tone brogues in brown and cream.

Personality: Coming across as a whimsical fool, using spoons as a musical instrument, and uttering the odd Dundrearyism (a nonsensical malapropism, which in itself is a quirky adaptation of an aphorism), this is a Doctor that appears curious and thoughtful, but perfectly harmless. His playful exterior masks both the extent of his intelligence and his calculating nature. He projects a subtle but powerful authority, easily pulling people into orbit around him, getting them to tell him things, or do things for him, without really knowing why. This is also a Doctor who holds secrets, frequently giving the impression that any information he divulges is scant in comparison to what he actually knows. He always tries to avoid force, preferring to use his quick wits and talking to confuse, manipulate, and disarm opponents.

Actor: Percy James Patrick Kent-Smith (1943–), known professionally as Sylvester McCoy, is a Scottish actor. His professional moniker is an adaptation of a character he played, Sylvester McCoy, while part of an experimental theater troupe. Having a love of physical comedy, he has portrayed Stan Laurel and Buster Keaton in one-man stage shows. He brought his penchant for physical comedy into the role of the Doctor and continued to play the part until the series was canceled in 1989.

THE EIGHTH DOCTOR

Paul McGann, 1996

Appearance: Having regenerated while in a morgue drawer, and having only a sheet to cover him, this Doctor's preliminary outfit was less about choice and more about convenience, appropriating it from a hospital locker where staff were about to hold a fancy dress party to celebrate the millennium. Thus, his costume had a Wild West gambler feel to it, with the owner intending to dress up like Wild Bill Hickok. The outfit is comprised of a forest green double-breasted frock coat, a silvery-gray double-breasted waistcoat, a silvery-gray cravat, and moss-green trousers. In a later appearance, the Doctor's outfit changes, although it still retains design references to the original. It features a bottle green moleskin coat, a single-breasted brocade waistcoat, a dark blue neckerchief worn under a crumpled white wide-collared shirt, a snake-clasp belt, brown trousers, and boots with leather lace-up gaiters. This Doctor has a longer face with sculpted, noble features, and while he starts with long brown wavy hair with a center parting, in a later appearance, it was cut much shorter.

Personality: This Doctor never got to have the luxury of a properly fleshed-out personality, due to appearing in a one-off attempt to reboot the series in the mid-1990s and having only a minor appearance after this. He starts as a charming and romantic figure, enthusiastic and full of hope, but when we meet him again, toward the end of his eighth regeneration (and with the Time War well and truly underway), he has become war-weary, his ceaseless fight against evil having taken its toll. When fate returns him to the planet Karn, and an encounter with the Sisterhood there, in a heartbreaking scene, he comes to terms with the fact that in a time of war, the universe needs not a doctor, but a warrior, giving rise to the War Doctor (more on that later).

Actor: Paul John McGann (1959–) is an English actor and part of a family of actors. His first foray into the performing arts was when he appeared in a school production of Gilbert and Sullivan's *The Gondoliers*. Still in his teens, he was working in a shoe shop when he was persuaded to apply for a place at the Royal Academy of Dramatic Art. He gained attention for his part in the cult black comedy *Withnail & I* alongside Richard E. Grant (who would go on to play a webcast version of the Doctor). His stint as the Doctor in the failed 1990s reboot may have been brief, but his portrayal is remembered far more fondly than the reboot itself was.

THE NINTH DOCTOR

Christopher Eccleston, 2005

Appearance: This Doctor has a very pared-back look. Gone are the eccentric, flamboyant costumes of Doctors past, replaced with a battered black leather jacket, a dark-colored V-neck jumper, black trousers, and boots. This is a man who has seen war and who has come out the other side, having defeated the most terrible evil, but at great personal cost. He has chiseled features, a pronounced nose, prominent ears, and very short hair.

Personality: This Doctor wears a mask of confidence, but there is a faltering, self-doubting side behind it. His previous self has seen terrible things, *done* terrible things, and this Doctor is all too keen to put that behind him. He is lonely, perhaps the loneliest he has ever been, and not only seeking, but *needing* a companion, someone to remind him of what he has lost, and what he can hopefully have once again. He does not suffer fools gladly and is sometimes a little harsh in his reactions. When confronted by a Dalek, believed to be the last of its kind, he takes a perverse pleasure in tormenting it, and when he tells it to kill itself, it tells him, "You would make a good Dalek," psychologically wounding him.

Actor: Christopher Eccleston (1964–) is an English actor. Growing up as part of a working-class family, he took up acting, inspired by the works of British film Director, Ken Loach, as well as gritty down-to-earth dramas, such as the 1960 film *Saturday Night and Sunday Morning* and the 1982 television series *Boys from the Blackstuff*. Having established himself as a serious actor, it may have been a surprise to some when it was announced that he would play the Doctor in the refresh of the series in 2005. Taking the view that his Doctor was more approachable and egalitarian, he left the show after a single series after taking a dislike to the way that things were being run behind the scenes.

THE TENTH DOCTOR

David Tennant, 2005–2010

Appearance: Tall, thin, with dark brown hair styled in a spiked quiff with narrow sideburns. He has youthful, boyish features. He wears a very long light brown coat and underneath he wears either a brown or blue pinstriped suit over plain shirts of different colors and a variety of ties. As to footwear, he wears a multitude of different Converse sneakers in different styles. He has been known to wear rectangular framed spectacles at times. Overall, his outfit has become one of the most iconic in modern-era *Doctor Who*.

Personality: This Doctor is exuberant, energetic, and regularly has a cheeky grin on his face. He is not averse to running, either toward danger or away from it, and the sight of his easily recognizable coat billowing out behind him is one that is very memorable. Even though he can be lighthearted and filled with hope, he is not without his dark side. When an enemy threatens what he holds most dear, he has been known to act without mercy or remorse.

Actor: David John McDonald (1971–), who legally changed his name to be professionally known as David Tennant, is a Scottish actor. Tennant has said that it was his love for *Doctor Who* growing up that encouraged him to pursue a career in acting. Having taken on many noteworthy roles in classical theater and television drama, he stumbled into the role of the Doctor after having worked with Russell T. Davies in the BBC series *Casanova*. Tennant gave up the role, admitting that he loved the part so much that if he did not move on he would be playing it forever.

THE ELEVENTH DOCTOR

Matt Smith, 2010–2013

Appearance: This Doctor's regeneration has the youngest appearance so far, with a shock of floppy brown hair and a prominent brow and jawline. He initially dresses like an Oxford or Cambridge professor—a brown tweed jacket with elbow patches, a scroll-striped shirt, braces, a bow tie, black jeans with turned-up bottoms, and ankle boots. The styles of tweed jacket, shirt, and bow tie vary slightly over time, but the biggest change comes when he moves to wearing longer coats, particularly his green double-breasted greatcoat and his purple frock coat. The latter of these is worn along with light or dark purple waistcoats, a gold double Albert watch chain, and brown and purple brogue boots. Aside from his quintessential bow ties, one of the other items of wear most associated with this Doctor is a red fez with a black tassel.

Personality: This Doctor has an almost childlike level of curiosity and enthusiasm, but he has the boundless energy to accompany it. He seems to take delight in his eccentricities, but he is also prone to mood swings, going from happy and playful to sullen and frustrated when things do not work out for him. Of all the modern-era Doctors, he needs companionship the most, to remind him of how reckless and dangerous he can be. After all, he is the one who describes himself as, "a madman in a box."

Actor: Matthew Robert Smith (1982–) is an English actor. Initially set on pursuing a football career, he suffered a serious back injury, meaning he was unable to keep playing. Finding a place in acting, he took on several theater roles before gaining prominence in the 2007 BBC political drama

Party Animals, in which he played Danny Foster, a parliamentary researcher. At twenty-six, he is the youngest actor to ever play the Doctor, and while some believed he was too young for the part, his energetic and enthusiastic portrayal swayed opinions.

THE TWELFTH DOCTOR

Peter Capaldi, 2014–2017

Appearance: Tall, thin, with craggy features and prominent bushy eyebrows. He has gray hair, short to start off with but which grows much longer, giving him very much a classic *Doctor Who* look. He starts off wearing a dark blue Crombie coat with red lining, a white spearpoint collar shirt, buttoned up to the top with no tie, a dark blue cardigan, dark blue chinos, and black brogue ankle boots. He is known to switch between a black velvet frock coat with blue lining and a burgundy velvet frock coat with red lining. Over time, his style shifts from being quite formal to having an offbeat punk vibe, wearing several different colored hoodies, jumpers, and T-shirts under his coats, with combinations of these giving a layered flair. His shirts have longer unbuttoned cuffs, extending out from under his coat sleeves, and he starts wearing different types of checked trousers. He sporadically carries—and plays—an electric guitar, and for a while his sonic screwdriver is replaced with sonic sunglasses.

Personality: This Doctor is a complex character, repeatedly coming across as brusque and sarcastic, although his hard edges soften over time. He often suppresses his emotions, knowing that he has to make difficult choices, and the more he appears to care, the harder those choices become. But he *does* care, and he is fully prepared to break all sorts of rules to prove it. The Doctor has always been a renegade, but this regeneration is one of the most rebellious of all. His visage is of someone he met in the past, someone who was in danger and whom the Doctor would have abandoned without the intervention of his companion. He decides that he adopted this face as a reminder to himself that saving people is what he does.

Actor: Peter Dougan Capaldi (1958–) is a Scottish actor. Born into a family of Scottish, Irish, and Italian descent, he too shared a love of *Doctor Who* growing up. He attended the Glasgow School of Art and while a student, he became the lead singer and guitarist in a punk rock band, The Dreamboys, alongside drummer and future comedian Craig Ferguson. He enjoyed a multitude of roles on stage and screen before becoming famous for his portrayal of the infamously foulmouthed spin doctor Malcolm Tucker in the BBC political sitcom, *The Thick of It*. Having achieved his dream role of playing the Doctor, Capaldi eventually left the part, feeling he had brought all that he could to it.

Chapter 2

THE THIRTEENTH DOCTOR

Jodie Whittaker, 2018–2022

Appearance: Most notably, this regeneration is female, the first in the series, with a blonde bob hairstyle and an off-center parting. She wears a long gray hooded coat with rainbow trim at the edges of the lining, a blue T-shirt with a rainbow stripe across it, yellow braces, blue culottes, blue socks with white stripes, and brown boots. It is quite an understated and minimalistic style with the odd splashes of color here and there. She wears an earring and cuff on her left ear, both attached by a chain, the lower detail which features two hands meeting, as in the act of shaking, and the upper detail which is a small cluster of stars. Apart from the odd event-appropriate change of wear (such as a tuxedo top with black culottes), her outfit remains static throughout her run.

Personality: An energetic ball of energy—running, talking rapidly, and habitually fidgeting—she seems to struggle to keep her attention focused on anything for longer than fleeting moments. Her relationship with her companions is on a different level from that of previous Doctors; she calls them her "fam" (a colloquialism for family). She is brave and selfless, willing to throw herself headlong into danger without a second thought. Her Doctor is forced to confront painful revelations about her past but she does not let them break her inimitable upbeat nature.

Actor: Jodie Auckland Whittaker (1982–) is an English actor. Having caught the acting bug, she decided she did not want to go straight to drama school and traveled the world for a year. Upon her return, she attended the Guildhall School of Music and Drama, graduating with a coveted gold medal in acting. She took on various radio, television, film, and theater roles before taking lead roles in the 2013 ITV drama *Broadchurch* and the 2017 BBC drama *Trust Me*. During her audition for *Doctor Who*, Whittaker thought that the role of the Doctor might not be for her, but series producer Chris Chibnall persuaded her to go with it. She is the first woman to play the lead role in the series.

THE FOURTEENTH DOCTOR

David Tennant, 2023

Appearance: In a bizarre twist of fate, this Doctor looks just like the Tenth Doctor, only older—a sort of reprise regeneration. He wears a long dark blue double-breasted tweed coat with wide lapels, matching waistcoat and trousers of brown, blue, and white checked wool (with the waistcoat having only the topmost button done up), a white poplin shirt, a silvery-gray knitted skinny tie, rounded off with light colored Converse footwear. He dons Wicklow tortoiseshell glasses with round frames when required.

Personality: The Doctor himself asks why *this* face has come back. He may retain all the energy of his look-alike predecessor, but now he is more melancholic, reflective, and sentimental. All things point to him having unfinished business. This Doctor also experiences something never encountered before—bigeneration! As he is dying, his body emits regeneration energy, but then it burns off. Rather than be replaced, his body is healed, and it bisects, leaving his fourteenth regeneration intact and creating the Fifteenth Doctor.

Actor: David John McDonald . . . Wait, hold on! If you think you might be experiencing some déjà vu here, it is because Tennant's love for the role was so great that he agreed to return in three *Doctor Who* specials to celebrate the show's sixtieth anniversary. Since then, series producer Russell T. Davies has been quite adamant that Tennant will never again return to the show. We shall see. . . .

THE FIFTEENTH DOCTOR

Ncuti Gatwa, 2023–Present

Appearance: This Doctor is a younger Black man with short hair and a thin mustache. At the time of writing, we have only seen him in two different stories, but from promotional teasers, there is already a suggestion of a lot of outfit diversity. His first solo outing sees him in a long brown double-breasted leather coat with a belt, a zip-up polo top with vertical stripes in various hues of orange and blue, blue trousers, and a pair of hip men's sneakers. It is a striking look, blending the best of retro and contemporary styles. We also see him in a white vest, a kilt, and a black biker-style jacket. This Doctor seems to have an affection for jewelry, wearing necklaces and rings.

Personality: This Doctor exudes confidence and charisma, with a smile that could light up an overcast day. He is very fit and energetic, engaging in a game of catch with the Toymaker, dancing in a nightclub, and running along rooftops. He comes across as someone who has finally liberated himself from the baggage that has weighed down a lot of his past selves, choosing to look to the future rather than be held back by the past.

Actor: Mizero Ncuti Gatwa (1992–) is a Scottish actor. Rwandan by birth, Gatwa's family fled from the genocide perpetrated against the Tutsi in 1994, moving to Scotland. After living in Edinburgh and Dunfermline, Gatwa moved to Glasgow to study at the Royal Conservatoire of Scotland, graduating with a Bachelor of Arts in Acting. He found prominence after being cast as Eric Effiong in the Netflix comedy *Sex Education* (2019–2023), a role that has brought him numerous accolades. He is the first Black actor to fully play the lead role of the Doctor in the series.

SONIC SCREWDRIVER

One of the things that many—but not quite all—of the Doctors have in common is their trusty sonic screwdriver—a multifunctional device (think of it as a highly advanced electronic Swiss army knife) that has helped get them out of many a predicament. The First Doctor did not have one, and when the Fifth Doctor lost his, destroyed by a Terileptil (a reptilian alien) in 1666 (and starting the Great Fire of London), it was not replaced during his time, nor was a new one introduced for the Sixth or Seventh Doctors. This was because producer John Nathen-Turner felt that it had become a deus ex machina, providing the Doctor with an all-too-easy method of overcoming obstacles. When *Doctor Who* returned, albeit briefly, in 1996, the Seventh Doctor had somehow acquired one, which then got inherited by the Eighth Doctor. Since 2005, when the show made a full comeback, every Doctor in the modern era has had their own.

Most are conceptually similar in design, being broadly long and thin, with an emitter crystal at one end, although modern-era ones have an assortment of extendible and retractable parts, each with their own functions. In general use, the Doctor scans something with it, looks at the screwdriver, and automatically knows what the results are, despite there never being a visible onboard display (via telepathic link, perhaps?). When the fourteenth Doctor gets his sonic screwdriver, things were taken to a whole new level. He can use it to render a display in midair and create movable force fields. Of all the sonics up to that point, his is by far the most feature-rich.

The most recent version, for the Fifteenth Doctor, is quite unlike anything that has come before—larger and more curvaceous, in hues of blue, gold, and silver, with rotating segments, and controls on either side. It has Gallifreyan script on it, which translates to an old Rwandan proverb, "The sharpness of the tongue defeats the sharpness of the warrior," honoring Ncuti Gatwa's cultural heritage while remaining faithful to the tenets of the Doctor.

REPUTATION

The Doctor has always had a reputation—good *and* bad. Among his own people he is regarded as a rebel and a renegade, one who shunned their ways. To the people of Earth, he is regarded as an aberration. In the 2005 story "Rose," a man named Clive (Mark Benton) collects pictures and news articles, chronicling the Ninth Doctor's presence throughout Earth's history. As he tells Rose Tyler (Billie Piper), the Doctor's soon-to-be companion, "The Doctor is a legend, woven throughout history. When disaster comes, he's there. He brings the storm in his wake, and he has one constant companion. Death."[1]

In the 2007 two-part story "Human Nature/Family of Blood," Tim Latimer (Thomas Brodie-Sangster), talks of the Doctor, "I've seen him. He's like fire, and ice, and rage. He's like the night, and the storm, and the heart of the sun. He's ancient and forever. He burns at the center of time, and he can see the turn of the universe."[2]

To get a balanced view of the Doctor, and an insight into the darker side of his nature, we need to hear what his enemies have said about him. In the same story, the alien that took over the body of Baines (Harry Lloyd) says of the Tenth Doctor, "He never raised his voice. That was the worst thing. The fury of the Time Lord. And then we discovered why. Why this Doctor, who'd fought with gods and demons, why he'd run away from us and hidden. He was being kind. He wrapped my father in unbreakable chains, forged in the heart of a dwarf star. He tricked my mother into the event horizon of a collapsing galaxy, to be imprisoned there . . . forever. He still visits my sister, once a year, every year. I wonder if one day he might forgive her, but there she is. Can you see her? He trapped her inside a mirror. Every mirror. If ever you look at your reflection and see something move behind you, just for a second, that's her. That's always her. As for me, I was suspended in time, and the Doctor put me to work, standing over the fields of England as their protector. We wanted to live forever, so the Doctor made sure that we did."

In the 2008 two-part story "The Stolen Earth/Journey's End," Davros (Julian Bleach), faced with several of the Doctor's companions who are prepared to go to extraordinary lengths to stop him, tells the Tenth Doctor, "The man who abhors violence, never carrying a gun, but this is the truth, Doctor. You take ordinary people and fashion them into weapons. Behold your Children of Time, transformed into murderers. I made the Daleks, Doctor, but you made this."[3]

Such is the complexity of the character; you would not be mistaken in thinking that this all makes the Doctor sound rather ominous. However, the truth is that the Doctor is often forced to operate in morally ambiguous ways, at least from a human perspective. But he is not human, and it is very important to always remember that.

Chapter 3

The Tardis

Figure 3 The Tardis. BBC / Photofest © BBC

What would *Doctor Who* be without the Tardis? That magnificent vehicle that can travel in all of space and time, is larger on the inside, and looks like a battered old police box from 1960s Britain on the outside (a design decision prompted entirely by budgetary constraints when the program started, with a police box prop both cheap to reproduce and easy to pack away and rebuild on location). There is no doubt about it: It is utterly bonkers!

The name itself, TARDIS, is an acronym standing for Time and Relative Dimension In Space (with the "Dimension" part sometimes being pluralized). There is some debate as to the origins of this, with Susan (Carole Ann Ford), the granddaughter of the first Doctor (William Hartnell), telling her teachers, Barbara Wright (Jaqueline Hill) and Ian Chesterton (William Russell), that it was she who came up with the name. However, it is also the name that all other Time Lords use to refer to their time ships, so either Susan exaggerated, or she had a lot more influence back on Gallifrey than anybody realized.

BIGGER ON THE INSIDE

The reason why the Tardis appears bigger on the inside is that the exterior and the interior are dimensionally transcendental, meaning that both exist in separate dimensions, but are inexorably linked together. When one passes over the threshold, it is just like walking through a doorway into the room beyond, although it is not inconceivable that those who are sensitive enough might just experience a fleeting moment of dimensional adjustment. The phrase, "It's bigger on the inside" is one that the Doctor habitually hears from those who enter the Tardis, but in the 2012 Christmas story, "The Snowmen," Clara (Jenna Coleman) stuns the Twelfth Doctor by saying, "It's smaller on the outside," having him to admit that hearing that is a first.[1]

THE ZERO ROOM

The interior may be large, very large, with seemingly endless corridors and rooms, but that does not mean it is infinite. Just the opposite. In the 1982 story "Castrovalva," the newly regenerated Fifth Doctor (Peter Davison), experiencing an unstable regeneration, seeks out the Zero Room, a large pink-hued chamber deep in the Tardis that smells of roses. It is a place of tranquility, cut off from all external interference, where he can take some time to recuperate. But the Master (Anthony Ainley) has set a trap, hurtling the Tardis backward in time toward something labeled Event One—the largest explosion in history—the Big Bang!

With the Doctor seemingly incapacitated, Nyssa (Sarah Sutton) and Tegan (Janet Fielding) try to find a way to deflect the Tardis from its current trajectory, but neither of them knows how to operate it. The Doctor, recognizing the signs that something is wrong, and having found an electric wheelchair, makes his way to the console room and concocts a plan. Making his calculations, he determines that jettisoning a whole quarter of the Tardis interior will give them sufficient thrust to break free. He is successful but then realizes that the part of the Tardis he ejected contained the Zero Room.

A MUSEUM PIECE

The Doctor's particular Tardis is a very old model, a museum piece even, which is designated a Type 40 TT Capsule. When the Doctor (William Hartnell) meets another of his kind (Peter Butterworth) in the 1965 story "The Time Meddler," they compare Tardises, with the Doctor noting that the Monk has a "Mark 4." When asked what type he has, the Doctor gets quite crotchety, telling the Monk to mind his own business (although in the 2011 story "Let's Kill Hitler" scans reveal the Doctor's Tardis to be a Mark 3). Not only is the Monk's Tardis newer, with lots of changes, especially when it comes to safety features—as noted by the Doctor himself—but it also has a working camouflage unit, making it look like a perfect replica of a Saxon sarcophagus.

THE CHAMELEON CIRCUIT

The part of the Tardis that gives it its camouflage ability, changing the shape, color, mass, and texture of the exterior plasmic shell to fit in with its surroundings, wherever or whenever it lands, is called the Chameleon Circuit. The Tardis, in its natural external form, with no disguise in place, is tall and cylindrical, with double doors providing access. When the Doctor and Susan stole the Tardis, it was in for repairs. The Chameleon Circuit was one of the parts that was not functioning properly, so when the Doctor took refuge in 1960s London, it assumed the form of a Metropolitan police box—a common enough sight back then (incidentally, for those not in the know, a police box is like a miniature police station, allowing officers of the law to sit inside to read and fill out reports, take breaks, and hold detainees in until they can be transferred to a proper station—they even have a telephone that members of public can use to call for help). Once the Doctor's Tardis assumed that form, it stayed like that.

That is not to suggest that the Doctor has never tried to fix it. In the 1981 story "Logopolis," the Doctor is wandering around the Cloister Room of the Tardis (having the appearance of a vaulted chamber filled with stone columns, overgrown with ivy). He is verbally musing about the second law of thermodynamics—entropy—taking its toll on the Tardis, with parts of it crumbling away in his hand. He tells Adric (Matthew Waterhouse) that he should really be running a tighter ship, and where better to begin than by repairing the Chameleon Circuit?

That is when the Cloister Bell rings. To the Time Lords, the Cloister Bell is a worrying sound. It is an early warning system, an alert that reverberates throughout the Tardis in the event of an impending catastrophe. When it ceases after a short while, the Doctor dismisses it as just another potential malfunction of the ship's systems.

The Doctor wants to materialize the Tardis around one of the few genuine police boxes that remain, taking exact measurements so he can give them to the mathematicians of Logopolis. They, in turn, will convert those measurements into a precise mathematical model of the Tardis exterior using block transfer computation—an advanced form of space-time modeling, allowing for the creation and manipulation of solid objects through pure mathematics. Applying this technique would allow them to resolve the problem with the Chameleon Circuit—at least, that is the theory. Thanks to the evil maneuverings of the Master (Anthony Ainley), this plan is aborted, with Logopolis and all the Logopolitan people falling victim to an accelerated form of entropy.

The Doctor (Colin Baker) makes one other attempt to fix the Chameleon Circuit in the 1985 story "Attack of the Cybermen." Tinkering with the Tardis' systems, trying to fix it himself, he is only partially successful. This results in the Tardis temporarily assuming the form of an elaborately decorated clothes dresser, a large pipe organ, and a set of wrought iron gates, before reverting to the guise of a police box, there to remain—after all, what more iconic form could the Doctor's space-time vehicle ever take?

POLICE BOXES

Most of the active police boxes in Britain were phased out from the 1970s onward. In 1994, there was a review of trademark law in England, resulting in the Trade Marks Act 1994. In the wake of this, in 1996, the BBC applied for a trademark to use the image of the police box in association with official *Doctor Who* merchandise. The Metropolitan Police filed an objection in 1998, stating that they still retained all rights to the police box design.[2] Additionally, they argued that the police box was far more commonly associated with the Metropolitan Police, rather than the BBC or *Doctor Who*, and when consent was given to use the appearance of a police box back when the show first aired, it was never their intention to give up their rights to the trademark.

However, in 2002, the Patent Office (known as the Intellectual Property Office of the United Kingdom since 2007) ruled in favor of the BBC, citing a lack of evidence from the Metropolitan Police—or any police force in the United Kingdom—having ever registered the design of the police box as a trademark.[3] On top of that, the BBC had already been selling *Doctor Who* merchandise featuring prominent imagery of a police box for several decades prior without any complaint or objection from the police, further eroding their claim.

THE CONSOLE ROOM

Now let us move from the outside to the inside. Once over the threshold, the first thing that any visitor sees is the Console Room, where the Tardis console—the ship's main bank of controls—is located.

Traditionally (as in the classic era), the Tardis console is hexagonal, with six different control panels, each being responsible for different functions (for optimal flight operations, all six panels should be manned). This is raised off the floor by a hexagonal pedestal through which the electronics of the console run directly into the floor and then connect to the ship's wider systems. On the very top of the console is a cylindrical segment called the Time Rotor, which raises and lowers while the ship is traveling, giving a clear visual indication of flight status.

Also, traditionally, the Tardis console room is spacious and predominately white. Some walls have roundels of differing sizes on them, while other walls are obscured by equipment or storage. Other than the console itself, there is no hard-and-fast consistency to the layout of the console room, with the first three Doctors regularly reconfiguring it at their whims.

The design of the original console room was the brainchild of Kazimierz Piotr Brachacki (1926–1980), generally known as "Peter." He was a production designer for the BBC, working on multiple programs, although he is best known for being the first production designer on *Doctor Who*. Ironically, he did not enjoy working on the show and only stuck around for a very short time before being replaced by Barry Newbery.

Throughout the classic era of *Doctor Who*, both the Tardis console and the room it sits in would change many times, but all the while retaining a familiar high-concept style and layout. When *Doctor Who* returned, albeit briefly, in 1996, in the TV movie that was hoped would reignite interest in the show, the Tardis got its biggest-ever interior makeover. Gone was the gleaming white and futuristic design, replaced by something out of a Jules Verne or H. G. Wells novel, with wooden paneling, brass inlays, analog dials, crankshaft handles, and a much longer central time rotor that stretched up from the top of the console to a suspended housing above. The console room itself is filled with all manner of wonders—bookshelves, statues, ornaments, lamps, candleholders, throw rugs, and clocks of different shapes and sizes. There is even an ornate armchair and occasional table from which the Doctor can enjoy a cup of tea and a good book while listening to a vintage record player. It may be quite a radical departure from what came before, but it feels lived in and just the sort of thing a time traveler would embrace. It is a fantastic reimagining, feeling both technologically advanced and delightfully retro at the same time.

In 2005, when *Doctor Who* made its triumphant return to television, the Tardis interior had undergone further dramatic changes. The console room is now domed and has a grungy feel to it. The Tardis console still has an elongated time rotor, stretching from floor to ceiling, and six different control panels, but it is now rounded rather than hexagonal and sits on a raised metal grill platform. The controls are set into semiopaque green panels, and much of the instrumentation has a kitbash feel as if the Doctor had replaced faulty parts ad hoc with whatever he has to hand. The console is flanked on several sides by coral-colored stanchions which have a very organic look to them. All in all, this feels like a Tardis that is beat up and has seen better days, but then, it has. This is the Tardis that survived through the Time War, and it shows.

The Tardis interior did not see a significant change until the Eleventh Doctor (Matt Smith) and it was quite a feast for the eyes. The Tardis console, now back in its hexagonal format, is raised on a transparent platform, held aloft by a myriad of angled steel supports, with staircases branching up and down at various points. The time rotor is flanked by wooden panels and the interior has blown glass detailing. The walls are angled, some with gentle curves, some with more extreme curves, and roundels of different sizes are distributed irregularly. This Tardis represents the quirky, zany nature of the Doctor that is at the helm, and we get a very real sense of the symbiotic nature that exists between man and machine.

We see this again with the Twelfth Doctor (Peter Capaldi). His Tardis, like himself, is more austere in nature. The console and its panels are smaller and less frivolously populated with extraneous controls. The time rotor extends upward to a much larger housing, with tiered stages, decorated with Gallifreyan symbology, which rotate clockwise and anticlockwise when the Tardis is operating. Following the new trend, the console platform is elevated and has extra banks of controls at the periphery, as well as stairs leading up to a gallery level that encompasses the room, which features bookshelves and blackboards. Even the lighting itself is more somber, with the edges of the room disappearing into shadow and directed lighting highlighting where the focus should be drawn.

As I have stated before, although the design of the Tardis console room may change, it generally follows a very familiar blueprint. When the Thirteenth Doctor (Jodie Whittaker) comes along, the interior loses a lot of that consistency. We are back to a larger and rounder Tardis console, but the glass time rotor is gone, replaced by a giant, semiopaque glowing crystal, jutting straight up out of the top. The controls appear to be extremely stark, looking far more decorative than functional. Surrounding the console are six massive crystalline structures, segmented and angled inward, looking like giant crab legs reaching up out of the floor. They are not support structures, and they do not seem to have an important function, certainly not enough to validate the amount of space they take up. The walls and floors are a mishmash of interlocking hexagonal panels, with shaped segments cut out of them. Lighting is very low, and somewhat curiously for a machine that is meant to be bigger on the inside, the interior feels quite claustrophobic. Lastly, and in an utterly baffling design change, when entering the Tardis from the outside, the entire interior of the police box is now visible before crossing the dimensional threshold and entering the Tardis proper. Overall, the dim, cramped crystalline redesign, as well as the moving of the threshold boundary, feels like a conceptual misstep. Yes, it feels *alien*, but the design has little in common with any Time Lord aesthetic we have ever seen, coming across as different merely for the sake of change.

The most recent Tardis, as used by both the Fourteenth Doctor (David Tennant) and the Fifteenth Doctor (Ncuti Gatwa), is the best one yet, perfectly fusing classic-era and modern-era designs in a way that delights. The interior space is the biggest it has ever been, and nearly spherical in nature, with roundel panels on the walls that not only light up but which can change color too (mood lighting). The console is the closest that we have ever come to replicating the look and feel of the originals (complete with the return of a glass time rotor), and it sits on a raised platform midway up the space, with ramps curving up and down to circular doorways located at various heights in the walls. Talking of ramps, the Tardis now has a retractable one at the entrance to make it wheelchair accessible.

THE SECONDARY CONSOLE ROOM

The Tardis has a secondary console room in addition to the primary one, for emergency purposes. We first learn of this in the 1976 story "The Masque of Mandragora." The Fourth Doctor (Tom Baker) encounters it while showing Sarah Jane Smith (Elisabeth Sladen) around the Tardis. It is a wooden paneled room with lit-up stained-glass panels in some of the roundels. There is a small wooden console in the center, looking very much like a hexagonal writing bureau. As it turns out, the Tardis has a habit of archiving old console rooms into memory so, in theory, all the different console room designs and configurations from the past are saved and stored away. When the Tenth Doctor (David Tennant), the Eleventh Doctor (Matt Smith), and the War Doctor (John Hurt) are all present in the Tardis at the same time, the system glitches, causing each of their individual "desktop themes" (as their distinct interiors are amusingly referred to) to appear, before settling on the most recent one.

A LIVING MACHINE?

It is an established fact that Doctors old and new talk to the Tardis as though it is alive—but is it? Well, according to the Time Lords themselves, Tardises are *grown* rather than *built*, such is the process of interdimensional engineering that takes place. In the 2011 story "The Doctor's Wife," the Eleventh Doctor (Matt Smith), follows an emergency message sent by another Time Lord, leading him to a scrapyard asteroid in a bubble universe. Once landed, the Tardis loses all power because it is a trap. The asteroid is not an asteroid at all, but the outer shell of an entity called "House" (Michael Sheen). House has been luring countless Time Lords to his bubble universe, stranding them and feeding off the Artron energy produced by their Tardises. To prevent the Doctor from leaving—like he did with all the other Time Lords before him—House extracts the living "soul" of the Tardis and puts it in the body of a temporary host, in this instance, a young woman, Idris (Suranne Jones).

The Doctor's hopes of finding another living Time Lord are dashed when he learns that all those who were lured there by House are dead, their body parts having been used to "repair" House's assistants, Uncle (Adrian Schiller), and Auntie (Elizabeth Berrington). When House discovers that the Doctor is the last of the Time Lords, meaning his food supply is now endangered, he transfers his consciousness into the now-vacant Tardis systems and uses it to travel to the main universe to seek out a new source. Back in the scrapyard, the Doctor and Idris construct a partial Tardis out of the remains of those that House had consumed and give pursuit. When they catch up to the House-controlled Tardis, they board it, and the dying body of Idris releases the living essence of the Tardis, which floods back into the systems, regaining control and obliterating House's consciousness. The Tardis uses its fading link with Idris to have one last verbal exchange with the Doctor before the body of Idris gives out and disappears.

A couple of other useful insights into the Tardis emerge from the same story. The first is that the Tardis has always been rather unreliable in terms of going where the Doctor intends. This has been put down to one of the many faults that the Tardis was experiencing when it was put in for repair, right before the Doctor stole it. When the Doctor communicates with his Tardis through Idris, he scolds her for being unreliable, not always taking him where he wants to go. She replies by saying, "No, but I always took you where you *needed* to go."[4]

Whatever the reliability of course-plotting—whether accidental or intentional—there was a point in time when the Fourth Doctor (Tom Baker) installed a "randomizer" into the Tardis's navigation system to prevent the Black Guardian (Valentine Dyall) from finding him. After all, as the Doctor reasoned, how could the Black Guardian find him if he did not know where he was going himself? This was only a temporary measure, and it was eventually disconnected.

The second insight is that while the Doctor has always believed that he stole the Tardis, he did not realize that the Tardis *let* him. It wanted to see the universe as much as he did, and as he was the only Time Lord mad enough to steal a Tardis, it facilitated the ease of the theft, ensuring the doors were left unlocked. Add to that the fact that Clara Oswald (Jenna Coleman) moved through the Doctor's timeline in the 2013 story "The Name of the Doctor" and guided the First Doctor (William Hartnell) to the right Tardis to steal, it seems like there was no combination of events that would ever result in the Doctor and his Tardis not finding one another.

THE EYE OF HARMONY

The power source of the Tardis comes from the Eye of Harmony (a temporal status field around a collapsing star). There is one located in the Tardis, or at least, a subset of the main one on Gallifrey. They are inextricably connected, with the one in the Tardis drawing power directly from the one in Gallifrey. With the destruction of Gallifrey, such a link would have been severed, so there have been times when the Doctor has parked the Tardis on the site of a space-time rift, using the energy from that to recharge the systems.

DEFENSIVE SYSTEMS

The Tardis has a handful of other systems that do not always work as intended. One of these is HADS, or the Hostile Action Displacement System. This is meant to kick in when the Tardis senses danger, moving to a different location until it is recalled or it is deemed safe enough to return. Despite this sounding like an important safety feature, it is unpredictable, and there have been times when the Doctor has been stranded because of it, causing him to turn it off most of the time. The Tardis is also meant to be able to create a state of temporal grace, meaning that no weapons should ever work within its confines, but this has seldom functioned properly, with the Doctor once claiming the whole thing is nothing more than a cleverly constructed lie. Even the wheezing-groaning sound that the Tardis makes when landing or taking off only happens—or so River Song (Alex Kingston) claims—because the Doctor habitually leaves the brakes on!

Chapter 4

Controversy and Censorship

Figure 4 The Sixth Doctor behind bars. BBC / Photofest © BBC

From its earliest days, *Doctor Who* has been one of those shows that children would watch while peeking between the gaps of their fingers as they covered their eyes with their hands, or warily peering out from behind the sofa. With alien menaces like Daleks, Cybermen, and yetis appearing on-screen, *Doctor Who* could be *scary*. But that is part of the fun of watching—it is *exciting*, and it is *challenging*. Children enjoy a challenge. It helps them learn more about themselves and what their limits are. When they confront something that is frightening, it helps build confidence. It is the same reason why ghost stories around campfires are so popular; they push the boundaries of one's comfort zone while being in a safe environment.

In October 2021, Heather Greenwood Davies wrote an article in *National Geographic* titled, "Scary Good: Why It's OK for Kids to Feel Frightened Sometimes."[1] Citing the findings of experts like neuropsychologist Sam Goldstein and sociologist Margee Kerr, the article looks at the positives that can come from exposure to "safe scares," helping children to grow and develop and to learn to manage stressful situations that they might encounter in real life.

MARY WHITEHOUSE

In the mid-1970s, *Doctor Who* faced one of his biggest threats. It was not an insidious alien, or a murderous robot, but a retired art teacher from Nuneaton in England. Constance Mary Whitehouse (1910–2001) was the founder and first president of the "National Viewers and Listeners Association" (now known as Mediawatch-UK), in 1965. It was created to be the successor to an earlier Clean-Up TV Campaign that Whitehouse had founded with her husband, Ernest, along with the Reverend Basil Buckland and his wife Norah, the previous year.

A devout Christian, Whitehouse took it upon herself to become Britain's guardian of moral rectitude when it came to publications and broadcasts. She regularly sent letters to Harold Wilson (1916–1995), the British Labour prime minister, but as he was a liberal and a social reformist, she would not find much support there.

Her biggest target was Sir Hugh Greene (1910–1987), director-general of the BBC, whom Whitehouse described as "the devil incarnate" and who was "responsible for the moral collapse in the country."[2] According to the manifesto of the Clean-Up TV Campaign, the BBC, under Greene's leadership, spread a message of "promiscuity, infidelity and drinking" when they should really be sending out a message to "encourage and sustain faith in God and bring him back into the hearts of our family and national life."[3] In response to this, in a speech that Greene gave in 1965—in which he did not mention

Whitehouse by name—he denounced the critics of his liberalisation of broadcasting, complaining that they promoted "a dangerous form of censorship."[4]

At a time when Christianity was still actively observed by the majority of people in the United Kingdom, Whitehouse was not without her supporters, including several strongly conservative politicians and ex-politicians who would speak at her events, and her petitions could get up to five hundred thousand signatories. However, the 1960s saw a cultural upheaval with the rise of the sexual revolution and feminism. Younger people no longer saw premarital sex as immoral, welcomed the freedoms that contraception brought, and questioned traditional relationship dynamics with women being subservient and expected to stay at home or to take up low-level, menial jobs.

From 1974 to 1981, Tom Baker's portrayal of the Doctor was not only the longest but also the most recognizable. During his time, and under the auspices of Philip Hinchcliffe (1944–) and scriptwriter Robert Holmes (1926–1986), *Doctor Who* enjoyed a period of darker, more frightening stories, taking influence from elements often found in Gothic stories. Naturally, this caught the attention of Whitehouse, and *Doctor Who* became a focus of her moralistic vitriol.

In an article in *The Independent*, writing an obituary for David Maloney (1933–2006), who directed many stories during the Hinchcliffe and Holmes era, writer Anthony Hayward talks of the ire that such stories invoked in Whitehouse, "Most notable was 1975's 'Genesis of the Daleks,' which featured the programme's first freeze-frame cliffhanger."[5] Both the new script editor, Robert Holmes, and producer Philip Hinchcliffe—not keen on yet more Daleks stories and steering the program toward Gothic, psychological horror in the Hammer Films vein—wanted to explore a darker side of the writer Terry Nation's creations, showing their Nazi-like origins. The result was a tale in which the Doctor is taken back in time to Skaro to prevent the Daleks' development, during a long war between the planet's two humanoid powers, and moments of violence that included Tom Baker convulsing in pain as an electric fence sends a current through him. Mary Whitehouse described it as "Teatime brutality for tots."

In focusing on the frightening elements alone, Whitehouse completely missed the important allegory of the Dalek's predecessors—the Kaleds—being like the Nazis, and the cautionary tale that it entreated to viewers on the dangers of zealotry and fascism.

The 1976 story "The Brain of Morbius" was met with similar scorn by Whitehouse, who proclaimed that it contained, "some of the sickest and most horrific material seen on children's television."[6] One suspects that if Whitehouse had been alive in the time that Mary Shelley (1797–1851) had released *Frankenstein* (from which "The Brain of Morbius" draws heavy influence), she would have campaigned to have the book withdrawn from publication.

By far, her biggest complaint about *Doctor Who* came with the 1976 story "The Deadly Assassin." While in a simulated environment (one that appears quite real to the viewer), the Doctor faces off against a foe who, at the end of the third episode, is seen holding the Doctor's head underwater. Before the end titles play, and for dramatic effect, the submerged Doctor's face is seen in a prolonged freeze-frame scene, suggestive of him having drowned. Whitehouse's reaction was, "The final shot of the episode was *Doctor Who* drowning," adding, "and this sort of image was left in the mind of the child for a whole week. I think it's extraordinary that people with the brilliance in many ways of making a programme of that kind couldn't extend their awareness to the effect of what they were doing on the children who were receiving it."[7]

For once Whitehouse had a point, Hinchcliffe and Holmes had taken things too far. It led to the director-general of the BBC, Sir Charles Curran (1921–1980), a man who was far more conservative than his predecessor, to personally apologize for the violent content depicted in the episode. In a statement, Curran said, "The television service was not totally satisfied with the way 'The Deadly Assassin' developed. With hindsight, the service does accept that one or two viewers may have imagined that Dr. Who's dreams were reality. What actually happened was the that head of department felt, before these episodes were transmitted, that some of the sequences were a little too realistic for a science-fiction series. Accordingly, several of them were edited out before transmission." He added, "The result was what you saw on the screen, and which I myself think was reasonably acceptable. However, with hindsight, the head of department responsible would have liked to have cut just a few more frames of the action that he did."[8]

Hinchcliffe was soon replaced as series producer and Graham Williams was brought in with instructions to lighten the tone of the series. Hinchcliffe subsequently spoke about the controversial scene, stating that it was intended to make the end of that episode *less* disturbing. The original scene was shown to Bill Slater, head of series, and there was an agreement that the drowning was too protracted. As Hinchcliffe notes, "There was a conversation with him and David Maloney said, 'Well, we could shorten it, but I could freeze-frame?'—actually, I think that made it worse myself." Speaking at a BFI screening in 2018, Hinchcliffe reflected on Whitehouse's attitudes to *Doctor Who* during his time, "She didn't quite understand that it was a family show and there was a wide age range of audience members."

In all subsequent airings of this episode, either on network television or on streaming services, the freeze-frame scene has been removed, being commonly referred to as 'the Whitehouse Cut."

Whitehouse was noted for having a particularly blinkered view of what was and was not acceptable. Portrayed violence would be met with indignation, but implied violence would not. As David Stubbs, a writer and journalist, noted, "Conversely, look at the shows she did like, including Dixon of Dock Green. Here's a show in which friendly Sergeant Dixon once uttered words to the effect of, 'Why, if the police were called out every time a bloke was giving his wife a good clobbering, we'd never get anything done.' This didn't trouble Whitehouse at all; she gave it a special award in 1967."[9] As Stubbs notes, "Explicitness, not implicitness, was her bugbear."

Stubbs also points out that gross racial stereotyping such as the "Black and White Minstrel Show," a prime-time "light-entertainment" show on the BBC that ran from 1958 to 1978, featuring white performers with their faces painted black (more commonly referred to as "blackface") singing a variety of songs, never once concerned her.

Whitehouse stepped down from her role as president of the National Viewers and Listeners Association in May 1994, eliciting differing opinions from those in influential roles connected with broadcasting. William Rees-Mogg (1928–2012), then chairman of the Broadcasting Standards Commission (now replaced by Ofcom, a portmanteau of the Office of Communications) and a former member of the BBC's Board of Governors, described her as, "a force for the good, an important woman."[10]

Michael Grade, former controller of BBC1, and then Chief Executive of Channel 4, said of her, "I don't think she has had any effect at all. She never sees things in context. She will see something in an exploitation video and condemn it in the same breath as she will condemn a Dennis Potter classic. I respect her fortitude in fighting the battles over the years, trying to get her point of view across, but it is a point of view which would have totally destroyed British television if it had become the set of values by which we had commissioned programmes."

Whitehouse died in November 2001. Although her views on morality may have been narrow-minded and hypocritical, and she may have been fervently homophobic, she still did important work in highlighting the issue of pedophilia and child pornography which led to the passing of the Protection of Children Act of 1978. Perhaps for this alone, history may not judge her quite so harshly.

VIOLENCE IN THE EIGHTIES

Doctor Who continued to find controversy throughout the 1980s, particularly in its depiction of violent scenes and its handling of them. The 1984 story "Resurrection of the Daleks" opens in London's Docklands area, where three men, dressed as British police officers, use submachine guns to mow down a group of fleeing men, before executing a homeless man who witnesses the scene. There are many deaths in this story, so much so that it gives longtime companion Tegan Jovanka (Janet Fielding) pause, and she decides that she no longer wants to travel with the Fifth Doctor (Peter Davison).

Famously, in the opening episode of the 1984 story "The Twin Dilemma," the Sixth Doctor (Colin Baker), having trouble adjusting to his new regeneration, and being accordingly paranoid, accuses his companion Peri (Nicola Bryant) of being an alien spy, and attempts to strangle her. In the 1985 story "Attack of the Cybermen," the character of Lytton (Maurice Colbourne, 1939–1989), makes a return from his appearance in the 1984 story "Resurrection of the Daleks," where he is tortured by Cybermen who crush his hands, having blood oozing out of them. The same story also features men dressed as British police officers wielding silenced pistols and pointing them at the Doctor and Peri (echoes of the "Resurrection of the Daleks"), and the Doctor himself gunning down several Cybermen. All in all, its reliance on violence, seemingly for the sake of excitement, has frequently been described as gratuitous and unnecessary. In the same year, the story "Vengeance on Varos" has the Doctor playing a part in causing two guards to fall into a large vat of acid, which he brushes off with the nonchalant quip, "Forgive me if I don't join you."[11]

Part of the problem with *Doctor Who*'s depiction of violence in the 1980s relates to the carrying and use of firearms, which were then, and still are now, heavily regulated in the United Kingdom, a country whose gun laws have been some of the strictest in the world, and which have only grown more strict over time. According to BBC News, the most important laws on gun control came into effect in the wake of two rare gun-related mass shootings— the 1987 Hungerford massacre, where twenty-seven-year-old Michael Ryan killed sixteen people in England, leading to a ban on modern semiautomatic rifles; and the 1996 Dunblane massacre, where forty-three-year-old Thomas Hamilton, killed sixteen pupils and one teacher in a primary school in Scotland, leading to a ban on handguns.[12] There was, understandably, concern in the 1980s that *Doctor Who* was following an American trend of including gun use in television dramas to heighten excitement and a sense of danger. However, according to statistics sourced from the FBI and the Home Office in the same news article, gun killings in the United States, as a percentage of all homicides, stood at 73 percent, compared to just 4 percent in England and Wales. This only highlighted just how out of place the featuring of conventional firearms in *Doctor Who* was (quite aside from the many alien or futuristic weapons that have been shown).

That is not to say that firearms never had reasonable representation in *Doctor Who*. With the introduction of military organizations in the series, particularly United Nations Intelligence Taskforce (UNIT), such armed forces would use all manner of munitions to fend off alien aggressors, but these were professionals using weaponry for the necessary defense of humanity. When

Doctor Who started showing what were ostensibly police officers—trusted establishment figures of law and order—brandishing firearms and killing innocents, or threatening the Doctor and his companion with them, things had gotten well and truly out of hand.

CONTEMPORARY CONCERNS

Modern-era *Doctor Who* has not been without its controversies either. The British Board of Film Classification (BBFC) issued a 12 rating (for viewers twelve and up) to the 2005 story "Dalek," which has the Doctor (Christopher Eccleston) torturing a Dalek by repeatedly electrocuting it. They issued a statement to accompany the rating, saying, "We are concerned about role models for children using the sort of tactics that *Doctor Who* used against the Dalek."[13] Of course, such a viewpoint is taken without context, with the Doctor being psychologically scarred by the events of the Time War and having developed an overwhelming hatred toward the Daleks for the obliteration of his people.

Another 2005 story, "The Unquiet Dead," saw the BBC receiving complaints from concerned parents who felt that its Victorian zombies (cadavers possessed by and resurrected by noncorporeal alien entities) were too scary for young children. The BBC justified the episode, saying that it was never intended for children as young as those whose parents were complaining. Further furor was raised when writer Lawrence Miles (1972–), who has written several original *Doctor Who* novels, both for the Virgin New Adventures and BBC Books series, posted an online review of the episode.[14] In it, he claims that the "evil" Gelth are a political subtext, warning of the dangers of immigrants and asylum seekers looking to exploit compassion. He received a lot of backlash for his views, along with emails from his publisher, who was concerned that he was damaging future sales. Despite deleting the original review and reposting a "toned down" version, he appears unrepentant for what he perceives as a thinly veiled political agenda from Mark Gatiss, the writer of the episode.

The most controversial episode of modern-era *Doctor Who* came with the 2014 two-part series finale, "Dark Water"/"Death in Heaven," where it is suggested that the dead are still conscious and fully aware of what is happening to their physical bodies. They can feel pain, even that of their own cremation. To reinforce this point, an audio excerpt of a telepathic communication is played, revealing a recently deceased person begging not to be cremated. This distressed people who had lost loved ones, especially those who had had them cremated, and a torrent of complaints followed. The BBC, in response, defended using this story device, especially as it turns out to be a cleverly constructed lie, and noted that several times before the so-called revelation, it is mentioned that what is about to be divulged could be distressing.

CENSORED EDITS

Many of *Doctor Who*'s earlier stories have been lost because the BBC had no official policy of content retention or archiving. Tape was expensive, and because repeat viewings were few and far between, once a show had been broadcast, tapes were often reused to record new shows. The shortsightedness of this is staggering, resulting in a remarkable loss of popular culture material before 1978, when the BBC finally abandoned the practice of "junking" tape. The classic era's third, fourth, and fifth seasons have suffered the most in terms of missing episodes, and in some cases, entire stories have been lost to time. The advent of modern-era *Doctor Who* reignited interest in the series, and stories that had been partially lost (i.e., an audio recording existed, but the film footage was missing) have been "restored" using animation to re-create them.

As it stands, ninety-seven episodes of early *Doctor Who* are still missing and it is believed that many, if not all of them, are still out there somewhere. Various stories have been recovered from all over the world from stations that originally broadcast them and then kept ahold of the tapes. Over the years fans have spent time searching for them, and in some cases, they have been successful (there used to be 137 missing episodes). One of the people who has played an important role in recovering lost episodes is director and producer Paul Vanezis, a valuable member of the *Doctor Who* Restoration Team, a collection of fans, many of whom work in or are associated with the television industry, working to source and restore lost episodes.

Curiously, and pertinent to this theme of this chapter, some of what original footage that had been thought lost has surfaced over time. Not whole stories, or even whole episodes, but censored clips that were cut from the original footage before broadcast. The Australian Broadcasting Corporation had purchased *Doctor Who* stories from the BBC, but before they were transmitted, they were sent to the Film Censorship Board for classification. As part of the process, cuts were made to episodes that were deemed too violent. In the autumn of 1996, Australian fan, Damian Shanahan, tracked down a number of these clips through the Australian Archives in Sydney. Shanahan's clips eventually found their way into a BBC video release of material from lost *Doctor Who* stories titled, "The Missing Years."

Hopefully, with the continuing passion of fans such as Vanezis and Shanahan, the possibility of recovering further lost *Doctor Who* material remains high.

In closing, it must be noted that while some of the things that have been highlighted as controversial in this chapter may seem quite tame by today's standards, in the context of the social and cultural environment of the time, they were considered quite shocking. Old films and television shows may contain material that is regarded as offensive and unacceptable by today's standards, but they are time capsules of the views and values of the era in which they were made.

These are by no means the only controversies that have surfaced regarding *Doctor Who*. Topics such as race and gender portrayals, as well as attempts to rewrite the show's own history, have arisen, but these will be dealt with in context later in the book.

Chapter 5

The End?

Figure 5 The Seventh Doctor and Ace. BBC / Photofest © BBC

John Nathan-Turner (1947–2002) took over as series producer from Graham Williams (1945–1990) in 1980. He already had a history with the show, having been a floor assistant on it in 1969, during Patrick Troughton's time as the Doctor. He then worked as an assistant floor manager on two stories during Jon Pertwee's time—"The Ambassadors of Death" (1970) and "Colony in Space" (1971)—before finding himself in the role of production unit manager under Graham Williams. When Williams decided to step down after three years, BBC management wanted George Gallaccio (1938–) to take on the role, but he declined, opening the way for Nathan-Turner.

Nathan-Turner was critical of his predecessor's time on the show, particularly how much latitude he had given Tom Baker, whom he felt had developed too much influence. He was also scathing of the direction the show had taken, with over-the-top plots and a focus on comedic elements, which he thought had become more parodic than serious (something which Nathan-Turner himself would come to be accused of in time).

He implemented significant changes, tasking Peter Howell (1949–) of the Radiophonic Workshop with creating a brand-new and more contemporary arrangement of the title music to accompany new Starfield title graphics that had been created by Sid Sutton (1939–2023).

Nathan-Turner did not have as much experience as a producer as the BBC would have liked, so they assigned former series producer Barry Letts (1925–2009) to be executive producer for the first season. Christopher H. Bidmead (1941–) was brought in as script editor and along with Nathan-Turner, they conspired to downplay the quirky, lighthearted elements of Tom Baker's portrayal of the Fourth Doctor. Nathan-Turner's intention to rein in some of the more flamboyant impulses of Baker led to a lot of tensions on set.

Baker disliked Nathan-Turner's changes, which he felt diminished him as an actor, and he detested the costume change that saw the addition of question marks on the Doctor's shirt collar, which he thought were "insufferably vulgar and cheap."[1] In an interview included with *Doctor Who: The Collection*, Season 12 Blu-ray set, Baker said, "He nudged me towards the realisation it had run its course, and I should go somewhere else. I think, in a way, when I said I wanted to go, he was relieved that he wouldn't have to have that fight. He could get his stamp on it." Baker remained for a single season before bowing out, and Nathan-Turner, wanting someone who would not only be a stark contrast to Baker, but someone who was already a household name, picked Peter Davison for the role. Davison (born Peter Malcolm Gordon Moffett) became famous for portraying Tristan Farnon in the BBC's adaptation of *All Creatures Great and Small*, based on the books of British veterinarian James Herriot. The youngest actor (at the time) to play the Doctor, he signed a three-year contract.

The End?

The show was to find more changes than just a new Doctor. Alan Hart (1935–2021), who became controller of BBC1 in 1981, decided to shift the program from its long-standing autumn transmission slot to a spring transmission slot. In an even more divisive move, he decided to move the show from its traditional Saturday-evening airtime to being shown twice a week, with weekday evening airtimes, something that was lambasted by fans who felt that its Saturday-evening slot should have been sacrosanct.

Nathan-Turner was successful in bringing back some of *Doctor Who*'s most well-known villains, including the Master, the Cybermen (who returned to screens after a seven-year absence with the 1982 story "Earthshock"), the Daleks and their creator Davros, the Black and White Guardians, and even the Silurians and the Sea Devils. This focus on prominent enemies from the franchise proved to be difficult for the scriptwriters and new script editor Eric Saward (1944–), who felt that the show's increasing reliance on ties to the past was hindering interesting new storytelling opportunities.

Something else Nathan-Turner was successful at was breaking into the American market, with PBS now showing stories from the Tom Baker era. Nathan-Turner himself became a recognized face among the many stars of *Doctor Who* who appeared at PBS fundraising events, allowing them to continue purchasing more stories for broadcasting.

Taking advice from Patrick Troughton on avoiding being typecast, Davison hung up his cricketing hat after his contract came to an end, choosing not to renew it. Nathan-Turner cast Colin Baker (1943–) in the role, someone who was already familiar with the series having appeared as Gallifreyan Commander Maxil in the 1983 story "Arc of Infinity." His first appearance broke with tradition by having his premiere story appearing at the end of a season, rather than beginning a brand-new season with a brand-new Doctor, as had been done in the past. Davison's congenial take on the Doctor was gone, replaced with a far ruder, far more arrogant version. Although it had now returned to its once-a-week traditional Saturday-evening slot, this was to be the beginning of a turbulent time for the series.

Ever one for publicity, Nathan-Turner had taken to casting several light-entertainment celebrities in roles on the show, thinking that easily recognized household names would appeal to a much wider audience. Generally, it was recognized for the crass stunt-casting exercise that it was, with many of the celebrities adding little to the show with their token performances. To make matters worse, Nathan-Turner amped up his cheap marketing stunts by first casting Janet Fielding as companion Tegan Jovanka, then Nicola Bryant as Peri Brown, in the hope that they would increase appeal to Australian and American audiences alike.

Such tactics had poured scorn on what had been a beloved show, with outpourings of criticism from the press, the public, and even those who had been a part of it. Eric Saward thought that Colin Baker did not have the qualities necessary for the Doctor, particularly in the "energy and eccentricity" departments.[2] Former series producer Philip Hinchcliffe said that the show had become a bit "pantomime,"[3] and former script editor Terrance Dicks believed that, "there was a decline, without a doubt."[4]

MICHAEL GRADE

This had not gone unnoticed by Michael Grade (1943–), the new controller of BBC1. Grade had joined the BBC in 1984, and had quickly established himself as a contentious figure, canceling shows that he felt cost too much and/or were of little merit. A man who has since come to admit that he is contemptuous of science fiction in general, he set his sights on *Doctor Who*, and in early 1985 he announced that the show would be put on an eighteen-month hiatus, having decided that its budget could be better spent on quality productions, providing better value for money for license fee payers.

To elucidate, as part of a legacy system that started with the Wireless Telegraphy Act 1904, implemented by the General Post Office (GPO), a license fee was required to own and operate broadcast receiving equipment. In 1922 the British Broadcasting *Company* was set up to provide radio programs that were funded by the sale of radio sets and sponsorship deals. In 1927, when it transformed into the British Broadcasting *Corporation*, by means of a royal charter, the annual license fee that must be paid by every television owner became the principal means of funding the BBC's shows and services.

Over the years Grade has repeatedly recounted a meeting he had with Nathan-Turner, saying, "I hated *Doctor Who*. I said to the producer, have you seen *Star Wars* or *ET*? He said Yes. I said, so has our audience. What we were serving up as science fiction was garbage."[5] This, however, did not incentivize him to increase the budget, allowing them to afford better sets and effects, so he was effectively condemning them for things that were largely out of their control.

After the hiatus, *Doctor Who* returned with a revamped—albeit a shortened—season, featuring a singular plot arc encompassing several individual stories under the umbrella title of "Trial of a Time Lord," something that had not been done since 1978–1979 with the "Key to Time" arc. The results were mixed, with fairly consistent viewing numbers throughout, having a high of 5.6 million viewers and a low of 3.7 million viewers, but which were notably lower than the previous season that had a high of 8.9 million viewers and a low of 6 million viewers.[6] The biggest criticism of the season was levied at the overall story, which was a disjointed mess. This can largely be attributed to two things that occurred—the first was that veteran writer Robert Holmes, who was tasked with creating the opening and closing stories of the season, passed away before his work was complete, leaving other writers to finish what he had started, but who had no idea as to how he intended wrapping up the story. The second was that Saward repeatedly clashed with Nathan-Turner over the direction the overall story was going in, particularly the climax, and he handed in his notice, leaving Nathan-Turner to temporarily take over the role of script editor. The finished results speak for themselves, having not just the Doctor on trial, but the future of the show itself.

In the wake of this, Grade agreed that *Doctor Who* could return, but with one big caveat—that Colin Baker was replaced. Grade made no attempt then, or subsequently, to hide the fact that he thought Baker's performance was "God awful."[7] There was discontent behind the scenes as well, with BBC executives unhappy with Nathan-Turner, but unable to find anybody to replace him. Ironically, Nathan-Turner had been thinking about resigning, but he was instructed to stay for the survival of the show.

Casting for a new Doctor began, and Scottish actor Sylvester McCoy (1943–) was chosen to replace Baker. Baker was asked to return for one four-part story as a handover between the two Doctors, but he refused. In an interview with the *Sun* newspaper in 1987, Baker said of his being ousted, "It was such a shock. I'd fought so hard for the show, I was stunned. What I couldn't accept was the Grade didn't have the guts to tell me man-to-man. If I knew why I was sacked, then I would feel better about it all. But I got fobbed off with excuses about Grade thinking three years as Dr. Who was long enough."[8] He also went on to say, "Grade didn't want me to say I had been fired. My boss, Jonathan Powell, the head of Series and Serials, said that the BBC would stand by any statement I made. He strongly suggested to me that I should claim to be leaving for personal reasons. They actually wanted me to come back and do four more episodes, just so I could be killed off and fit in with their plans! I told them what they could do with their offer."

Baker has subsequently said that he regrets his decision not to have a proper ending for his Doctor, saying it was a selfish and emotive decision and one that let fans down. Still, as it stood, Sylvester McCoy had to film the regeneration scene, donning Baker's garish costume and wearing a ridiculous curly blond wig before lying face down on the ground, apparently mortally wounded. As his body is turned over, the regeneration sequence begins.

McCoy was a comedic actor who rose to prominence in experimental theater, and who excelled in physical comedy. Largely unknown to television viewers, he started off portraying the Doctor as a whimsical fool, playing to his strengths, but that was about to change.

Chapter 5

ANDREW CARTMEL

Nathan-Turner had brought in new script editor, Andrew Cartmel (1958–), whom he was very excited to work with. In his recollections, Nathan-Turner said, "He's a writer, relatively young—in his twenties—and I read an awful lot of his stuff which I thought was smashing. We then met, to find out if he'd be interested in finding out more about television as a script editor, and he leapt at it. If you're going to have a new script editor, you want to capitalise on him, and what was most exciting about Andrew was that we sat there and chatted about *Doctor Who* and a sparky conversation happened—there were things we agreed on, things we disagreed on, and things that sent us off on tangents, and that's the best kind of environment for a producer to work in."[9]

Cartmel had a strong "vision" for the Doctor, one that harkened back to the mysterious origins of the character, something that had largely been forgotten about. This "vision" has since been dubbed the "Cartmel Masterplan" by fans, although the term "masterplan" is a bit of an overstatement, being more of a loose assemblage of ideas that were yet to be fully fleshed out. Even Cartmel has acknowledged that a lot of the details would have been down to writers Marc Platt (1953–) and Ben Aaronovich (1964–). The gist of the vision was that the Doctor was actually a figure from the distant past of Gallifrey, from the time of Rassilon and Omega, and who had had a much greater hand in the shaping of Time Lord society than had been recognized. Consequently, the Doctor harbored a great many secrets.

Hints to this end were introduced throughout McCoy's stories. Aaronovich's 1988 story "Remembrance of the Daleks" features a slip of the tongue by the Doctor, implying his presence at the creation of the remote stellar manipulator known as the Hand of Omega, and also, in a scene where he is addressing Davros, he asserts that he is "far more than just another Time Lord" (this scene was edited out of the original BBC broadcast at the request of Nathan-Turner, but other regions around the world got to see it intact). The 1988 story "Silver Nemesis" sees Lady Peinforte (Fiona Walker) claiming to have knowledge of the Doctor's actions during the Dark Times of Gallifrey's distant past, reinforcing the notion that he is far older than he claims.

Following Cartmel's suggested direction, McCoy changed to playing the Doctor, still with an air of whimsy, but with a much darker edge, suggesting the former was used as a means to cover up the latter, and acting like he was playing a much larger game than the viewer was ever let in on. The Doctor was not the only one playing games though, as Grade repositioned *Doctor Who* to a Monday-evening slot, opposite the most-watched soap opera on rival channel Independent Television (ITV), *Coronation Street*, which had retained a massive and loyal following since its inception in 1960. In 1987, Grade left the BBC to take up the position of Chief Executive at Channel 4, but *Doctor Who* remained languishing in its poor time slot, facing off against its unconquerable soap opera rival.

TIME RUNS OUT

In the same year, BBC1 got a new controller, Jonathan Powell (1947–). He shared a hatred of *Doctor Who* with his predecessor, and he had nothing but contempt for Nathan-Turner. In 1989, Peter Cregeen (1940–), left ITV to become head of series at the BBC. Through no fault of its own, ratings for *Doctor Who* remained poor, due to its challenging time slot, and production budgets remained woefully inadequate, frequently resulting in unconvincing sets and props and special effects that were well behind the curve. Fans were increasingly positive about the stories, and the performances of McCoy and Sophie Aldred (as companion Ace), but the damage had been done.

At the time, according to Cregeen, *Doctor Who* was not *canceled* per se, just being given a *rest*. In November 1989, he told the *Radio Times*, "There are no plans to axe *Doctor Who*," adding, "There may be a little longer between this series and the next," although everybody on the show knew what such a declaration really meant—the writing was on the wall.

In 2019, Cartmel told *Radio Times* that *Doctor Who* was, "held universally in contempt by the powers-that-be," adding, "People ask me about the cancellation . . . we weren't really cancelled, it's just like ghosting your girlfriend, they just never phoned us back."[10]

The final story to be aired, 1989's "Survival," was to have featured an extended showdown between the Doctor and the Master (Anthony Ainley). Continuing Cartmel's plan of hinting that the Doctor was more than he appeared to be, it was to have featured a scene where the Master challenged both the Doctor's identity and his nature. Fearing, rightly, that this was the end, the scene was cut so as to go out on a more definitive climax.

After the end of the series, Nathan-Turner continued to be actively involved in the ongoing *Doctor Who* community, regularly appearing at fan conventions. Nathan-Turner was a long-term smoker and drinker, the latter of which developed into alcoholism, taking a toll on his health. He contracted an infection and succumbed to liver failure in the Royal Sussex County Hospital on May 1, 2002, at the age of fifty-four.

In 2013, Richard Marson, a writer, television producer, and director (and a man who is no stranger to controversy himself) released a biography of Nathan-Turner.[11] In the book, he alleges that Nathan-Turner, a man who was openly gay, and his long-term partner, Gary Downie (1940–2006), exhibited sexually predatory behavior toward male teenage fans at conventions, and that he himself was on the receiving end of such unwanted advances.

Chapter 6

A Return

Figure 6 The Ninth Doctor. BBC / Photofest © BBC

In 1996, as part of a collaboration between Universal Studios and BBC Worldwide, a *Doctor Who* television movie was released. It was intended to be a reboot, breathing new life into the defunct franchise and kickstarting the opportunity for new stories to be made. Sadly, it failed to hit the mark with audiences, and the hopes of everybody who genuinely wanted to see it return for good were at their lowest ebb. Few television shows get a second chance, and having blown it, it seemed unlikely it would get another opportunity.

In 1997, Mal Young (1957–), took up the post of controller of continuing drama series at the BBC. He had expressed an interest in reviving *Doctor Who* and found support from then controller of BBC One (a rebrand of the older BBC1), Peter Salmon (1956–). Russell T. Davies (1963–), a screenwriter and television producer, had been petitioning for ages for the show to be revived, and his name invariably became linked with *Doctor Who*, bringing him to the attention of Young's department. A meeting was arranged, and discussions were held, but ultimately nothing came of it because BBC Worldwide still retained the rights to the franchise and they had tentative plans for another *Doctor Who* movie.

In 2000, Salmon took up the post of Director of BBC Sport, leaving the position of controller of BBC One open. Lorraine Heggessey (1956–) became BBC One's first female controller, and she was just as enthusiastic about a potential return of *Doctor Who* as her predecessor. This was an opinion that was echoed by Jane Tranter (1963–), the BBC's head of drama, but BBC Worldwide still stood in the way of this happening. Heggessey spoke with them, telling them that she wanted *Doctor Who* to return to BBC One, but they kept insisting that they were going to make a movie.

There were ways to bring *Doctor Who* back to fans, just not official ways through BBC One, as Heggessey wanted. In July 2001, on the BBCi website (which was originally called BBC Online, and which has subsequently reverted to that branding), a webcast *Doctor Who* drama was released, written by Dan Friedman under the pseudonym "Colin Meek." It was essentially an audio drama accompanied by limited animated visuals. Although it featured the voices of several cast members reprising their roles—Sylvester McCoy as the Seventh Doctor, Sophie Aldred as Ace, and Nicholas Courtney as Brigadier Lethbridge-Stewart—the story deviates from canonical lore and is not considered official.

It was, however, successful enough to inspire the making of further *Doctor Who* webcasts, and a second, titled "Real Time" was released in December 2002. Written by Gary Russell (1963–) former editor of *Doctor Who Magazine*, and coproduced with Big Finish Productions, it featured Colin Baker reprising his role as the Sixth Doctor. Like the story before it, this too falls outside of canon.

This was followed in May 2003 by a webcast of the unfinished *Doctor Who* story from Tom Baker's era, "Shada" (it was intended to be the final story of the 1979–1980 season seventeen but was never completed due to industrial action which was happening at the BBC at the time). The premise of the story was dusted down and overhauled, featuring Paul McGann's Eighth Doctor instead of Tom Baker's Fourth Doctor, and with Lalla Ward and John Leeson reprising their roles as Romana and K9.

In July 2003, the BBC announced another animated *Doctor Who* special, but this one was different. Written by Paul Cornell (1967–), it was intended to be a fortieth-anniversary story, meaning it should be regarded as canonical. With a planned November release, and with no sign of *Doctor Who* making a return to BBC One, BBCi announced that Richard E. Grant (1957–), was to play the Ninth Doctor in "Scream of the Shalka." Grant had previously had a brief, albeit quite unofficial, stint at the Doctor in the Comic Relief charity special, *Doctor Who and the Curse of Fatal Death* in 1999, written by Steven Moffat (1961–). The story also featured Derek Jacobi (1938–) in the role of the Master, four years before he would once again find himself playing the same role in the revived *Doctor Who* series (the 2007 story "Utopia").

While this was going on, Heggessey was further incentivized to move forward with her plans to bring *Doctor Who* back to BBC One. Helen O'Rahilly, deputy controller of BBC One, and a massive fan of *Doctor Who*, kept a model Dalek on her desk, one that could be made to utter several different phrases, such as the famous, "Exterminate!" Whenever Heggessey would come into the office, O'Rahilly would activate it, making the Dalek talk. This was intended to get under Heggessey's skin, and it worked, motivating her to instruct O'Rahilly to organize a meeting to see what could be done.

In her time as controller of BBC One, Hennessey had received several proposals for a revived *Doctor Who*. One had come from Dan Freedman, the writer, director, and producer of the webcast story "Death Comes to Time." Another proposal was submitted by Mark Gatiss (1966–), in collaboration with screenwriter Gareth Roberts (1968–) and the editor of *Doctor Who* Magazine, Clayton Hickman (1977–). Screenwriter Matthew Graham (1968–), who would go on to cocreate and cowrite for another BBC time-traveling drama, *Life on Mars*, also put forward a pitch.

By September 2003, Heggessey had managed to resolve her issues with BBC Worldwide, pushing ahead with her goal of bringing *Doctor Who* back to its traditional home on BBC One, and its traditional slot of Saturday evenings. Once more Russell T. Davies's name came up, and Heggessey and Tranter approached him with an offer, which he eagerly accepted.

Julie Gardner (1969–), head of drama for BBC Wales, was brought on board, and she worked with Davies to figure out the details. Davies had been given two stipulations about the series—that the episodes were to be forty-five minutes long, and they wanted six or eight of them. Gardner worked out budgets, including the cost of building the Tardis set, and figured out that spreading the cost over more episodes, say twelve or thirteen, would be more cost-effective, so she asked if they could do thirteen episodes instead, and that was quickly agreed upon.

In that same month it was officially announced that *Doctor Who* would be returning, set to air in 2005. Davies was to be the executive producer and chief writer, and it would be produced by Phil Collinson (1970–) as part of BBC Wales. Because of this change in circumstances, a planned sequel to "Scream of the Shalka" was shelved, but there was media speculation as to whether Richard E. Grant would be continuing as the Ninth Doctor or if the new series would skip to a Tenth Doctor. Clarification came in April 2004 when, in an interview with *Doctor Who Magazine*, Davies announced that the next—and *ninth*—Doctor would be played by Christopher Eccleston (completely bypassing any canonical legitimacy of Richard E. Grant's Doctor, who would then be referred to simply as the "Shalka Doctor"). When Davies was asked about this move by *Doctor Who Magazine*, he said, "I thought he was terrible. I thought he took the money and ran, to be honest. It was a lazy performance. He was never on our list to play the Doctor." The "Shalka Doctor" would have one last outing in a short story published on BBC Online as part of a feature focusing on vampires, titled, "The Feast of the Stone," written by Cavan Scott and Mark Wright.

Davies's plan for the revival of *Doctor Who* was simple, be faithful to the show's past, but not be shackled by it. Consequently, the Tardis and the sonic screwdriver returned, but some of the more lore-heavy elements, such as Gallifrey and the Time Lords, were brushed aside. As it turns out, the way this was handled was quite brilliant, introducing the concept of the Time War, a fierce battle that had raged across all of space and time, and which had ended up with the annihilation of both species, save for the Doctor, now the last of his kind. Of course, it was inevitable that the Daleks would find a way to return, for what would *Doctor Who* be without its most enduring and popular enemy? The revival also reset the clock, designating it season *1*, a controversial choice among some fans, but which made a lot of sense, drawing a line under the past and marking this as a fresh start—classic-era Who and modern-era Who (or "New Who" if you prefer).

It is no secret that Davies is a huge fan of the work of Joss Whedon (1964–) and has mentioned on several occasions that he credits two of his series, *Buffy the Vampire Slayer* (1997–2001) and *Angel* (1999–2004), as major inspirations for his reimagining of the format of *Doctor Who* (and later its spin-off, *Torchwood*).

With a distinguished actor like Eccleston (1964–) as the Doctor, there was a feeling that he would add some welcome gravitas to the character. What was less clear was how well the casting of Billie Piper (1982–) would go down as new companion, Rose Tyler. In the late 1990s and early 2000s, Piper was a pop star, being the youngest female singer to enter the UK singles chart at number one when she was fifteen years old. Would this be a repeat of the kind of stunt casting that was common in the latter years of Classic Who? As it turns out, not at all. Piper proved herself to be extremely capable in the role, winning the most popular actress category in both the 2005 and 2006 British National Television Awards, as well as BBC News naming her as one of the Faces of the Year in 2005.

A copy of the first episode was leaked online three weeks before it officially premiered. This was done by an employee of an undisclosed company that had ties to the Canadian Broadcasting Company and, unsurprisingly, they were fired. While it was a prerelease version that was leaked, the lack of any watermarks or time stamp codes led some to speculate that the leak was secretly sanctioned by the BBC to generate media hype, of which there was a lot.

The first episode, "Rose," was broadcast on BBC One on March 26, 2005, to critical acclaim, and a show that had once been derided by the BBC was suddenly propelled to being one of its flagship properties, with a peak audience of 10.5 million viewers.[1] On March 30, the BBC confirmed that a second series had been commissioned, but on the same day, they also released a statement to the effect that Eccleston would not be returning after season one.

Eccleston was livid that the BBC had released such a statement without clearing it with him first. He also felt that the tone of the statement was incorrect, implying that he was unable to keep up with the pace of the work. Being a consummate professional, he did not make a thing of it at the time, but he has subsequently spoken about his experiences on the series. In an interview with *Radio Times* in 2021, Eccleston said, "I left because my relationship with Russell T. Davies, Julie Gardner and Phil Collinson completely broke down during the shooting of the first series."[2] He added, "I agreed with Russell that I would go, quietly and respectfully, and I would look after the show publicity-wise, in terms of publicising it. And then, without saying anything to me, they announced that I was leaving. They didn't tell me they were going to do that. I was walking down the street, and suddenly I got quite a lot of aggression. And more importantly . . . they created a quote, and they attributed it to me, which said I was tired."

At the For the Love of Sci-Fi convention in 2023, held in Manchester, England, Eccleston and Piper attended a panel. Eccleston was asked how he felt being associated with the character, to which he replied, "I love being associated with the character, just don't like being associated with those people and the politics that went on in the first series. The first series was a mess, and it wasn't to do with me or Billie, it was to do with the people who were supposed to make it, and it was a mess."

In response to Eccleston's criticisms, Davies talked about his "duty of care" to Eccleston, "He's free to say and explore whatever he wants—that's fine. This duty of care involves respecting him and listening to him at all times."[3] On Eccleston's portrayal of the Doctor, Davies said, "It's a magnificent, never-to-be forgotten Doctor, and it was an honour to work with an actor delivering a performance like that." He added, "I think the darkness is off the scale with him—when the Doctor's angry, it's spectacular."

At the Wizard World convention in Madison, Wisconsin, in 2016, David Tennant (born David John McDonald) told the audience how he had ended up being offered the role of the next Doctor, "Russell asked me round to his house in Manchester, which is where we'd been filming *Casanova*, because he had a couple of rough cuts of the first series of *Doctor Who* and he knew that I was a bit of a fan, and that I might want to see how the show was looking. So, he invited me over and he showed me a rough cut of 'Rose,' the first episode, and I was very excited, and then he showed me a *really* rough cut of 'Dalek,' the first Dalek episode—without any special effects or anything—but you could tell it was all very exciting. And then they told me that they wanted me to take over. This was before the show was even transmitted, so that was the slightly weird bit. Would you take over, and can you film a scene for the end of episode 13, kind of in about 10 minutes. It was a bit like that. Which was odd, because the show hadn't been out yet, so you were thinking, what if I film a little bit for the end of episode 13, the show doesn't ever go again, and I'm the person who played the Doctor for 35 seconds?"

Tennant did not get to play the Doctor for only thirty-five seconds. In fact, he is second only to Tom Baker in terms of actors who played the Doctor the longest. He has frequently been at the top, or near the top, of polls conducted asking viewers who their favorite Doctor is. And a fan he truly is, telling *Radio Times* in August 2023 that his earliest television memory is John Pertwee's Doctor regenerating into Tom Baker's Doctor (from the final episode of "Planet of the Spiders" in 1974), "It's weirdly specific, especially considering the things that have happened in my life since. I remember thinking, that man just turned into another man. That's wild."[4]

If there is one criticism that could be made of Davies's *Doctor Who* stories, it is that they tend to escalate to the point of going completely over the top—from London being in danger, to the world, to the universe, to all of time itself—there seems to be a lack of control, a recognition of when to dial things back a bit, rather than giving in to an impulsive need to scale up the danger to be bigger and more deadly each time. Nevertheless, all *Doctor Who* fans, from the ardent Whovians like myself to the more casual watchers, owe Davies a debt of thanks for helping to bring the show back to television.

A Return 65

In May 2008 it was announced that Davies would be stepping down as he wanted to do other things. Tennant decided it was also time for him to move on, saying, "I have loved every day of it. It would be very easy to cling on to the Tardis console forever and I fear that if I don't take a deep breath and make the decision to move on now, then I simply never will. You would be prising the Tardis key out of my cold dead hand. This show has been so special to me, I don't want to outstay my welcome."[5]

It was announced that screenwriter and producer Steven Moffat (1961–), having written some of the best stories during Davies's time ("The Empty Child"/"The Doctor Dances," 2005; "The Girl in the Fireplace," 2006; "Blink," 2007; and "Silence in the Library"/"Forest of the Dead," 2008), would be taking over as executive producer and lead writer. Matt Smith (1982–) was cast as the Doctor and at twenty-six years old, Smith would be the youngest person to portray him. Although Moffat had been anticipating casting someone older, the strength and quality of Smith's audition seriously impressed him.

With strong writing talent and an unbridled imagination, Moffat delivered smart and exciting stories. He became known for crafting long, complex narratives, and many callbacks to the history of the show. The latter might have been something that delighted long-term fans, but it made the show a bit more impenetrable for newer viewers, especially the younger ones. When interviewed by the *Guardian* newspaper in 2012, Moffat talked about *Doctor Who*, and *Sherlock* (an up-to-date retelling of Sir Arthur Conan Doyle's Sherlock Holmes stories, cocreated and cowritten with Mark Gatiss), "They are very clever shows, but they also fetishise cleverness. Cleverness is the superpower. So I get irritated when people say on Twitter: 'It's too complicated. I'm not following it.' Well, you could try putting your phone down and watching it."[6]

On June 1, 2013, it was announced that Matt Smith would be turning in the keys to the Tardis after that year's Christmas special. On August 4, 2013, the BBC held a special publicity event where it was revealed that Peter Capaldi (1958–) would be the next Doctor. Prior to that, Capaldi was best known for playing the foulmouthed government spin doctor Malcolm Tucker in Armando Iannucci's masterful political satire *The Thick of It*. Like Tennant before him, Capaldi was a lifelong *Doctor Who* fan and as a teenager he used to send letters to the production team, as well as the *Radio Times* and the Official *Doctor Who* Fan Club.

In January 2016, Moffat announced that he was stepping down as executive producer for *Doctor Who* and that Chris Chibnall (1970–) would be the next executive producer and lead writer. On January 30, 2017, Capaldi confirmed that he was leaving *Doctor Who*, coinciding with Moffat's departure. In May 2017, in an interview with Newsweek, Capaldi said of Moffat,

"He's an astonishing talent, but he's a human being, and I don't think he can continue working at this rate." He added, "He loves this job so I think it's very, very difficult for him to leave. But I think he has to, otherwise he might have a heart attack."[7]

Chibnall, who had written several episodes of *Doctor Who* ("42," 2007; "The Hungry Earth"/"Cold Blood," 2010; "Dinosaurs on a Spaceship," 2012; and "The Power of Three," 2012), and who had also been head writer for the first two series of spin-off *Torchwood*, also professed to being a lifelong fan. On July 16, 2017, it was revealed that Jodie Whittaker (1982–) would be the show's first-ever female Doctor.

On July 29, 2021, the BBC announced that Chibnall would be stepping down, along with Whittaker. On September 24, the BBC announced that Chibnall's replacement would be none other than Russell T. Davies, making a surprise return. Modern-era *Doctor Who* had, it seems, come full circle.

PART II

CHARACTERS AND SPECIES

Chapter 7

The Time Lords

Figure 7 The Master in ceremonial Time Lord robes. Fox Television Network / Photofest © Fox Television Network, photographed by Joseph Lederer

The plant Gallifrey in the constellation of Kasterborous (coordinates: ten-zero-eleven-zero-zero by zero-two from galactic centre), is the home of the Gallifreyan people, more commonly known as the Time Lords. The history of Gallifrey is a long and fascinating one, stretching back billions of years, and like much of history, is full of conflicting information.

The planet Gallifrey itself has a yellowish-orangey appearance when seen from space. It is surrounded by an impenetrable barrier known as a quantum force field, which prevents unauthorized planetfall by ships, and a transduction barrier, which prevents teleporter incursions. Given that they are one of the most powerful species in the galaxy, and masters of time, it is unsurprising that they take security very seriously.

THE CAPITOL AND ARCADIA

Most of Gallifrey is undeveloped, a wilderness of snowcapped mountains and vast plains of red grass stretching off as far as the eye can see. The Time Lords have two cities in which the majority of them dwell, the larger of the two being their principal city, the Capitol (comprising of large shining towers protected by a mighty glass dome), and the smaller city being Arcadia. There is no obligation to live within either city, with the Third Doctor (Jon Pertwee) once recounting in the 1972 story "The Time Monster," "When I was a boy, we used to live in a house that was perched halfway up the top of a mountain."[1] Both Susan (Carole Anne Ford) and the Tenth Doctor (David Tennant) have mentioned burnt-orange skies and silver-leafed trees. In the 2007 story "Gridlock" he explains, "The second sun would rise in the south and the mountains would shine. The leaves on the trees were silver. When they caught the light every morning, it would look like a forest on fire."[2] In the 2007 two-part story "The Sound of Drums"/"Last of the Time Lords," he gave a further recollection, "It was beautiful. We used to call it the Shining World of the Seven Systems, and on the Continent of Wild Endeavour, in the Mountains of Solace and Solitude, there stood the citadel of the Time Lords, the oldest and most mighty race in the universe, looking down on the galaxies below, sworn never to interfere, only to watch."[3] (Although noninterference was an official policy, the Time Lords had a Celestial Intervention Agency, a covert group that could violate that rule under the most drastic of circumstances.)

RASSILON

One of the most revered characters in their civilization is Rassilon, a member of the High Council and the founder of Time Lord society. He devised a plan that would allow them to suspend time around a dying star, just as it is forming a black hole, letting them harness the energy of that permanent state of decay. It was captured in a crystalline structure known as the "Eye of Harmony" which was then buried under the floor of the panopticon in their principal city, the Capitol. Such a process required fine-tuning with an endlessly dynamic equation that is balanced against the mass of the planet. Any attempt to remove it would result in the destruction of Gallifrey (as demonstrated when the Master attempted to do so in the 1976 story "The Deadly Assassin"). Rassilon utilized this power to make them lords of time, and he was rewarded with the title of Lord High President.

Although generally venerated among his people, there are contradictory opinions of Rassilon. While many saw him as their savior, some regarded him as a tyrant. He was the holder of the Black Scrolls of Rassilon, containing the only source of terrible and forbidden knowledge from a barbaric period of Gallifrey's past known as the Dark Time (when they used to kidnap other species and make them fight to the bitter end in an arena called the Death Zone, located out in the wastelands of Gallifrey). Although it is thought that Rassilon put a stop to these gladiatorial games, they might have ended because he is rumored to have been deposed around the same time.

He is also alleged to have unlocked the key to immortality, coded within the Ring of Rassilon. His tomb sits within the Death Zone, and those who seek immortality must venture there, playing the Game of Rassion to find and claim the ring. However, it is a trap, and those who seek the ring, and the immortality it brings, are imprisoned in stone, conscious and aware for all eternity. Whether or not this is a benevolent move by Rassilon, believing that those who desire immortality are too dangerous to wield it, or whether he merely wishes to jealously guard this knowledge against aspirants, is unclear, but it begs the question—if he really knew the secret of immortality, what need would he have for a tomb? It seems more likely that he was biding his time, letting the controversies of his legacy fade from memory, and waiting until his people needed him once again (something that does indeed come to pass with the advent of the Time War).

Some of the most important artifacts in Time Lord society are eponymously linked to him (just like the ring and scrolls that we have already mentioned). They are the Sash of Rassilon (protecting the wearer from the immense gravitational forces of the Eye of Harmony), the Crown of Rassilon (providing a mental link between the wearer and the Matrix), the Rod of Rassilon (also known as the Great Key of Rassilon, permitting the bearer to have access to the containment controls of the Eye of Harmony), and the Coronet of Rassilon (allowing the wearer to amplify their will to overcome and dominate others). Other things named after him include the Harp of Rassilon (which unlocks a secret passage to a hidden chamber containing the controls of the Time Scoop, the device that was used to abduct species and deposit them in the Death Zone), and the Seal of Rassilon, the renowned symbol of Time Lord society.

THE MATRIX

The Matrix, as mentioned earlier, is one of the Time Lords' finest achievements. It is a vast supercomputer which is the repository of all Time Lord knowledge. When a Time Lord reaches their last regeneration and is close to death, their consciousness is uploaded and becomes a part of the Matrix, storing all their memories and experiences. While the Matrix can be interfaced with, where the person interacting with it appears within a virtual environment, its physical hardware is located deep within the Cloisters. It is protected by Cloister Wraiths, phantomlike apparitions of deceased and uploaded Time Lords, who act as a sort of firewall, protecting the Matrix from physical intruders. The Cloisters are also where the Cloister Bells are located, which ring out when Gallifrey is in great peril.

OMEGA

Omega, another member of the High Council, and their most gifted stellar engineer, worked with Rassion to bring his plan to capture the energy from a black hole to fruition. He created a remote stellar manipulator, called the "Hand of Omega," that could be used to control the reactions inside of a star. When conducting his experiment, he was believed to have been killed when the star went supernova and collapsed into a black hole. But he didn't die, having passed through the event horizon into an antimatter universe where he was trapped. He survived through the strength of his will, which also allowed him to shape the antimatter universe to his whims. His lengthy solitude saw him slowly descend into madness and he built up quite a resentment toward the Time Lords, believing that he had been abandoned by them. In the 1972–1973 story "The Three Doctors," Omega (Stephen Thorne) finds a way of extending his influence out into the normal universe, intending to take retribution against the Time Lords. Omega tries to capture the Doctor and have him take his place maintaining the antimatter universe while he escapes, but two things impede his plan. The first is that the Time Lords break their own First Law of Time to allow all three regenerations of the Doctor (William Hartnell, Patrick Troughton, and Jon Pertwee) to work together against him. The second is that Omega has been in the antimatter universe for so long that he hadn't realized his physical self had simply faded away to nothing, leaving only his force of will and his hatred of the Time Lords remaining.

Omega attempted one more return to the normal universe in the 1983 story "Arc of Infinity." A traitorous Time Lord, Councillor Hedin (Michael Gough), steals the biodata of the Fifth Doctor (Peter Davison) and gives it to Omega (Ian Collier) in the hope of restoring him to his rightful place among the Time Lords. Omega uses it to try to bond with the Doctor, perfectly replicating his body and forsaking the antimatter form that he has been using. This is only partially successful, leaving him in an unstable state, slowly reverting from matter to antimatter. When Omega realizes this, he would rather accelerate the process, destroying himself and the Earth, rather than having to return to the antimatter universe. The Doctor is forced to use a matter converter weapon on him, evidently destroying him.

In the Time Vaults of Gallifrey, there is a section named after him, the Omega Arsenal, where all their forbidden weapons are locked away. This includes "The Moment" (also referred to as the Galaxy Eater), the final work of the ancients of Gallifrey. It is a weapon so powerful its operating system became sentient and, according to legend, it developed a conscience. As the Time Lord known as the General (Ken Bones) says to fellow Time Lord Androgar (Peter De Jersey), in the 2013 Sixtieth Anniversary Special, "The Day of the Doctor," "How do you use a weapon of ultimate mass destruction when it can stand in judgment on you?"

THE TIME LORDS

While it is a truism that all Time Lords are Gallifreyan, not all Gallifreyans are Time Lords, that title being conferred on those who pass through the academy. Children are taken from their families at the age of eight to attend the academy, which organizes the students into chapters, of which only a few are canonically known. These are the Arcalian Chapter, with their green robes, the Patrex Chapter, with their heliotrope robes, and the Prydonian Chapter, with their scarlet and orange robes (to which both Rassilon and the Doctor belonged). Not all Gallifreyans submit to this way of life, with a subset of them, known as "Outsiders," preferring to live a simpler, more primitive existence out in the wilderness.

RENEGADE TIME LORDS: THE TIME MEDDLER

It is also true that while the Time Lords have adopted a strict policy of non-interference, renegade Time Lords, although uncommon, are not unheard of.

Some are driven by different tenets, some by misplaced loyalties, and others by selfish ambitions.

The first time we encounter one of these is in the 1965 story "The Time Meddler." In England in 1066, a Monk (Peter Butterworth), with access to technology far beyond the era, is plotting to destroy an incoming Viking fleet, thereby averting the Battle of Stamford Bridge, leaving Saxon soldiers fresh and free to defeat William of Normandy at the Battle of Hastings. When the First Doctor (William Hartnell) visits a nearby monastery, he is lured in by the Monk and discovers the sounds of chanting are coming from a recording being played back by a gramophone. When he stops the gramophone, the Monk traps him, but the Doctor finds a way to escape.

When the Doctor's companions, Stephen (Peter Purves) and Vicki (Maureen O'Brien), go looking for him, they arrive at the monastery, and although the Monk claims not to have seen the Doctor, Steven tricks him into revealing that he had. They wait until after dark and sneak into the monastery. While searching the crypt, they find a power cable that extends from a sarcophagus. Finding a way in, they enter it, discovering that it is really a Tardis in disguise. They locate the Monk's private collection of artifacts from all the different eras he has visited. Vicki finds evidence that he tried to influence Leonardo da Vinci while Steven uncovers the neutron bombs that the Monk plans to bombard the Viking fleet with.

The Doctor confronts the Monk and learns of his plans to accelerate mankind's development through his meddling. When the Doctor forces him to take him to his Tardis, they find Steven and Vicki there. The Monk gives them the slip, but by that time his plans have begun to unravel. The Doctor sabotages the Monk's Tardis by removing the dimensional controller, leaving the Monk a letter to say that he has taken precautions to stop his time meddling. When the Monk returns, intending to make himself scarce, he finds that his Tardis interior has shrunk down to a size where it is no longer usable.

RENEGADE TIME LORDS: THE WAR CHIEF

We first learn of the term "Time Lords" in the 1969 story "The War Games." The Second Doctor (Patrick Troughton) reluctantly reaches out to his people when he discovers that another renegade Time Lord, known as the War Chief (Edward Brayshaw), has colluded with an aggressive race of aliens, led by the War Lord (Philip Madoc). They have been kidnapping soldiers from various eras of Earth's past, hypnotizing them, and putting them into simulated war zones where they continue their bloody conflicts, unaware that they are no longer on Earth. The goal of this endeavor is to take the survivors, the ones who have proven themselves worthy in the brutal art of warfare, and to form an army out of them that the War Lord will use to conquer the galaxy.

The War Chief has been providing the War Lord access to Time Lord technology, but without the direct knowledge and resources of his own people to hand, such technology turns out to be a second-rate copy. This can be seen with the Space and Inter-time Dimensional Robot All-purpose Transporter (SIDRAT), a Tardis-like remote-controlled space-time vehicle used to kidnap soldiers and transport them to their replicated zones of conflict. They are to become instrumental in carrying the War Lord's new army around in his pursuit of galactic conquest.

When the Doctor points out that the SIDRAT machines are fundamentally flawed, and only have a limited lifespan, the War Chief confesses that he knows this, and implores the Doctor to join him in seizing control. When this betrayal is discovered, the War Lord has the War Chief killed (for reasons unknown, the War Chief does not appear to regenerate). The Doctor reluctantly admits that he needs the help of the Time Lords to return all the kidnapped soldiers to where and when they came from, even at the risk of his own capture.

When the Time Lords appear, they arrest the War Lord and prevent the Doctor and his companions from escaping. The War Lord is put on trial, and a list of his heinous crimes is recounted. When asked if he has anything to say in his defense, he declines, remaining steadfastly silent, so the Time Lords torture him to loosen his tongue. When he does speak, he refuses to recognize the authority of the court, stating that the humans would have killed themselves anyway. Some of the War Lord's comrades use a SIDRAT to follow him and during their attempt to free him, they murder two Time Lords. When the doctor prevents their escape, the Time Lords capture them and deliver their final verdict. A force field is erected around the War Lord's home planet so that his warlike race will remain prisoners forever. As for the War Lord and his murderous associates, they are to be dematerialized, with one of the Time Lords indicating that it will be as though they never existed.

RENEGADE TIME LORDS: MORBIUS

In the 1976 story "The Brain of Morbius," the Time Lords redirect the Fourth Doctor (Tom Baker) to a strange planet for reasons unknown. There he and Sarah Jane Smith (Lis Sladen) discover a collection of crashed spaceships. When they find the headless body of an insectoid being, the Doctor realizes that it was killed *after* it had crashed, which means it was murdered. The planet is Karn, home to a cult known as the Sisterhood of Karn, where the sacred Flame of Life is used to create the Elixir of Eternal Life. In the past, they had shared the Elixir with the High Council of Time Lords, but now the flame is waning, and no Elixir has been produced for over a year. When the Doctor arrives, the Sisterhood is suspicious, wondering if the Time Lords have been sent to claim what little reserves there are.

The Doctor and Sarah Jane make their way to a nearby castle where they meet Doctor Mehendri Solon (Philip Madoc), a brilliant neurosurgeon, an expert in microsurgical techniques for tissue transplant, and his servant, Condo (Colin Fay). Solon invites them to dine with him, but he has laced the wine with sedatives, and the Doctor recognizes a sculpted bust of Morbius, a renegade who once led the High Council of the Time Lords, describing him as, "one of the most despicable, criminally minded wretches who ever lived," before he passes out. Solon intends on using the Doctor's head to house the brain of Morbius, which he has kept alive, looking for a suitable transplant subject.

Solon comes to learn that the Doctor has a secondary cardiovascular system, recognizing him as a Time Lord, noting that there will be no problems with tissue rejection. Condo is afraid of the Time Lords, but Solon dismisses his fears, saying, "The Time Lords are spineless parasites. Morbius offered them greatness once, but he was betrayed and rejected. They'll pay for that mistake, Condo. These pacifist degenerates will be the first to feel the power of his revenge."[4] Solon and Condo leave the laboratory, but having teleported the Tardis to them, the Sisterhood does the same to the unconscious Doctor. Solon returns, quickly grasping that the Doctor has been taken by Maren (Cynthia Grenville), leader of the Sisterhood.

When the Doctor regains consciousness, he finds himself among the Sisterhood. They are still suspicious of him. The Doctor remembers seeing the statue of Morbius, comprehending that their minds briefly made contact before he passed out. The Sisterhood is dismissive of this, saying that Morbius is dead, asserting that Morbius was executed by the Time Lords for leading a rebellion. His body placed was in a dispersal chamber and atomized to the nine corners of the universe for overrunning Karn with his followers, trying to seize control of the Elixir and immortality.

The Sisterhood begins a ritual to sacrifice the Doctor in the hope of reigniting the flame but is interrupted by Solon, who beseeches them to spare him, or at the very least, his head. They will have none of it, knowing of Solon's unnatural experiments. While they are distracted, the Doctor escapes. Morbius's brain communicates with Solon, using a speech synthesizer, telling him that he grows weary of such slow progress, urging Solon to hurry up and complete his work.

Solon tricks the Doctor into returning to the Sisterhood, believing he has struck a deal with them for his head. The Doctor arrives but surprises them, cutting through their mumbo jumbo and rectifying the problem of the waning

Flame of Life. Solon and Morbius recognize that their plan has failed and knowing that the combined wrath of the Time Lords and the Sisterhood of Karn now face them, Morbius insists that Solon complete his work using an artificial brain casing on the monstrous body he has already created. During an argument, Condo knocks over the container containing Morbius's brain and a furious Solon shoots him. Concerned about the damage that Morbius's brain has sustained, Solon urgently proceeds with the transplant. Morbius is ambulant once more, but when he catches sight of himself in a mirror, comprehending what a truly horrific form he is now in, he goes mad, turning on Solon.

Telling the Doctor that Morbius's brain is only operating on a basic level, and that he had not fully completed the operation, he implores the Doctor to help find him so he can restore his higher brain functions. The Doctor agrees but with the intention of stopping Morbius and returning his brain to the Time Lords. They find and immobilize Morbius, but not before he has murdered one of the Sisterhood and the sisters march on Solon's castle. The Doctor is deceived by Solon, who restores all of Morbius's brain functions, but dies when he inhales cyanide gas that the Doctor releases into the venting system.

The Doctor challenges Morbius to a mind-bending challenge—a combat of wills—and while Morbius is defeated, the Doctor is badly hurt and dying. The Sisterhood arrive, brandishing flaming torches, and force the fleeing Morbius off the edge of a cliff, where he plunges to his death. In gratitude for helping to vanquish the evil of Morbius, Maren gives the Doctor the last of the Elixir, saving him.

RENEGADE TIME LORDS: CHANCELLOR GOTH

Morbius was not the only high-ranking Time Lord to fall from grace. In the 1976 story "The Deadly Assassin," Chancellor Goth (Bernard Horsfall) becomes a pawn of the Master, trying to kill the Doctor (Tom Baker) within the mental landscape of the Matrix. The Master, in turn, leaves Goth dying when he fails in his task. It is in the same story that we first meet Cardinal Borusa (Angus Mackay), who was the Doctor's tutor at the academy. He alters records to make it look like Goth died a hero, rather than let the scandal of his betrayal get out.

RENEGADE TIME LORDS: COUNCILLOR HEDIN

Borusa (John Arnatt) made a return in the 1978 story "The Invasion of Time," helping the Doctor to defeat the Sontaran invasion of Gallifrey. We see a promoted President Borusa (Leonard Sachs) in the 1983 story "Arc of Infinity," in which he is framed and the rest of the High Council are manipulated by the real villain, Councillor Hedin (Michael Gough), trying to bring about the return of Omega.

RENEGADE TIME LORDS: PRESIDENT BORUSA

President Borusa (Philip Latham) appears for the last time in the 1983 story "The Five Doctors." Borusa's ambition and ego have finally got the better of him, and he is seeking immortality and the title of President Eternal, intending to rule over the Time Lords forever.

RENEGADE TIME LORDS: SALYAVIN

The prison planet of Shada was where the Time Lords imprisoned the most feared criminals, including Salyavin, a Time Lord whose mental aptitude to read and manipulate minds was considered a dangerous aberration. In the 1979 story "Shada," a student, Chris Parsons (Daniel Hill), of St. Cedd's College in Cambridge, visits doddering old Professor Chronotis (Denis Carey). He reminds the professor that they had met at a faculty party and the professor offered to lend him some books on carbon dating. Chronotis turns out to be a Time Lord who sends a signal to the Fourth Doctor (Tom Baker), asking him to come as soon as possible. Being rather forgetful at times, Chronotis initially has no recollection of sending such a request, but then remembers that he wanted the Doctor to return a book that he "borrowed" from Gallifrey. The Doctor agrees, knowing that Gallifreyan books can be dangerous in the wrong hands. When Chronotis is asked what the title of the book is, he replies, "The Worshipful and Ancient Law of Gallifrey." The Doctor is shocked, saying the book is an ancient artifact from the panopticon archives, dating back to the times of Rassilon, and potentially imbued with powers and secrets that none of them fully understand. Unable to locate the book, Chronotis realizes that Chris Parsons must have borrowed it by accident.

Not only has Parsons inadvertently taken the book, but he has come to learn that there is something strange about it. It is written in a language he does not understand, and while the pages look and smell like paper, they do not behave like paper. As far as he is concerned, it appears to have a nonatomic structure, which he deems impossible. When he tries to x-ray the book, the X-ray machine blows up. He is convinced that it is of extraterrestrial origins, and he shares this knowledge with Clare Keightley (Victoria Burgoyne).

But Parsons is not the only person interested in the book. Skagra (Christopher Neame) is a mad research scientist who wants to find and exploit the powers of Salyavin to unite all life into a singular universal mind, where individuality no longer has a place. The book has been written in a code that Skagra is unable to decipher, and he needs the Doctor to help him do so.

Keightley goes in search of Chronotis, and while looking through his room, she finds hidden equipment, which she activates. Chronotis's room is a Tardis in disguise! She passes out, but when she regains consciousness, she finds Chronotis, who admits that it is an ancient Tardis that he recovered from a scrap heap since he is not allowed to have one, although he does not explicitly state why. He confesses that the book is really the key to Shada, a dirty secret of the Time Lords that they have been induced to forget about. He figures out that Skagra is after Salyavin and resolves to stop him. He works with Keightley to repair his Tardis, but being human, her skills in such matters are inadequate, so Chronotis mentally projects the information she needs into her mind.

Skagra works out that the location of Shada is not just a case of where, but also when, and because time runs backward over the book, by flicking through it in reverse while near a Tardis console, it will lead them to the point in time where Shada is hidden. Having done so, he begins to release the prisoners from their cryogenic cells, but Chronotis follows him in his repaired Tardis. Skagra finds Salyavin's cell, but when he opens it, he finds it empty, and Chronotis is revealed to be Salyavin.

Thanks to the Doctor, Skagra's plans are unraveled, and though he escapes, he finds himself imprisoned on his own vessel. The Doctor acknowledges that Salyavin was never really all that dangerous and the Time Lords overreacted and imprisoned him more out of fear than due to anything that he ever did, and so he promises to keep Chronotis's secret.

RENEGADE TIME LORDS: THE RANI

The last renegade Time Lord we will focus on, at least in this chapter, is the Rani (Kate O'Mara). She is a brilliant biochemist, one of their finest scientific minds, but she is also utterly amoral, ruthlessly putting the importance of her research above everything else.

We first meet the Rani in the 1985 story "The Mark of the Rani." Her experiments on the population of the planet Miasimia Goria resulted in them having drastically heightened awareness, but at the cost of their ability to sleep, plunging their society into violent chaos. She seeks to counter this by extracting the neurochemical that promotes sleep in humans, and doing so in periods of Earth's history where the resulting aggression of her victims will go largely unnoticed. Between the meddling of the Master (Anthony Ainley) and the interference of the Sixth Doctor (Colin Baker), her foul scheme is prevented.

She returns in the 1987 story "Time and the Rani," in which she fools a newly regenerated Seventh Doctor (Sylvester McCoy) into believing that she is his companion, Mel Bush (Bonnie Langford). She wishes to convert the planet Lakertya into an enormous time manipulator, drawing on the combined intelligence of abducted geniuses. She intends to use it to control evolution on a cosmic scale, even contemplating going back and preventing the extinction of the dinosaurs on Earth to see how they advance. She has enslaved the Lakertyan people, going so far as to put explosive anklets on them to ensure their cooperation. The Doctor and Mel devise a means of safely removing the anklets, and they take them and put them around the Time Brain. When the Rani thinks she is being betrayed and wants to punish the Lakertyans, she activates the anklets, blowing up her own creation.

THE FATE OF THE TIME LORDS

Since the return of *Doctor Who* in 2005, we have witnessed mixed fortunes for Gallifrey and the Time Lords. With Russell T. Davies at the helm, we are told that Gallifrey was lost in the Time War against the Daleks and that the Doctor was now the last of them. After an aborted attempt by a resurrected Rassilon to bring his people back from the brink of annihilation, it seemed like the Time Lords were gone for good. During Steven Moffat's tenure, in the 2013 fiftieth-anniversary special, "The Day of the Doctor," all the Doctor's regenerations work together to shift Gallifrey into a pocket dimension just before its destruction, ensuring its survival. If one of their own, the Doctor, was to be their savior, then another of their own, the Master, was to be their ruin. Under Chris Chibnall's direction, the Time Lords are once more wiped out, and using Cyberman technology, transformed into "Cyber Masters," a hybrid race of Time Lords and Cybermen.

The inability of the showrunners to have a consistent vision for Gallifrey and the Time Lords has been one of the most confusing and disappointing elements of modern-era *Doctor Who*, each of them seeking to undermine the choices made by their predecessors. Gallifrey is lost. Gallifrey is saved. Gallifrey is lost, again.

Chapter 8

Companions

Figure 8 The Fourth Doctor and Leela. BBC / Photofest © BBC

If we have any hope of knowing and understanding the Doctor better, we need to see him through the lens of human perspective, so enter the companions. Originally referred to as assistants, the term was later changed to companions to reflect a more equitable association between the Doctor and them.

SUSAN FOREMAN, BARBARA WRIGHT, AND IAN CHESTERTON

When we meet the First Doctor (William Hartnell) in the 1963 story "An Unearthly Child," he effectively kidnaps two teachers, Barbara Wright (Jaqueline Hill), and Ian Chesterton (William Russell), because they have stumbled upon his secret. They both work at Coal Hill School, which Susan (Carole Ann Ford), attends as a student. Perplexed by inconsistencies in Susan's knowledge (she is a genius when it comes to science and history yet she mistakenly thinks that Britain operates on a decimal currency system—something that does not come into effect until 1971), they resolve to speak to her grandfather about her education. Turning up at what Susan gives as her home address, 76 Totter's Lane, they find only a junkyard and a strange old police box that is vibrating with energy. The Doctor arrives, there is a confrontation, and hearing Susan's voice from within the police box, the two teachers force their way in. Faced with the option of letting them go and them alerting the authorities or kidnapping them, the Doctor opts for the latter. It is hardly an endearing introduction to the Doctor, but that choice, made in the heat of the moment, would have a profound and lasting effect on him.

When the series was devised, Barbara was intended to be the levelheaded companion, while Ian was to be more action-focused, dealing with scenes that were too physical for the older Doctor. In truth, as the series progressed, there was quite a crossover between their roles. Barbara was very much a roll-the-sleeves-up-and-get-on-with-it kind of woman, while Ian would often take the Doctor to task for putting them all in danger for the sake of appeasing his curiosity.

As the 1960s saw an increase in the number of jobs available for single young women, more female students went on to higher education than before, and feminism gave rise to ideals of liberation and equality, it is disappointing that it was Susan's character that evolved the least. Being related to the Doctor, and having an extensive knowledge of the Tardis, hers was intended to be a much bigger part, but it was decided that she should portray something closer to an average teenager so the younger viewers could more easily identify with her. As such, she became the show's very first "screamer" (a character whose function is largely to scream, both to draw attention to a perilous situation and to heighten tension for the viewers). This was not appealing enough to keep Carole Ann Ford in the role, and the character of Susan departed. In the 1964 story "The Dalek Invasion of Earth," realizing that Susan has fallen in love with a freedom fighter, the Doctor locks her out of the Tardis, telling her that she deserves to have a normal life, and they exchange emotional goodbyes.

By the time the Doctor bids Barbara and Ian farewell, he does so with a heavy heart. He has come to admire and respect them. Their compassionate nature, along with their ability to rein in a lot of his reckless and selfish impulses, makes him a better man. This leaves him with a newfound sense of fondness for and interest in the human species.

It is worth noting that despite flaws in the early characters' development (or lack of same) the first two female characters on *Doctor Who* were still a supremely smart young girl and her teacher, eschewing more familiar gendered television roles of the period, such as girlfriend, wife, mother, or secretary.

JAMIE MCCRIMMON, VICTORIA WATERFIELD, AND ZOE

As William Hartnell bowed out of the series due to his failing health, the Second Doctor stepped in (Patrick Troughton). One of his longest-running companions is Jamie McCrimmon (Frazer Hines), a piper from eighteenth-century Scotland. Although this primitive highlander is a far cry from the more contemporary companions the Doctor had become used to traveling with, he admires Jamie's open-mindedness and ability to translate complex technical matters into more relatable terms that he (and, by proxy, the viewers) can easily grasp. When Victoria Waterfield (Deborah Watling) arrives on the scene, Jamie is strongly protective of this sheltered young Victorian lady. It is a good job too, as Victoria ends up doing very little other than look pretty, be confused, scream a lot, and need to be rescued on a fairly regular basis.

After Victoria leaves the Tardis, she is replaced by another female companion, Zoe Heriot (Wendy Padbury), and she could not be more different. Zoe is an astrophysicist from the twenty-first century, holds a degree in pure mathematics and, as well as having an eidetic memory, has the capacity to solve complex mathematical equations in her head. She worked on a space station and a large part of the appeal of joining the crew of the Tardis—drawing parallels with the Doctor himself—was the desire to escape from the restrictive confines of her life. However, her uneventful existence onboard the space station leaves her unprepared for many of the experiences she comes to face. With Jamie and Zoe, we see some gendered role reversal compared to what mainstream media of the time was used to portraying. Zoe is fiercely intelligent, her intellect being on par with the Doctor's, and it was certainly rare in the late 1960s to have a woman depicted as being as smart as, or smarter than, her male on-screen counterparts. Jamie, on the other hand, counters Zoe's logic-based approach with instinct and common sense.

At the end of Patrick Troughton's tenure, in the 1969 story "The War Games," the Doctor finds he has no choice but to appeal for help from the Time Lords, the same people he has been running away from for so long. In doing so, he reluctantly acknowledges that he will receive punishment from them, but he is distraught when the Time Lords not only return Jamie and Zoe to their respective eras but cruelly remove all traces of their time spent with him from their memories. The Time Lords force a regeneration on the Doctor and exile him to the planet he has become so fond of—Earth.

LIZ SHAW

The dynamic between the Third Doctor (Jon Pertwee) and those he spends time with changes while he is in exile, if for no other reason than he can no longer just run away when things become difficult or when he wants to avoid responsibility. He becomes a scientific adviser to UNIT, the remit of which is to protect the Earth from alien threats. In doing so, he meets fellow scientific advisor, Liz Shaw (Caroline John). Liz has been drafted into UNIT from the University of Cambridge, where she holds degrees in multiple subjects. She is initially skeptical of UNIT, and of the Doctor, but after dealing with several extraterrestrial dangers, she quickly comes to realize their importance. Her time with the Doctor is limited but significant in that when she resigns from UNIT, she tells Brigadier Lethbridge-Stewart (Nicholas Courtney) that all the Doctor really needs is someone to pass him test tubes and tell him how brilliant he is. It is the first time it is acknowledged that the Doctor's ego drives someone away from him. In real life, Caroline John left because she became pregnant, but she already had conflicted feelings about the role, stating that she was glad to be playing someone with brains, but frustrated that the directors at the time still wanted her to come across as sexy and glamorous.

JO GRANT

If sexy and glamorous became prerequisites of what was required from a companion in the early 1970s, they were delivered with aplomb by Jo Grant (Katy Manning) who arrived on the scene with significantly less knowledge and experience than Liz Shaw, but with endless amounts of enthusiasm. Jo Grant's principal function was for the Doctor to explain what was going on, making it easier for the audience at home to keep up (Pertwee's Doctor loved using scientific jargon, which was largely gibberish, but sounded impressive). While the character of Jo Grant was hardly a progressive move in how women were represented on the show, her character's bubbly, affable persona, good heart, and loyalty to the Doctor ensured that she became a fan favorite.

SARAH JANE SMITH AND HARRY SULLIVAN

In the 1973 story "The Time Warrior," during Pertwee's last season as the Doctor, we are introduced to Sarah Jane Smith (Elisabeth Sladen), a plucky investigative journalist. She is determined, quick-witted, and not shy about voicing her opinion. She embodies the essence of the growing feminist movement, stating, "I'm not afraid of men. They don't own the world. Why should women always have to cook and carry for them?" She stays around, even when the Doctor regenerates once more into the Fourth Doctor (Tom Baker). As Harry Sullivan (Ian Marter) joins the series as a Royal Navy medical officer who becomes attached to UNIT, Sarah Jane takes exception to his outdated, old-school, English phraseology, particularly when he repeatedly refers to her as "old girl" or "old thing," which she finds deeply patronizing.

Just as the previous companion, Ian Chesterton, was meant to deal with the more physically demanding parts of a shoot, Harry Sullivan's character was intended to perform a similar purpose, but when Baker was cast as the Doctor, he was perfectly capable of undertaking a lot of action scenes himself and, consequently, Harry's role was severely diminished. It wasn't long before he was written out of the series.

Sarah Jane Smith remained with the Doctor for a while, but even Sladen felt that her character never got to develop enough, admitting that Sarah Jane had a lot of potential, but had become a bit of a "cardboard cutout" figure. She left the series in the 1976 story "The Hand of Fear," with Sarah Jane being unceremoniously dumped back on Earth when the Doctor states he needs to return to Gallifrey, where outsiders are not welcome.

LEELA

The Doctor's subsequent traveling companion, Leela (Louise Jameson) raised a lot of eyebrows with her appearance. A female warrior, scantily clad in animal skins, she was envisioned to be an Eliza Doolittle–type character, coarse and unsophisticated, who would learn and grow from her time spent with the Doctor. Although it was never stated, it was unofficially acknowledged that Leela's skimpy attire was hugely popular with the fathers who watched the show with their children.

Despite the high concept, and the Doctor's repeated attempts to civilize her, Leela's character never grew much beyond her signature "noble savage" identity; she remains superstitious and all too eager to draw her weapon when feeling threatened. In her final outing, the 1978 story "The Invasion of Time," the Doctor takes Leela to Gallifrey (somehow ignoring his previous assertion that outsiders are not welcome), where she meets and falls in love with Andred, commander of the Chancellery Guard, choosing to remain with him.

ROMANA

When the Doctor is recruited by the White Guardian (Cyril Luckham) to recover all six pieces of the Key to Time, he is given the help of fellow Time Lord Romanadvoratrelunder (or Romana for short) played by Mary Tamm. This is the first time since Susan that the Doctor had traveled with another of his own kind. Romana is conceited, considering the Doctor to be academically inferior, and she is scathing about his lax attitudes and unorthodox approaches. As they spend time together, Romana comes to understand the Doctor's desire to break free from the overbearing restrictions imposed by Gallifreyan society. It makes her acknowledge her own yearning for a sense of adventure, and she is in no hurry to return to her old life.

Feeling that she had taken the role as far as she could go, Mary Tamm opted to leave, but with the producers unwilling to lose the character entirely, it was decided that Romana, being Gallifreyan, would regenerate. This particular regeneration was a contentious move, with the character seen trying on new bodies akin to trying on new outfits, completely bypassing the often physically and mentally traumatic experience of regeneration (a move that was put down to script editor Douglas Adams's attempt to introduce some humor to the proceedings). Eventually she settles on her new form (played by Lalla Ward).

The new Romana enjoys a much more relaxed relationship with the Doctor, emulating his sense of style with long coats and scarves, and even crafting a sonic screwdriver of her own (which the Doctor resentfully acknowledges as superior to his). At this stage, she is every bit the Doctor's equal. The easy on-screen relationship between the two was no doubt a reflection of the very real off-screen relationship that was going on between Baker and Ward, culminating in their short-lived marriage in 1980. The breakdown of their real-life relationship meant the writing was on the wall for Romana as far as the show went.

Eventually, Romana receives word that the Time Lords are recalling her to Gallifrey, and she asserts her reluctance to return. When the Tardis becomes trapped in a parallel universe known as E-Space, Romana chooses to stay there rather than acquiesce to the Time Lords' summons.

ADRIC, TEGAN JOVANKA, AND NYSSA

During his time in E-Space, the Doctor meets Adric (Matthew Waterhouse), a young native of the planet Alzarius. Adric is young, but he is technically brilliant and wears a star-shaped badge for mathematical excellence. He is quite immature and habitually adopts a sullen disposition, leading him into frequent conflict with those around him (the main reason Adric is cited as one of the Doctor's least favorite companions).

The Doctor takes Adric with him when he escapes from E-Space, and it is not long before the Doctor picks up two new companions, Australian air stewardess Tegan Jovanka (Janet Fielding) and Traken-born Nyssa (Sarah Sutton), who end up joining Adric and the Doctor when they all become caught up in an insidious trap set by the Master. In the process of stopping him, the Doctor becomes fatally injured and regenerates into a new body (Peter Davison).

Not since the time of William Hartnell's Doctor with Susan, Barbara, and Ian, had the Tardis been this busy, and it made the show seem livelier. There were meaningful attempts to give a greater depth to the characterization of the companions, making them seem more like real people, and to embody a deeper rapport between themselves and the Doctor. However, there were concerns on set that with such a large regular cast, not everybody was getting a sufficient amount of screen time. This was resolved, to some degree, in the 1982 story "Earthshock" where Adric dies while attempting to stop a Cyberman attack on Earth.

Nyssa was originally intended to feature only in the 1981 story "The Keeper of Traken," in which the body of her father, Tremas (Anthony Ainley), is taken over by a ravaged Master, replacing the usual regeneration process (he had already squandered all his available regenerations). The production team, feeling that she was a character with a lot of potential and ongoing narrative options, brought her back as a companion. She is an aristocrat of Traken by birth but can no longer return home when she discovers that, as a consequence of a larger plan by the Master, her home world has been utterly destroyed. Nyssa is quiet and contemplative and technically astute. She develops a firm friendship with Tegan, and her help is greatly valued by the Doctor.

On the surface, Tegan is loud and abrasive, describing herself as "a mouth on legs." She complains a lot and doesn't ever feel the need to hide her displeasure. Regardless, she is loyal and has a strong moral compass, and the death of Adric affects her quite strongly. Tegan has already suffered some psychological trauma from when she was possessed, not once, but twice, by a vile entity called the Mara that manifests itself through the subconscious, and which desires corporeal form. When she is temporarily left behind at Heathrow by the Fifth Doctor (Peter Davison), due to a misunderstanding, she realizes just how much she misses traveling with him and Nyssa, and when they meet up again (roughly a year later in story terms), she eagerly returns to the fold. When Nyssa determines to leave the group to establish a hospital in an old space station in the 1983 story "Terminus," feeling that her skills would be essential, Tegan is dismayed. At the conclusion of the 1984 story "Resurrection of the Daleks," Tegan finally comes to accept that in the time she has been part of the Tardis crew, she has witnessed too much death and experienced too much loss, and bids a painful, final farewell to the Doctor, who is genuinely saddened to see her go.

VISLOR TURLOUGH

The 1983 story "Mawdryn Undead" sees the introduction of a different companion, Vislor Turlough (Mark Strickson). Appearing to be nothing more than a student at Brendon Public School, it swiftly becomes clear that there is more to him than meets the eye; he is an alien who is stranded on Earth. He becomes a pawn of the Black Guardian (Valentine Dyall) who wishes to use him to destroy the Doctor. When Turlough requests to join the Tardis crew, he does so with treacherous duplicity, seeking only to find a way to carry out the Black Guardian's demands. It is the first time in the show's history that a companion intentionally means to do the Doctor harm (other than being mind-controlled by some external source).

Turlough comes across as a deeply unlikable character, displaying both cowardly and selfish attributes, but as he gets to know the Doctor, he begins to doubt the twisted account the Black Guardian paints of him. In essence, Turlough is not a bad person, but he has backed himself into a corner and fears reprisal, not only from the Black Guardian, but from the Doctor, should he find out the truth. In the end, Turlough believes the Doctor to be a good man and chooses to side with him, rejecting the Black Guardian and breaking the malevolent hold he has over him.

In the 1984 story "Planet of Fire," we learn that Turlough came from the planet Trion, where there had been a civil war. Turlough's family were regarded as political dissidents, and he had been exiled to Earth as punishment. When he finds out that, in his absence, the political situation on Trion has stabilized and that former dissidents are no longer persecuted, he chooses to rejoin his people.

PERI BROWN

The last story for Turlough also introduces us to a brand-new companion, Perpugilliam—mercifully truncated to "Peri"—Brown (Nicola Bryant). Peri is an American from Baltimore, Maryland, only the actress who played her hailed from Surry in England. Bryant had been talent-spotted by an agent who had mistaken her for an American during a performance where she was using an accent. Given that John Nathan-Turner, then producer of *Doctor Who*, was looking for an American companion to generate more appeal toward a growing fanbase in the United States, the agent arranged for an audition, and Bryant secured the role. Unfortunately for her, to keep up the premise, she had to speak with an American accent whenever she was in public, and also in and around the BBC television studios, even when she wasn't filming.

When viewers first get to see Peri, she is in a bikini, because filming took place amid the scorching temperatures of Lanzarote, an island off the coast of Spain. This made such a splash with British newspapers that even when back filming in the far more reserved English weather, Peri continued to be decked out in costumes that exposed as much leg, cleavage, and bare midriff as they could get away with. Bryant even suffered from frostbite and caught pneumonia due to this.

If things were not already bad enough, Bryant came to realize that Peri not only had the flimsiest of backstories, but that she was not changing in any meaningful way. Indeed, Peri became a very stereotyped female character, the kind who would go off and get into trouble just so the hero could come and rescue her. In terms of the portrayal of female companions, this was a massive step backward, the like of which viewers had not seen since the 1960s.

When Nicola chose to depart the role, she was asked how she wanted to be written out and she said she wanted to go "out with a bang." In the 1986 story "Mindwarp," part of the larger "Trial of a Timelord" story arc, the Sixth Doctor (Colin Baker) and Peri arrive on the planet Thoros Beta. There they discover that a scientist, Crozier (Patrick Ryecart), is in the employ of an arms dealer, Sil (Nabil Shaban) to find a host for the mind of the dying Lord Kiv (Christopher Ryan), and they rescue the warlord King Yrcanos (Brian Blessed) from his machinations. After the Doctor is abducted by the Time Lords to stand trial for interference, it is revealed to him that Peri became the victim of Crozier's plans and she had her mind wiped and replaced with that of Kiv. When Yrcanos discovers this, he guns down both Crozier and the Kiv-controlled Peri, fulfilling the dramatic end that Bryant wanted, but upsetting a lot of younger viewers in the process.

Eventually, it is discovered that evidence being presented against the Doctor has been tampered with. The truth is exposed that Peri did not die and went on to be betrothed to King Yrcanos. This displeased Bryant, for not only did it diminish the impact of the end she wanted for Peri, but she felt it made no sense as there was not even the remotest hint of romantic interest between Peri and Yrcanos during the story.

At this point Colin Baker is ousted from his role as the Doctor by BBC management. They feel that he failed to click with audiences and that stories have become both violent and farcical. They want a refresh and so arrives the Seventh Doctor (Sylvester McCoy).

ACE

Ace (Sophie Aldred) has the distinction of being the very last companion of the classic *Doctor Who* era. She is a sixteen-year-old girl from Perivale, a suburb of London, and had a troubled upbringing. She committed arson at an old abandoned Victorian property in Perivale, known as Gabriel Chase, burning it to the ground because it frightened her (we learn this is because she sensed the presence of an alien entity there).

Ace, whose real name is Dorothy (we are never given a surname), is a refreshing return to a complex and dynamic female character. She outwardly displays a streetwise resilience, although she does so mostly to mask her own insecurities. She carries a baseball bat to defend herself (when confronted by danger she is more likely to hit than scream) and she likes to experiment with explosives, especially a concoction of her own that she calls Nitro-9.

The Doctor and Ace have a strong relationship, albeit a challenging one at times. She refers to him as "Professor" rather than "Doctor" and develops a loyal and protective stance toward him. He, in turn, encourages her natural curiosity, and knowing about her problematic history wants her to become more than she has been, realizing that she has huge amounts of untapped potential.

Of course, the Doctor knows certain things that Ace does not, like how she is from a genetic dynasty that has been manipulated through many generations with the ultimate aim of freeing an evil from the dawn of time that had been imprisoned. The Doctor helps her defeat Fenric, ending the influence it had over her. He even takes her back to Gabriel Chance in the past, so she can confront her fears. Although she is angry that he has taken her to the one place she dreads the most, she uncovers what it was that frightened her and frees herself from its crippling hold. Regrettably, we never get to see how their relationship evolves for, in 1989, *Doctor Who* was canceled.

ROSE TYLER

Thankfully, after far too long a hiatus, *Doctor Who* returns to television with the 2005 story "Rose," named after the newest companion, Rose Tyler (Billie Piper). Rose lives in London with her mother, Jackie (Camile Coduri). She has a boyfriend called Mickey Smith (Noel Clarke). Hers is a very unremarkable life, and it is the first time we get to see a companion in a normal, everyday family environment before she's whisked off by the Ninth Doctor (Christopher Eccleston).

Rose is all too easily swept up in the excitement and adventure of traveling with the Doctor, neglecting her relationship with Mickey, and often leaving her mother worrying for her safety. The Doctor is addicted to Rose, and he is caught up in her enthusiasm, encouraging him to do more and more things to impress her. In truth, he has been alone for so long that he is enjoying the attention and the ability to show off, and he fails to acknowledge the dangers that he might be putting her in.

In the 2005 story "The Parting of the Ways," when the Doctor attempts to save Rose's life by sending her back home to Earth in the Tardis when he is faced with an overwhelming force of Daleks, she refuses to accept this. Trying to find to way to get back to him, she opens up the Tardis console, absorbing the raw energy of the time vortex. Infused with this newfound power, she returns to save the Doctor and wipe out the Daleks. Realizing that no one person can hold so much vortex energy without dying, the Doctor extracts the power from her, taking it into himself, and he regenerates into the Tenth Doctor (David Tennant).

Skeptical that he is essentially the same man, Rose continues to travel with the Doctor, slowly coming to terms with the fact that she has fallen in love with him. Up until then, there had never been any suggestion of romantic interest between the Doctor and any of his companions, but now, perhaps not quite appreciating the impact he has on Rose, the Doctor openly reciprocates her flirting. In the 2006 story "Doomsday," while attempting to defeat an army of Cybermen and Daleks, Rose is pulled into a parallel Earth, trapping her there, giving a very emotional end to their time together.

MARTHA JONES

The Doctor meets his companion, Martha Jones (Freema Agyeman), a medical student, when he detects strange emanations around the hospital where she works. He takes to her quickly, realizing that she is capable and smart. Awkwardly, it was decided that her character would also fall hopelessly in love with the Doctor, and although she travels with him for a while, even seeing him through some very difficult times, he is still reeling from the loss of Rose. Martha finally decides she can no longer bear her unrequited love and she departs.

It is interesting to note that Martha Jones is the Doctor's first black companion, although some have questioned this. After all, Mickey Smith traveled with the Doctor for a short time, but as that was motivated by his desire to spend more time with Rose, and not the Doctor, he is generally not considered a proper companion.

DONNA NOBLE

Impending companion Donna Noble (Catherine Tate) doesn't start as one. She appears, quite without warning, in the Tardis in a wedding dress in the 2006 Christmas story "The Runaway Bride," and the Doctor is presented with the conundrum of figuring out how such a thing could have happened. He soon ascertains that her wedding was a trap, and he saves Donna from being devoured by the hungry offspring of the Empress of the Racnoss, wiping them all out in the process and showing the full force of his fury. Having lost her job and her fiancé, the Doctor asks if she wants to travel with him. She declines but notes that he really does need someone to keep him in check.

When the Doctor and Donna next meet, in the 2008 story "Partners in Crime," she realizes just how dull and ordinary her life has been without him, and she leaps at the chance to travel with him. Donna is one of the few companions who calls out the Doctor for his lack of compassion at times, even convincing him to save a family from certain death when Mount Vesuvius is about to erupt, killing everyone in Pompeii.

For all the fun and excitement being with the Doctor brings Donna, it leaves its traumatic legacy too. In the 2008 two-part story "Silence in the Library" and "Forest of the Dead," Donna is uploaded into a virtual network, as part of an emergency protocol, when a planet-sized library is infected with the carnivorous Vashta Nerada. In the network, she has no memory of her life before she ended up there, and she falls in love with a man that she meets. Because her sense of time is distorted, she perceives that many years pass, and she ends up having two children with him. When the Doctor eventually frees her, along with others who were trapped in the virtual network, Donna has the heartbreaking realization that she's lived a life that was nothing more than a fantasy construct. She and the Doctor leave, just missing the man she fell in love with, who, as it turns out, was a real person.

In the 2008 story "Turn Left," Donna is tricked into creating an alternative timeline where she makes a small life change that means she never meets the Doctor (who dies). She has to live through the consequences of multiple events that take a destructive course because the Doctor wasn't there to save the day. With the help of UNIT, Donna travels back to the point just before she makes the fateful change but being unable to get to her past self in time to warn her, Donna elects to sacrifice herself, walking out in front of a truck, causing a traffic jam which forces her past self to choose a different path—the one where she meets the Doctor—thereby restoring the original timeline.

In the season finale two-part story "The Stolen Earth" and "Journey's End," Donna fulfills a misunderstood prophecy (one surrounding the "DoctorDonna") when she absorbs a huge amount of siphoned-off regenerative energy from the Doctor, imbuing her with all of his knowledge. She uses this to foil a Dalek plan, but her mind quickly begins to deteriorate under the burden of all the information it now carries—that of a Time Lord who has lived many lifetimes. The Doctor is forced to impose memory blocks on her, including wiping out all recollection of her time with him, to prevent her from accessing the part of her mind which still holds all of his knowledge, and which would kill her if let out.

AMY POND

With the Eleventh Doctor (Matt Smith) we get a new companion, Amy Pond (Karen Gillan). He first meets her when he crashes the Tardis (damaged by the intense energy output he gives off during his regeneration) outside her house. She is seven years old, and he tells her that he will be right back, but he miscalculates and returns twelve years later. By now, Amy has been receiving psychiatric help to deal with memories of her "imaginary" friend, the Doctor. On top of that, and unbeknown to her, Amy's life has been affected by a huge crack in her bedroom wall, something which becomes a repeating motif throughout her time with the Doctor. This is caused by a future event where the Tardis is destroyed, exploding, and creating multiple rifts—or cracks—throughout Amy's timeline.

Throughout Amy's tenure, a lengthy and complex narrative unfolds under the watchful eye of showrunner, Steven Moffat. Although such an intricate storyline does work, and even makes total sense in retrospect, overall, it is regarded as being too complicated for more casual viewers. Moffat likes to drop in lots of callbacks to the show's lengthy history such as Matt Smith's Doctor showing an identity card that still has a picture of the original Doctor's face on it. While these are fun and appreciated by longer-term fans of the show, they tend to confuse and alienate more spontaneous viewers, along with newer fans, especially those picked up since the show's return in 2005, who are unfamiliar with the show's past.

CLARA OSWALD

If there were lessons to be learned about making things too convoluted for less committed viewers, they were not necessarily heeded when we were introduced to Clara Oswald (Jenna Coleman). The Twelfth Doctor (Peter Capaldi) meets her, not once, but twice, and although she has the same voice and the same face, she presents herself as two separate identities, each having no knowledge of the other. Both of these versions of her die, and the Doctor goes in search of any others that might exist, and that's when he finds Clara, the "impossible girl."

The answer to the mystery of Clara presents itself when a malevolent alien entity called the Great Intelligence lures the Doctor to the plant Trenzalore (the location of the Doctor's eventual grave) with the intention of having the Doctor provide access to his time-stream so it can enter it and undo all the victories that the Doctor has ever had. Wanting to save the Doctor, and thwart the Great Intelligence, Clara enters his time-stream, resulting in multiple echoes of her herself appearing throughout his life.

In the 2015 story "Face the Raven," Clara attempts to save someone by taking their death sentence tattoo and transferring it to herself. The tattoo counts down until it reaches zero when a quantum shade, in the guise of a raven, takes the bearer's life. The Doctor fights to prove that the person wasn't guilty of the crime he was accused of but is horrified to learn that when Clara willingly took the tattoo, it changed the circumstances of the contract made with the shade and the death sentence can no longer be revoked. Clara begs the Doctor not to seek vengeance for her impending passing and walks out to face the raven.

Feeling intense remorse about Clara and her unjust end, the Doctor returns to Gallifrey and uses their technology to snatch her moments before she is killed by the shade. He escapes with her in another stolen Tardis, which he then gives to her so she can run away in it to avoid her fate. He plans to use a device to wipe her memory of him, making it harder for the Time Lords to track her down and reverse what he has done, but she tricks him and wipes his memory of her, relieving him of the burden of guilt he has been carrying.

YASMIN KHAN, RYAN SINCLAIR, AND GRAHAM O'BRIEN

As Jodie Whittaker takes the helm of the Tardis as the Thirteenth Doctor, she does so with a cohort of companions, which she cringingly refers to as her "Fam" (a colloquial contraction of "family"). These are probationary police officer Yasmin Khan (Mandip Gill), warehouse worker Ryan Sinclair (Tosin

Cole) and his step-grandfather, the retired bus driver, Graham O'Brien (Bradley Walsh). This is, by far, the most packed the Tardis has been since the days of Adric, Nyssan, and Tegan, and the same problems that occurred back then rear their ugly heads once more. All three characters show possibilities for development, but there is simply not enough screen time for each, so they are left feeling incomplete.

We first meet Yasmin when she is handling a situation in her role as a police officer, showing that she can take charge of a confrontation and deftly handle it without escalation, but it is not long after she meets the Doctor that she is suddenly quite subservient to the Doctor's authority and seldom draws upon her valuable skill set. She remains with Jodie Whittaker's Doctor the longest, but her character is also one who falls into the rather tired modern-era trope of finding herself in love with the Doctor.

With Ryan Sinclair's character, we are shown that he has a disability in the form of dyspraxia, a developmental coordination disorder. This means that Ryan has trouble riding a bicycle or climbing a ladder, but it never truly hinders the character to any significant degree or is forgotten about entirely when it is convenient to do so. It would have been nice to have had a character whose disability was more meaningful, one that really defined them through the struggles they faced, rather than feeling like a tacked-on issue.

Graham turns out to be the most interesting of the three companions. He is an older man, a cancer survivor who falls in love with, and marries, his chemotherapy nurse, Grace (Sharon D Clarke), who sadly dies in the 2018 story "The Woman Who Fell to Earth." This leaves Graham with a lingering guilt, feeling that it should have been him who died as he has already cheated death once. He is the most down-to-earth and thoughtful of the three, but inadequate screen time means that any additional depth remains frustratingly unrealized.

THE EX-COMPANIONS SUPPORT GROUP

At the end of the 2022 feature-length episode "The Power of the Doctor," marking the hundredth anniversary of the BBC (which is also the final story for Jodie Whittaker's Doctor), we learn that a number of those who have traveled with the Doctor have sought each other out and formed a support group where they can share their recollections and talk about their experiences. It is a very telling scene because it gives a tangible sense of what it is like to have been whisked away in the Tardis and to have had the most amazing adventures, only then to have returned to life, both enhanced, yet somehow diminished, in the Doctor's wake.

Chapter 9

Recurring Characters

Figure 9 The Brigadier. BBC / Photofest © BBC

The Doctor has had many companions who have traveled with him over the years, that much is indisputable. There are, however, certain characters that have appeared time and time again that do not technically meet the criteria to be regarded as full companions. That does not mean that they are in any way any less important, either to the narrative or to him, just that they have other commitments that preclude them from being regular travelers in the Tardis.

ALISTAIR GORDON LETHBRIDGE-STEWART

One of the most prominent recurring characters in all of *Doctor Who* is Brigadier Alistair Gordon Lethbridge-Stewart. Played by Nicholas Courtney (1929–2011), he has met no less than six of the Doctors' regenerations, only being beaten by Sarah Jane Smith (Elisabeth Sladen) for the number of Doctors a single character has met.

Lethbridge-Stewart works for UNIT (originally the United Nations Intelligence Taskforce, later changed to the UNified Intelligence Taskforce), a military organization whose remit is to investigate extraterrestrial threats to Earth. He first meets the Second Doctor (Patrick Troughton) in the 1968 story "The Web of Fear." He is only a lieutenant-colonel, and not yet affiliated with UNIT, being part of a group of soldiers combating the yeti menace in the London Underground (the yeti, incidentally, being the robotic foot soldiers of an entity called the Great Intelligence).

This was not the first role that Courtney played in *Doctor Who*. In the epic twelve-part 1966 story "The Daleks' Master Plan," he plays Space Security Agent Bret Vyon, who was looking into the disappearance of another agent, and who is killed by his own sister when she is manipulated into believing he is a traitor.

We next meet Lethbridge-Stewart in the 1968 story "The Invasion," in which he has been promoted to brigadier and is working for UNIT, alongside another recurring character, Corporal Benton (John Levine). Together with the Doctor, they investigate an electronics company called International Electromatics. It is run by a man called Tobias Vaughn (Keven Stoney), who has created the "Cerebration Mentors," devices that are intended to be used as teaching machines. But Vaughn is working with the Cybermen, who plan to send a signal out through Vaughan's machines, nullifying resistance to their invasion.

The Brigadier (as he is generally referred to by the Doctor) meets the Third Doctor (John Pertwee) when he has been exiled to Earth in the 1970 story "Spearhead from Space." At first, he refuses to believe that this man is the Doctor, having had his appearance changed through regeneration, but he comes to accept it, offering him the position of UNIT's scientific adviser. The Brigadier, along with Benton, who gets promoted to sergeant, and newcomer Captain Mike Yates, played by Richard Franklin (1936–2023), works with the Third Doctor in several stories: "The Silurians," "The Ambassadors of Death," and "Inferno" (1970); "Terror of the Autons," "The Mind of Evil,"

"The Claws of Axos," "Colony in Space," and "The Daemons" (1971); "Day of the Daleks" and "The Time Monster" (1972); "The Three Doctors" and "The Green Death" (1973); and "The Time Warrior," "Invasion of the Dinosaurs," and "Planet of the Spiders" (1974).

Courtney got to play an alternative version of the Brigadier in the 1970 story "Inferno," when the Doctor ends up in a parallel Earth. There he discovers the sadistic Brigade Leader Lethbridge-Stewart, a man with a scarred face and an eye patch, who works for the fascistic British Republic.

With the words, "Well, here we go again," the Brigadier sees out the Third Doctor and the arrival of the fourth (Tom Baker).[1] They share just two stories, "Robot" and "Terror of the Zygons" (1975). Similarly, he appears with the Fifth Doctor (Peter Davison) only twice, in "Mawdryn Undead" and "The Five Doctors" (1983). By this point he retired from UNIT, became a teacher at Brendon Public School, and married a woman called Doris (Angela Douglas, having already had one marriage to a woman called Fiona, which failed as a result of his relentless dedication to his job).

He was recalled to action one last time in the 1989 story "Battlefield," when he fought alongside the Seventh Doctor (Sylvester McCoy) to defeat Morgaine (Jean Marsh), a sorceress who has summoned the Destroyer of Worlds (Marek Anton), in this take on Arthurian legends.

The last official appearance of Lethbridge-Stewart was in the 2008 episode of *The Sarah Jane Adventures* titled "Enemy of the Bane." He is now Sir Alistair, having received a knighthood. Ever a stickler for the rules, he notes that his full title is now Brigadier Sir Alistair Gordon Lethbridge-Stewart. It is clearly an honor that he is immensely proud of.

Overall, Lethbridge-Stewart is a resolute, no-nonsense, by-the-book military man. He takes his service very seriously, has a dislike for politicians and bureaucrats, and generally acts honorably, being the kind of officer who leads from the front, never asking his men to do anything that he is not fully prepared to do himself. He represents the calm assuredness and stiff upper lip of British mentality, standing in resolute defiance of any threat, be it domestic, foreign, or extraterrestrial.

There are only two occasions when he does not fully act in accordance with the best of his principles. The first is in the 1968 story "The Web of Fear," in which he acts impetuously, leading to the death of all the men under his command. The second is in the 1970 story "The Silurians," in which he disregards the Doctor's request to leave the retreating Silurians in peace, and following orders from his superiors, blows up their base, killing them all.

The 2001 story "The Wedding of River Song" saw the Doctor (Matt Smith) calling the nursing home where the Brigadier resides. The nurse says she did not know how to contact the Doctor, but she is sorry to inform him that the Brigadier passed away a few months ago. She added that he always spoke well of the Doctor, and always wanted an extra brandy poured, just in case he turned up. The Doctor is shaken at the news.

The connection between Lethbridge-Stewart and the Doctor does not end there, however. The Brigadier's daughter, Kate Lethbridge-Steward (Jemma Redgrave)—who generally drops the Lethbridge part of her name—carries on the family's legacy of service, becoming the chief scientific officer at UNIT, being introduced in the 2012 story "The Power of Three." Like her father, she too has worked with multiple regenerations of the Doctor, namely the Eleventh, Twelfth, Thirteenth, Fourteenth, and Fifteenth.

As well as her first story Stewart also appears in "The Day of the Doctor" (2013), "Death in Heaven" (2014), "The Magician's Apprentice" and "The Zygon Invasion"/"The Zygon Inversion" (2015), "Survivors of the Flux" and "The Vanquishers" (2021), "The Power of the Doctor" (2022), and "The Giggle" (2023).

In the 2017 story "Twice Upon a Time," the Twelfth Doctor (Peter Capaldi) meets up with the First Doctor (David Bradley) in the South Pole as they are both coming to the end of their respective regenerations. They encounter a British captain (Mark Gatiss) from World War I who has been displaced in space and time after being in an armed standoff with a German soldier in a crater in December 1914. As it turns out, he was meant to die in the crater, with an entity called Testimony stealing him just before that moment to capture a record of his memories, before returning him to meet his death. Testimony asks the Doctor to return the captain, which he agrees to, but the Doctor cheats and moves him slightly forward in time, into Christmas Day. Before he departs, the captain identifies himself as Archibald Hamish Lethbridge-Stewart, strongly implying that he is Alistair's ancestor.

Faced once again at gunpoint with the German soldier, the moment is interrupted by the sound of Christmas carols being sung on both sides. Amid all the death and chaos, something remarkable happens. As the Doctor himself says, "If I've got my timings right—and clearly, I have—we should be right at the beginning. I adjusted the time frame, only by a couple of hours, any other day it wouldn't make a difference, but this is Christmas 1914, and a human miracle is about to happen. The Christmas Armistice. It never happened again. Any war, anywhere, but for one day, one Christmas, a very long time ago, everyone just put down their weapons, and started to sing. Everybody just stopped. Everyone was just kind."[2]

RIVER SONG

Another of the most prominent noncompanion figures is one that only came along in the modern era, but who has left a lasting—if divisive—impression on the show. This is the indomitable River Song (Alex Kingston) who has a far more complicated relationship with the Doctor than any Lethbridge-Stewart ever had.

Song first turns up in the 2008 two-part story "Silence in the Library" and "Forest of the Dead." She is a professor and an archaeologist, one who has been hired to be part of a team that is investigating why a planet-sized library sealed itself one hundred years ago with no word of what happened to the 4,022 occupants present at the time. When she meets the Tenth Doctor (David Tennant), she greets him with the words, "Hello Sweetie," suggesting a familiarity, although as far as he is concerned, he has never met her before.[3] She carries a diary, with an embossed leather cover that is blue and detailed like the Tardis exterior, but she will not let him look at it, saying that it contains spoilers. She seems distressed that the Doctor does not appear to know who she is, as though such a revelation has a far deeper significance than she is prepared to acknowledge.

One of the group is killed, their body reduced to a skeleton in mere moments, and Donna Noble (Catherine Tate) is shocked to find that they can still hear her. That is because the neural link in her environment suit holds a Data Ghost—an impression of living consciousness—for a brief time after death, at least until the power in the buffer has fully run out. The Doctor warns that not all shadows in the library are as they appear, some are swarms of Vashta Nerada—tiny piranhas of the air!

Song even has her own sonic screwdriver, telling the Doctor that at some point in the future, he will give her his own. To prove that he can trust her, she whispers something in his ear—and whatever it is, it changes his opinion of her.

In the end, Doctor prepares to hook himself up to the planetary data core to save everybody—the remaining members of the party, and all the people that he discovers have been stored in the library's system memory when the Vashta Nerada attack first began, existing in a virtual environment. The process will kill him, and Song begs him not to do it, but he is prepared to sacrifice himself to save so many lives. She knocks him out and handcuffs him, swapping positions because she cannot bear to lose him. When he regains consciousness, she tells him about the last time she saw him, when he took her to Darillium to see the singing towers. She says that he cried, but she could never figure out why, until now. She acknowledges that he knew she was going to die.

He confirms that she whispered his name, his *real* name, into his ear, and says there is only one reason he would *ever* trust someone with information like that.

With that, she sacrifices herself, freeing all 4,022 people who had been trapped in the system memory. The Doctor realizes that there must have been a reason why he gave her his sonic screwdriver, and when he opens it, he finds there is a neural link inside, holding her consciousness in its buffer. He races to upload it into the library's system memory and succeeds. Song is saved as a digital version of herself in the virtual environment.

At this point, Song seems like an intriguing character, but not someone that we are ever likely to meet again, after all, she is dead. However, this is *Doctor Who*, a show about an alien that travels in time, so death is no barrier to entry.

She returns in the 2010 two-part story "The Time of Angels" and "Flesh and Stone." The Eleventh Doctor (Matt Smith) has taken Amy Pond (Karen Gillan) to look around the Delirium Archive, the biggest museum ever. He scampers around the exhibits, proclaiming, how wrong many of them are. He is distracted by a black box in a glass display cabinet, which he states is a Home Box—like the black box of a plane, but which flies home in the event of a disaster—from an old category four starliner. What has really captured his attention is that there is something etched into the surface of the box, which he says is Old High Gallifreyan, the lost language of the Time Lords. He goes on to explain, "There were days, there were many days, these words could burn stars and raise up empires, and topple Gods."[4] When Amy asks what it says, the Doctor looks sheepish and replies, "Hello Sweetie." It is an invitation, one for the Doctor to come and find Song twelve thousand years in the past.

When the Doctor finds her, she demonstrates that she has a remarkable knowledge of how the Tardis works, further deepening the complexity of their relationship. Pond is intrigued by Song, wondering who this remarkable woman is. When the Doctor introduces her, he lets slip that she has become a professor (she is not at this point) which she thinks is exciting. When Song takes out her diary, and Pond asks what it is, the Doctor indicates that Song's past is his future and that they keep meeting in the wrong order. Song acknowledges that he does not yet fully know who she is, and when he asks her how she knows who he is, as his appearance changes over time, she tells him that she has pictures of all his faces—what she calls her spotters' guide. But Song has been hiding something, and we learn that she has been in the Stormcage Containment Facility, a maximum-security prison, for killing a man, a good man, and that she is currently on a mission to earn a pardon. When the mission is over, she tells the Doctor that he will see her again quite soon.

Song knows Gallifreyan, and she can pilot the Tardis, yet she does not appear to be a Time Lord herself. Also, she knows far more about the Doctor than he knows about her, a fact that clearly perplexes him. We begin to get our first inkling that not only is Song much more than she appears, but she is dangerous.

True to her word, Song appears again in the 2010 two-part story "The Pandorica Opens"/"The Big Bang." The Doctor ends up healing a space-time rift and ends up trapped outside of the known universe. With all memory of his existence erased, he has no way back. It is the day of Amy's wedding to Rory Williams (Arthur Darvill), and she cannot help but feel that something is missing. At the reception, she sees Song pass by a window, sparking a flash of memory. She should be joyous because of the occasion, but she is sad, feeling that someone is missing. Rory gives her something, a present that he says came from a woman. It is Song's diary, and it is the final piece of the puzzle that helps her remember the Doctor and the Tardis—*something old, something new, something borrowed, something blue*—allowing him to return.

The Doctor and Song have a complicated verbal exchange, leaving the Doctor uncertain as to whether he asked her if she is married, or if he is asking her to marry him. Either way, the answer from her is yes. He asks her, once again, who she is, and she tells him that he is going to find out very soon, but it is when everything will change.

The words that Song leaves the Doctor with are clearly a warning. And, perhaps, a veiled threat? Despite all the banter and the flirting, there is a shift in the dynamic between the two that hints at a deeper and darker level of interaction yet to come.

In the 2011 two-part story "The Impossible Astronaut" and "Day of the Moon," Pond, Williams, and Song each receive invitations in envelopes that are Tardis blue. There is a date, a time, and a map reference. They arrive in America in 1969 to find the Doctor, who takes them for a picnic by Lake Silencio. An astronaut with a tinted visor emerges out of the water. The astronaut shoots the Doctor, initiating the regeneration process, then shoots him again in the middle of it, terminating the process and killing him. After the astronaut has left, they push the deceased Doctor out on the lake on a boat, setting it on fire, like a Viking funeral. They then arrive at a nearby diner, to find *the Doctor*, very much alive. It seems that it was a future version of the Doctor, the one who died, who sent the invites, leaving his past self with no knowledge of what was going on. Pond, Williams, and Song try to hide the Doctor's impending death from him.

As the story unfolds, the characters encounter aliens who can only be seen when someone is looking directly at them. The moment they look away, all memory of them is wiped away. They also end up looking for a young girl who is somehow caught up in what is going on. Song reveals that she and the Doctor travel through time in opposite directions and each time they meet, she knows him more and he knows her less.

Following clues, Amy finds an old, abandoned children's home, Greystark Hall, where she finds a room with photos of a young girl on a bureau, along with one of herself holding a baby. The astronaut appears once again, revealing a little girl inside the suit, asking for help. The home is also filled with the memory-stealing aliens, who identify themselves as the "Silence," who seem to be part of a silent occupation of the Earth. When the others catch up with Amy, they find both her and the child missing, with only the empty astronaut suit remaining. An examination of it reveals that it is filled with twenty different kinds of alien technology, turning it into an exoskeleton survival suit, although the child's connection to it remains a mystery.

The Doctor splices footage of one of the Silence, caught on Amy's camera phone, into the broadcast of Neil Armstrong landing on the moon—one of the most watched events ever—planting their presence in the minds of all the viewers, meaning their secret occupation is no longer a secret. Amy reveals that she is pregnant, or at least she thought she was. The Doctor secretly runs a scan on her, but the results are inconclusive.

In New York City, the young girl walks down a back alleyway. She encounters a homeless man who asks if she is alright. She reveals that she is dying, but she says she can fix that, and *she begins to regenerate*!

Narratively we are at a point where the Doctor, River Song, and even the little girl all appear to be linked, but *how*? If Song and the Doctor do indeed travel through time in opposite directions, and his future is her past, then she must surely have an idea of how this all plays out. What is she hiding?

In the 2011 story "A Good Man Goes to War," it has been revealed that the Amy that the Doctor and Rory have been traveling with is not the real Amy; she has been replaced by a duplicate. The real—and very pregnant—Amy has been abducted by someone called Madame Kovarian (Frances Barber) and held in a place called Demon's Run. Amy gives birth to her infant girl called Melody Pond.

Williams visits Song, who is breaking back into Stormcage. She tells him, "It's my birthday. The Doctor took me ice skating on the River Thames in 1814, the last of the great frost fairs."[5] Song works out that the Doctor is going to Demon's Run, and only she knows what that means. She tells Rory that she cannot be there, right until the very end, because this is the day that the Doctor finally finds out who she is.

The Doctor, Rory, and an assortment of his allies storm Demon's Run and recover Melody. The Doctor retrieves a cot from the Tardis, his *own* cot from when he was a baby, for Melody to lie in. Now the Doctor needs to figure out why somebody has gone to such lengths to get ahold of her. Kovarian has been scanning the baby, revealing traces of Time Lord DNA. Melody, it seems, was conceived on board the Tardis while traveling through the time vortex, and it has had a profound effect on her and altered her physiology. Kovarian discloses that she intends to use Melody as a weapon against the Doctor and that the child they recovered is not the real Melody, merely a duplicate, which then dissolves.

Song turns up and the Doctor berates her for not coming earlier when he needed her most. She tells him that she could not have changed things, no matter how much she might have wanted to. Song finally reveals her true identity—she is Melody Pond, all grown up!

The pieces of the puzzle that have been scattered throughout the show since River Song's arrival are finally coming together. One big question remains, however. Who is the good man that she kills, the murder of whom sees her incarcerated in Stormcage?

Song returns in the 2011 episode "Let's Kill Hitler." Pond and Williams have a reckless friend called Mels (Nina Toussaint-White) who takes the Doctor hostage at gunpoint. With the sound of police sirens approaching, she says to him, "You've got a time machine, I've got a gun. What the hell—let's kill Hitler."[6] There follows a sequence of flashbacks of Amy and Mels growing up together throughout their school years and beyond, with Mels constantly getting into trouble.

Being her irresponsible self, Mels ends up shooting the Tardis console, so their arrival in 1938 Berlin is a rather abrupt one, crash-landing in Hitler's office. In all the confusion, Hitler shoots Mels in the gut, mortally wounding her. As she lies dying, Mels confesses to the Doctor that after all the stories Amy used to tell her about him, she used to dream about marrying him. The Doctor, trying to give her a reason to live, tells her that if she lives then he will marry her. When Mels suggests that the Doctor gets her parents' permission, he says that he will, as soon as he can contact them. Mels tells him he can do it now since they are both there. There is a sudden realization, and Mels regenerates *into River Song!*

But she is different. She is now the product of all the conditioning given to her by Kovarian, programmed, trained, and weaponized to kill the Doctor. After several thwarted attempts to kill him with handguns and a letter opener, she deals the final blow with a fatal kiss—her lipstick laced with poison. An analysis by the Tardis indicates that the Doctor has been infected with the poison of the Judas Tree, his regenerative abilities have been disabled, and he will be dead in thirty-two minutes.

Throughout the episode, having learned who she will become, and what she and the Doctor will mean to one another, she bitterly regrets her actions and opts to channel all the power of her remaining regenerations into him, saving his life, but at the expense of this now being her last one.

The end of the 2011 story "Closing Time" sees Kovarian and the silence track down Song, place her in an astronaut's suit, and submerge her in Lake Silencio, waiting for the arrival of the Doctor when, following a historic event already established, she will be forced to kill the Doctor.

The 2011 story "The Wedding of River Song" closes a story arc that began with "The Impossible Astronaut." By now it has been revealed that Silence is not a species, they are a religious order, dedicated to stopping a prophecy coming true, namely, "On the fields of Trenzalore, at the fall of the Eleventh, when no living creature can speak falsely or fail to answer, a question will be asked, a question that must never, ever be answered."[7]

The question is the first question. The oldest question in the universe, hidden in plain sight—Doctor *Who*? The Silence is determined that the Doctor must never reach Trenzalore so the question can never be answered.

As history repeats itself and the group gathers to picnic by Lake Silencio, the astronaut suit, containing Song, emerges from the water, and the Doctor approaches it. Song is bereft, saying the suit is in control and she cannot stop it. But she is cleverer than that and has drained the suit's weapons systems, so the Doctor lives. However, since the perceived death of the Doctor was regarded as a fixed point in time—one that cannot be changed or rewritten—time itself breaks. Two different versions of the same momentous event have started a chain reaction, and it will continue until all of reality falls apart.

The Doctor knows that both he and Song are vital elements in the change, and that physical contact with one another will cause events to reset and replay as they were supposed to. The Doctor and Song arrange a wedding ceremony. He whispers something in her ear and when they kiss, time is restored, and for them, it is reset. The dramatic events at Lake Silencio play out once again. It has been established that time cannot be rewritten, but that does not mean that the Doctor cannot cheat, so while he appears to die, he remains very much alive (such is the paradoxical nature of time travel).

Another piece of the puzzle falls into place. She is believed to have killed the Doctor, and to maintain that illusion, she will serve out a sentence in Stormcage. Such is her devotion to him that not only has she saved his life once, and then attempted to avert his death on a separate occasion, but she is willing to go to prison for his apparent murder to stop others coming after him.

Song reappears in the 2012 story "The Angels Take Manhatten," in which Pond and Williams fall victim to Weeping Angels, being displaced in time to a point in 1938 where neither the Doctor nor Song can reach them. He has lost his companions, and she has lost her parents. A distraught Doctor asks Song if she will travel with him, and she indicates that she will, but only for a bit.

It is especially cruel that after all the disclosures that have brought the Doctor, River Song, Amy, and Rory together, and established their remarkable connection, the latter two are ripped away, leaving the Doctor and Song united in their grief.

She makes a reappearance in the 2013 story "The Name of the Doctor," in which her digital version from the library is summoned to participate in a conference call by allies who are concerned about the Doctor. After the call is ended, she maintains a link with Clara Oswald (Jenna Coleman) who can still see and hear her, although she appears to be the only one. Later it is revealed that the Doctor can see and hear her too, and when she asks him why he never spoke to her, he says he thought it would hurt too much. When she says he believes she could have coped, he corrects her, saying he thought it would hurt *him* too much—and he is right.

We meet Song one final time in the 2015 story "The Husbands of River Song," in which she is undertaking a caper to steal a rare diamond. The Twelfth Doctor (Peter Capaldi) learns that she occasionally *borrows* the Tardis in her mischievous schemes, and that while she really does love him, she is never sure how much he is capable of loving her back. They end up on Darillium, as indicated back when he first met her in the library, where he gives her a sonic screwdriver and tells her that he will spend the night with her—her *last* night—only, nights on Dariullium last for twenty-four years. What more of a romantic gesture could he make?

Song turned out to be a controversial element in *Doctor Who*. Moffat came under fire for the way that she, and other women, were written, outwardly appearing to be clever, strong, and independent, but who are mostly portrayed as little more than satellites caught in the Doctor's orbit. Certainly, the writing struggles to stand up to the scrutiny of the Bechdel Test (a test that is the measure of representation of women in film, asking if any of the women present can hold a conversation about anything other than a man). Song is a truly brilliant character, exceptionally portrayed by Alex Kingston, but to viewers, her entire life ends up revolving around the Doctor, far more than any companion's ever has, so it is understandable why some feminists have been up in arms about the way she has been written.

Some fans felt as though her story arc dragged on for far too long, while others could not quite accept the notion of the Doctor having a wife, and all the intimacies that are involved. Let us not, however, forget that while the Doctor may have been portrayed as fairly *asexual* in the classic-era series, he did have a granddaughter, so it is not as though he is unknowledgeable about such things.

Kingston, incidentally, was born in 1963, the same year that *Doctor Who* first aired, and has long been a fan of the show.

Chapter 10

A Bestiary of Nemeses

Figure 10 Daleks! BBC / Photofest © BBC

The Doctor has never had a shortage of foes, and in this chapter, we are going to examine some of his most well-known ones. Unlike many of his own kind, the Doctor is willing to interfere in the affairs of others wherever and whenever he sees injustice happening. This invariably creates adversaries, but as the Doctor (Sylvester McCoy) points out to Ace in the 1988 story "Remembrance of the Daleks," "You can always judge a man by the quality of his enemies."

Chapter 10

DALEKS

On the subject of Daleks, let us start there, with the oldest and most famous of the Doctor's foes. He first encounters them in a seven-part story that ran from December 1963 to February 1964, called "The Daleks." In it, the First Doctor (William Hartnell), Susan (Carole Ann Ford), Barbara (Jaqueline Hill), and Ian (William Russell) arrive in an outwardly dead world, in the middle of a petrified forest. As they explore, they spot a city off in the distance with no signs of life.

The planet is Skaro, and the city is the home of the Daleks, a race that would go on to become the scourge of every other life-form in the galaxy. While they are revealed to be horrifically mutated creatures lurking within armored casings, they were once humanoid. Called the Kaled (from which the name Dalek is an anagram), they had a bitter thousand-year war with the Thals, another race that they shared Skaro with, culminating in a neutronic war that devastated their world, leaving it a radioactive husk.

The war between the Kaleds and the Thals rivals some of the worst of humanity's own prejudices and atrocities. The hatred that the Kaleds feel toward the Thals is not dissimilar to that of the Nazis' attitudes regarding racial superiority over what they deemed lesser races. When we see Kaled society as it was in the 1975 story "Genesis of the Daleks," the war has already been in progress for a very long time, resulting in an attrition of resources and equipment on both sides. Fascistic parallels persist, with the upper echelons of the Kaled Military wearing black uniforms and giving Nazi-like salutes to one another. Security Commander Nyder (Peter Miles), head of the Special Unit, has a fanatical devotion to the cause of keeping the Kaled race pure, ensuring their survival through the complete eradication of the Thal people.

But even his fanaticism pales in comparison to that of their chief scientist, Davros (Michael Wisher), a gnarled and withered man with assistive implants who uses an electronically powered chair for mobility—one that looks exactly like the lower half of a Dalek. He has dedicated his life to the creation of ways to safeguard the continuation of the Kaled race, even if that means altering them by unthinkable means. Not all the science divisions are as zealous as he is and are misled as to the real purpose of what Davros calls his "Mark III Travel Machine"—a Dalek!

Since mutations among their people have already begun, as a result of chemical warfare, Davros convinces the other scientists that forced genetic mutation is inevitable and is the only assured means of survival in the long run. He develops his Dalek machines to encase these mutated forms, but the scientists are unaware that he had altered them to be without conscience or pity, or that their weapons are for more than self-defense.

Knowing that his immoral research might come under threat from his own government, Darvos leaks information to the Thals, allowing them to launch a rocket at the dome where they reside, killing them all. He and his cohorts are safe in their bunker, continuing their work on the Daleks, but his arrogance means he miscalculates the ruthlessness of his own creation. The Daleks take over the production of their machines and turn on their creator, exterminating him.

Time and time again, the Daleks suffer setbacks, but because survival is encoded into their very existence, they always manage to rise again. When they encounter another species, the android Movellans, with whom they go to war, they learn that both sides operate on the basis of cold unfeeling logic, so they keep encountering tactical stalemates. The Daleks seek out Davros from the underground bunker where they left him, hoping to use his mind to aid them in victory. It is the first of several occasions when the Daleks realize that they still need their creator, far more than they are willing to admit.

The Daleks form their own hierarchies, but this just exacerbates civil wars breaking out among them, each with divided loyalties. There are factions loyal to Davros, factions loyal to the Supreme Dalek, and factions loyal to the Emperor Dalek. On top of that, those with genetic links—however weak—to the Kaled race hate those without—the ones that have been created from other life-forms to swell Dalek numbers. Then some have completely pure Kaled lineage—referred to as the Dalek Paradigm—who hate all other Daleks in turn.

All infighting ceases when the Daleks and the Time Lords have a confrontation in what is known as the Time War, a horrendous battle that rages throughout all of space and time, devastating many other species caught up in the fighting, and leaving both Daleks and Time Lords alike on the brink of extinction.

The real creator of the Daleks is Welsh screenwriter and novelist Terry Nation (1930–1997) who invented them when he accepted an offer to write for *Doctor Who*. Not even he could have anticipated just how popular and enduring the Daleks would become, firmly cementing their place in pop culture and creating a science-fiction merchandise phenomenon. Instantly recognizable and looking quite unlike anything seen up to that point, they captured the imagination of viewers, holding them transfixed with a combination of terror and excitement. When they first appeared on television, young children in school playgrounds up and down the length of the United Kingdom could be heard shouting, "Exterminate!" and despite their lengthy absence from television screens, the same thing happened when they returned to the show in 2005, admirably demonstrating their lasting popularity.

CYBERMEN

Next on the list, certainly in terms of popularity and longevity, is the Cybermen. They first appear in the 1966 story "The Tenth Planet." They hail from Mondas, the twin plant of Earth that is knocked out of orbit by a cosmic cataclysm, becoming a rogue planet. The Mondasian people start replacing organic parts with cybernetic parts to help them survive the harsh conditions they face. Over time, this results in the loss of their culture, and they adopt the term Cybermen for themselves. They discover a means of piloting their planet, navigating it back toward Earth, where they intend to steal its energy and turn its inhabitants into Cybermen. Their plans go awry, and Mondas explodes.

Not all the Cybermen are destroyed by this, and those who survive relocate to Telos, making it their new home world. In the 1967 story "Tomb of the Cybermen," archaeologists travel to Telos to find and examine the remains of the Cybermen, believed to have perished centuries beforehand. Some of the group suspect that the Cybermen are not as dead as assumed, merely lying in a dormant state, and they intend on reviving them, thinking they will share their power. Once it becomes clear that there is no negotiating with them, the revived Cybermen are forced back into hibernation, and their "tomb" is sealed once more.

Like the Daleks, they are all about the survival of their kind, and with the ability to convert other life-forms into Cybermen, they keep finding ways to propagate themselves (they are not obsessed with genetic ancestry, wanting to transform *all* organic life into Cybermen). While early Cybermen are a mixture of organic and cybernetic, the more their species evolves, the less the organic parts are deemed necessary, culminating in the brain itself being regarded as the only important organ of preservation. Indeed, whenever we meet a Cyber Controller—one of their leaders—their brain is visible through semiopaque or transparent panels in their helmets.

Their ability to conquer and convert other species means that they have assembled huge fleets throughout their history but their biggest failing is in underestimating the lengths that others will go to avoid being turned into Cybermen. This leads to the discovery that Cybermen are allergic to gold, and when made into gold dust, it can clog up their respiratory systems, killing them (sadly, this is a weakness they eventually overcome).

One of the most interesting things about the Cybermen is that the Doctor has encountered them in different histories, even different dimensions, and the Cybermen always seem to find a way of coming into being, like their very existence is an inevitability. The Cybermen that the Tenth Doctor (David Tennant) encounters in a parallel version of Earth in the 2006 two-part story "Rise of the Cybermen"/"Age of Steel" are created by wheelchair-bound

John Lumic (Roger Lloyd Pack). He views his own condition as being symptomatic of organic weakness, seeking to "upgrade" humans into a stronger, more resilient form.

Throughout *Doctor Who*, the Cybermen change their design multiple times, but whatever form they take, the basic armored humanoid shape with handlebar "lugs" on either side of their head remains a characteristic element. Different versions have diverse attributes to distinguish them by—some with head-mounted weaponry, some with arm-mounted weaponry, some that can disassemble themselves (with each separate part having autonomy), and some even have rocket propulsion built into their legs. The one thing they all have in common is that their emotions are purged. There is no point in upgrading the body to be strong if the mind is prone to emotional weakness. Most of all, though, it is a form of self-defense, for if the conscious, feeling parts of the brain were to comprehend the butchery and pain that their bodies go through during the process of conversion, they would be driven mad enough to kill themselves.

Their most powerful form to date comes when the Master (Sacha Dhawan) converts the dead remains of the Time Lords of Gallifrey into Cybermen, what he dubs "Cyber Masters," retaining their regenerative abilities, resurrecting themselves whenever they are killed. Unfortunately, there is a huge narrative inconsistency here in that Time Lord regeneration repairs and even regrows damaged organic matter, so cyber-converted Time Lords should be restored to their former selves upon regeneration, not merely sustaining their hybrid form.

The Cybermen were invented by the combined talents of Kit Pedlar (1927–1981), an English scientist, screenwriter, and author, and Gerry Davis (1930–1991), also a screenwriter. Curious about what would happen if a person had so many prosthetics that it became impossible to distinguish between man and machine, they devised the Cybermen as a fictional terror that has some roots in scientific fact.

As it is, here in the twenty-first century, the science of bionics and assistive prosthetics is very real, giving people with disabilities a better quality of life. Medical science has created powered exoskeletons that give some mobility back to paraplegics. Even the small act of enhancing our senses using spectacles, contact lenses, or hearing aids is a form of augmentation we use to make up for physical weaknesses. There is a very real philosophical and intellectual movement called transhumanism, promoting the enhancement of humans through technological adaptation, and there is a grassroots movement that indulges in what is known as biohacking. While there might be an appetite for technological enrichment of our organic selves, let us hope that it never comes at the cost of our humanity, lest we too become Cybermen.

Chapter 10

SONTARANS

While they might not be as popular as some of the Doctor's other enemies, certainly in terms of the number of appearances they have made, the Sontarans (pronounced with an emphasis on the "tar" syllable) justify their position as next on our list. They are a mono-gendered, male-only species from the planet Sonar, in the southern spiral arm of the galaxy. They generally have a disdain for females, perceiving them to be weak and, therefore, unsuited to the rigors of warfare. Short, squat, muscular warriors with ugly domed heads, they were bred for war and created with the express purpose of dying in battle for the expansion and glory of the Sontaran Empire.

They propagate themselves using cloning technology. Since casualties in battle are usually extensive, cloning is the only way of keeping their active numbers remotely in balance with their fatalities, and it removes entirely the need for females in their society. They produce batches of up to a million embryos every four minutes, after which it takes only ten minutes for said embryos to grow to combat-ready adulthood.

Unfortunately, this leaves them with an inherent weakness, for while they are growing, their umbilical cords are attached to the back of their necks (located under the probic vent in their armor) leaving that area susceptible to damage. A heavy blow there can render them unconscious, and a blade inserted into the probic vent will kill them instantly. It is said that this weakness is the reason why Sontaran warriors never retreat in battle, turning their most vulnerable spot to face their enemy. The vent itself is necessary, having two purposes. The first is to allow a change of gases in their armor every twenty-seven hours while in an incompatible atmosphere, and the second is that long-term physical exertion can exhaust their energy reserves and they can recharge themselves through the vent.

Their bitter enemies, the Rutans (as seen in the 1977 story "The Horror of Fang Rock"), are a shape-shifting species who, in their natural form, are green, jellyfish-like creatures. They have been at war for tens of thousands of years, so long, in fact, that it is said they have forgotten the reason why the conflict started in the first place. Despite having an archrival in the Rutans, Sontarans are happy to spread out and conquer whatever planets and races they encounter, mostly for the strategic value they bring to their war effort.

As is befitting a warrior race, all their technologies are created primarily for militaristic purposes. They have huge motherships that can disperse hundreds of spherical capsules, each piloted by a single Sontaran, and a single mothership and its occupants are usually more than enough to subjugate a whole planet. Their field weapons are adapted to their physical form and the three stubby digits that they have.

They made their first appearance in the 1973 story "The Time Warrior," and it wasn't long before they returned in the 1975 story "The Sontaran Experiment," in which one of their warriors conducts physical and psychological testing on humans as part of an invasion stratagem, seeing how easily they might be conquered. It is in the 1978 story "The Invasion of Time" that we get to see them at their most audacious, invading Gallifrey to seize control over the power of space and time. Regardless of their defeats, Sontarans keep on coming, and many races throughout the galaxy live in fear of one day hearing their battle cry—"Son-tar-ha!"

Humanity is no stranger to warfare. Since our ancestors first learned to make tools and use them as weapons, we have been in conflict with one another, citing race, religion, and territorial lines on maps as perfectly virtuous reasons to do so. Humans, however, are not engineered for war, and as time has progressed, we have become increasingly reliant on new technologies to enhance our aggressive capabilities. From intercontinental ballistic missiles that can deliver devastating nuclear payloads, to drone warfare that allows for the killing of enemy combatants using joysticks and screens (not dissimilar to playing computer games), we have become very good at removing the up-close-and-personal element from fighting. But the more we distance ourselves from it, the easier it is to turn a blind eye to the sheer horror of warfare.

ICE WARRIORS

We are used to hearing about Mars being a dead planet, but it was not always that way. It was once home to the Ice Warriors, a cold-blooded reptilian species that encase themselves in biomechanical armor that has a reptilian, almost crocodile-like appearance, with wrist-mounted sonic weapons.

Despite their fearsome appearance, Ice Warriors are not inherently evil, even if their sibilant whisper-like speech gives off sinister overtones. In the 1972 story "The Curse of Peladon," the Third Doctor (Jon Pertwee) meets some Ice Warriors who have renounced violence and have become members of the Galactic Federation. In a sequel, the 1974 story "The Monster of Peladon," Ice Warriors act as a peacekeeping force for the Galactic Federation, although their leader, Ice Lord Azaxyr (Alan Bennion), has conspired to engineer a crisis because he longs to return to their warrior-like past.

It is quite something for a species like the Ice Warriors to forsake their violent history. Despite this, Ice Warriors are still dangerous and inherently mistrusting of other species, particularly humans. In the 1967 story "The Ice Warriors," the Second Doctor (Patrick Troughton) meets a group of scientists who have found Ice Warriors trapped in a glacier for millennia. Thinking of them only as an archaeological find, they cut one out and take it back to their base (reminiscent of the plot from the 1951 science-fiction horror movie *The Thing from Another World*).

The Ice Warrior, Varga (Bernard Bresslaw) thaws out and returns to the glacier to liberate his comrades still trapped in the ice. Despite the Doctor trying to convince them that he wants to help free their ship so they can leave Earth, they are skeptical of his offer. In the end, the scientist's ionizer, which they have been using to hold the unrelenting advance of glaciers at bay, preventing a new ice age, is trained on the Ice Warrior's ship as it is powering up, and it is destroyed.

After a lengthy hiatus, in the 2013 story "Cold War," a lone Ice Warrior trapped in a block of ice, is taken aboard a Soviet submarine in 1983. Their scientist, Professor Grisenko (David Warner), mistakenly thinks it is a frozen mammoth. When the Ice Warrior, General Skaldak (Spencer Wilding) thaws out, he tries sending a signal to others of his kind but is rendered unconscious by Lieutenant Stepashin (Tobias Menzies). Knowing that an Ice Warrior like Skaldak will seek retribution for the attack on him, the Eleventh Doctor (Matt Smith) tells him he has been trapped in ice for over five thousand years and that the assault was an error of judgment, that no further hostilities are necessary. Skaldak's warrior code convinces him that retaliation is obligatory, and believing he has nothing to live for, he plans to launch the submarine's nuclear payload, knowing that the paranoia of the era will spark off a global nuclear war. When an Ice Warrior ship arrives, answering Skaldak's distress signal, he shows mercy, deactivating the missiles. This story is notable in that it is the first time we ever get to glimpse an Ice Warrior out of their armor, utilizing modern CGI to portray the skinny, elongated frames of their organic selves in a way that would not have been possible in classic-era *Doctor Who*.

In the 2017 story "Empress of Mars," the Twelfth Doctor (Peter Capaldi) travels to Mars, following the discovery of the words "God Save the Queen" formed out of rocks under the Martian ice cap. Estimating the message to have been made in the past, he travels there in 1881, meeting a group of Victorian soldiers from Earth. They rescued and befriended an Ice Warrior they call "Friday" (Richard Ashton) when they discovered him in his crashed ship in Africa. Traveling with him to back Mars, and establishing a breathable base in an underground cavern, they intend on mining for resources. Friday has ulterior motives, using them to find, and hopefully resurrect, his queen, Iraxxa (Adele Lynch), and the other Ice Warriors from their dormant state. This happens, but when a nervous soldier accidentally fires off a shot at her, it is taken as a declaration of war. When a loathsome character, Captain Catchlove (Ferdinand Kinsley), takes Iraxxa hostage at knifepoint, Colonel Godsacre (Anthony Calf) kills him and begs the Queen to take his life but spare the lives of his men. She is impressed by this noble gesture and says she will spare them all if they pledge themselves to her service, which they do.

The Ice Warriors may have a fierce legacy, but it has not stopped them from working toward peaceful solutions. When Ice Warriors and the Doctor have found themselves at odds, it has usually come about because of wariness and miscommunication, but the fact that they can still find it in themselves to rise above their aggressive nature should be an example to us all, giving hope to the process of diplomacy to quell rising tensions.

AUTONS

The Autons, creatures made of living plastic, have long had the ability to unnerve viewers, turning everyday objects, such as mannequins, toys, and even chairs into potential means of killing humans. We first encounter them in the 1970 story "Spearhead from Space," in which the Nestine Consciousness, a hive-mind intelligence, uses them as its invasion force. They are brought to earth under the guise of a meteorite shower, but the polyhedrons that fall from the skies are plastic, not rock, and are power sources for the Nestine. Having taken over a toy factory, it is set up to produce duplicates of key government and public figures to help facilitate their invasion plans.

In episode four of the 1970 story "Spearhead from Space," there is a scene where mannequins in shop windows come to life, smashing through the glass, and using weapons concealed in their hands, start shooting passersby in the street. It is a scene that is shocking for its time, causing nightmares in children and adults alike, and I could imagine many a person walking down a shop-filled street after that episode aired, nervously glancing at the shop windows for any signs of movement from the mannequins.

The Third Doctor (Jon Pertwee) and Liz Shaw (Caroline John) confront the invading Nestine in a host form created for it, something resembling a cephalopod, and neutralize it, causing all the Autons under its influence to cease functioning.

The Autons return in the 1971 story "Terror of the Autons," in which the Master (Roger Delgado), assists them in their latest plan to invade Earth. This story also has its shocking scenes, particularly ones where a man is smothered to death by a plastic chair that engulfs him as he sits on it, and when Autons, disguised with carnival outfits, hand out fake daffodils that spray out a plastic film, covering the victim's face and suffocating them. Jo Grant (Katy Manning) almost loses her life to one of these.

So persistent is the legacy of the Autons that when Russell T. Davies brings the show back in 2005, they are the first enemy the Ninth Doctor (Christopher Eccleston) faces.

According to the Science History Institute's history of plastics, while early forays into synthetic polymers had occurred previously, the science of plastics took off after World War II. According to them, "The possibilities of plastics gave some observers an almost utopian vision of a future with abundant material wealth thanks to an inexpensive, safe, sanitary substance that could be shaped by humans to their every whim."[1] Plastic waste in our oceans was first observed in the 1960s but has grown to the point where we now have the Great Pacific Garbage Patch, a collection of plastic waste about the size of Texas floating in the Pacific Ocean. The National Geographic Society has even reported on a plastic bag having been discovered in the Mariana Trench—the deepest known part of the ocean—when examining the Deep-Sea Debris Database, a collection of undersea photos and videos logged from over five thousand dives over the past thirty years.[2] While we may not have to face Autons, plastic still poses a very real threat to humanity, along with all other species on our planet.

SILURIANS AND SEA DEVILS

Next up, and taking joint place in the list, are the Silurians and the Sea Devils. They are both a highly intelligent race of reptilian humanoids, native to planet Earth, whose scientifically advanced society rose to prominence long before mammals became the dominant species.

Predicting an impending cataclysm when a rogue body is detected approaching the Earth, they choose to go into hibernation deep underground to avoid atmospheric devastation, intending to revive themselves once things have settled. However, their predictions are inaccurate. The rogue body is captured by Earth's orbit and becomes our moon, and the mechanism the Silurians and Sea Devils create to awaken them fails to do so. Like the Ice Warriors, neither the Silurians nor the Sea Devils are fundamentally evil. They are just frustrated that their culture has been forgotten about and the Earth, which they still consider *their* planet, has been overrun by mammals.

When some of them are roused from their slumber in the 1970 story "The Silurians," they find a world that has moved on without them. The Third Doctor (John Pertwee) tries to broker peace, imploring their leader to find a way to coexist with humans. While he is receptive to this notion, a younger upstart among their number refuses to concede, killing the leader and assuming his position. The Doctor fools the Silurians into thinking there is going to be a catastrophic overload of the nuclear reactor they had been draining power from, and they descend back underground to return to a state of hibernation.

In the 1972 story "The Sea Devils," ships have been disappearing in the English Channel. Being used as pawns by the Master (Roger Delgado), the

Sea Devils attack shipping and take over a naval base. The Master forces the Doctor to help him build a machine that will revive the rest of the dormant Sea Devils, but the Doctor sabotages it, causing the base to be destroyed. Interestingly, in this story the Doctor points out that the name "Silurian" is a misnomer and that they should really be called "Eocines"—a response to the many scientists and geologists who wrote in to complain that reptilian life during the Silurian Era would not have been possible.

In a powerful antiwar story from 1984, "Warriors of the Deep," an underwater military base in 2084 is attacked by a combined force of Silurians and Sea Devils. They intend on launching the nuclear missiles stationed there, sparking a devastating war between the two dominant superpowers, clearing the planet of humans and leaving it free for them to retake. By the end of the story only the Fifth Doctor (Peter Davison), Tegan (Janet Fielding), and Turlough (Mark Strickson) are left alive, leaving an appalled Doctor to muse, "There should have been another way."

In 2018, American astrophysicist Adam Frank and British climatologist Gavin Schmidt created the Silurian Hypothesis, an experiment to evaluate science's ability to detect any advanced civilizations that may have existed prior to humankind.[3] Their hypothesis is named after the intelligent reptilian precursors from *Doctor Who*.

WEEPING ANGELS

Most of the creatures we have looked at in this chapter have their roots in classic-era *Doctor Who*, which speaks volumes about their popularity and longevity. But there is one monster from modern-era *Doctor Who* that is absolutely worthy of a mention, one that has the capacity to scare audiences in a way that few ever have—the Weeping Angels.

Resembling human-sized stone statues of angels, the kind that one might find in any number of cemeteries around the world, they are a predatory species, consuming the time-potential energy released by victims when the Weeping Angels displace them in time. They are often found with their hands covering their faces, but as a potential victim becomes aware of them, they transform from having a serene appearance into something far more bestial.

They are swift and silent, able to cover distances toward their prey very quickly, but when they are observed, they are caught in a quantum-locked state, turning to stone and quite unable to move. They can only move when their prey is not looking directly at them or is unable to see them. They can interfere with light bulbs, draining their energy, and causing them to flicker. Imagine, if you will, a corridor with a single light bulb. You see a Weeping Angel at the far end. The light goes out momentarily, and when it comes on again, the Weeping Angel is halfway down the corridor. The light goes out again, just for a second, and when it comes back on, the Weeping Angel is almost upon you, mouth open, baring its fangs, its clawed hands reaching out to grab you. Nothing short of terrifying, right?

When they first appear in the 2007 story "Blink," the Tenth Doctor (David Tennant) is stuck in 1969, and through a hidden recording embedded in DVDs, communicates with Sally Sparrow (Carey Mulligan) in the present, asking for her help in getting his Tardis back. He tells her about the Weeping Angels, that they cover their eyes with their hands, not because they are weeping, but because they cannot risk looking at one another. His most sage advice comes in how to stay alive, "Don't blink. Don't even blink. Blink and you're dead. They are fast, faster than you could believe. Don't turn your back, don't look away, and don't blink."

Sally finds the Tardis and gets into it, but not before being surrounded by several Weeping Angels. When the Tardis dematerializes, the Angels are left looking at one another, trapped by their own gazes.

There is more than one kind of Weeping Angel, such as the Cherubim that appear in the 2012 story "The Angels Take Manhattan." They are not silent, emitting childlike giggling and discernible footsteps as they move about, almost as if they take pleasure in distressing their quarry.

The Weeping Angels were created by Steven Moffat, inspired by seeing an angel statue in a graveyard in Dorset. He recounts taking his son back there, years later, but the statue was gone. He also drew inspiration from the children's game "Statues," also known as "Red Light, Green Light," or "Grandmother's Footsteps," where one child turns their back on a group of other children who advance upon them to tag them. When the lone child turns around, all the other children must freeze in place. Apparently, Moffat always found this game to be frightening. Wouldn't it be interesting if Weeping Angels were real and were the origin of humanity's collective fear of the dark?

Chapter 11

The Master

Figure 11 The Doctor's archenemy. BBC / Photofest © BBC

While the Doctor has faced many adversaries down through the decades, one stands out as being different from all the rest, one that not only knows the Doctor as well as he knows himself, but one who used to be his best friend. I am talking, of course, about the Master. Despite the rift that would grow between the two due to their differing ideologies, there is more in common between them than either might like to admit. They both resented the staid and rule-bound nature of life on Gallifrey, each wanting to escape out into the universe and engage with it, rather than merely being passive observers like the rest of their kind.

The concept of the Master came along during Jon Pertwee's tenure as the Third Doctor. Producer Barry Letts and script editor Terrance Dicks wanted to introduce a recurring villain, one who would be presented as an archenemy to the Doctor, in a similar way that Professor James Moriarty is to Sherlock Homes. The name, the Master, was agreed upon because, just like the Doctor, they wanted it to reflect an academic title (especially fitting as the Doctor and the Master attended the academy on Gallifrey together).

ROGER DELGADO

Barry Letts had a single name in mind for someone to play the role, someone that he had worked with previously and who was already a good friend of Pertwee. This actor was Roger Delgado, whose debonair and charismatic demeanor instantly brought the character of the Master to life with his intense eyes and a smile that cut sharper than any knife.

The Master made his first appearance in the 1971 story "Terror of the Autons," in which he aids in the invasion of the Earth by the Nestine, a hive-mind entity that controls a form of living plastic, often in the guise of an army of humanoid figures called Autons. When the Third Doctor (Jon Pertwee) points out a serious flaw in the Master's plan, one that would get him killed, the Master betrays his former allies and joins forces with the Doctor to repel the invasion. It is here that we get an important insight into the Master's psyche, that he is not above betraying those he has an alliance with, because when it comes right down to it, the Master's own goals and agendas, along with his personal survival, are more important than anything or anyone else. Delgado's Master treats everybody else as mere playthings, pawns to be used in his game of ultimate power.

Roger Delgado appears as the Master six more times, the 1971 stories "The Mind of Evil," "The Claws of Axos," "Colony in Space," and "The Daemons," as well as the 1972 story "The Sea Devils" and the 1973 story "Frontier in Space." During this period, we learn that the Master enjoys employing the art of disguise and using hypnosis to control and manipulate others. We are also introduced to a weapon that will go on to become his trademark, the Tissue Compression Eliminator (or TCE for short), which compresses the matter in a victim's body down to a doll-like size, killing them in the process. As is befitting of his arrogance, he likes to leave the shrunken bodies of his victims as a sort of calling card.

Delgado was due to appear in one more *Doctor Who* story "The Final Game," in which the Master and the Doctor would have a last confrontation, ending with the Third Doctor's regeneration. This never happened as, very sadly, Roger Delgado died, aged fifty-five, in a car accident while on location in Turkey, filming another series in June 1973.

PETER PRATT

That could have been it for the Master, except that nobody wanted to lose such a great character, and with him also being a Time Lord, he could always regenerate. When the Master appears once again, in the 1976 story "The Deadly Assassin" (played by Peter Pratt), he has a grotesque, living-corpse-like appearance, having squandered all his regenerations during his unscrupulous exploits, and is very near to the end of his final life. He seeks to harness the power of the Eye of Harmony to give himself a new set of regenerations, even if it destroys Gallifrey itself. While his plans are foiled by the Fourth Doctor (Tom Baker), he escapes.

The extensive makeup required for this ruined version of the Master meant that the actor was severely limited in his portrayal, resulting in much of the character's menace being projected through his voice alone.

GEOFFREY BEEVERS

The Master next turns up in the 1981 story "The Keeper of Traken." Still in his ravaged form (now played by Geoffrey Beevers), he seeks to access a powerful energy known as the Source, the very heart of a technologically advanced and peaceful empire called the Traken Union, which the Fourth Doctor describes as "A whole empire held together by people being terribly nice to each other."[1] The elderly Keeper (Denis Carey), who has a direct connection to the Source, reaches out to the Doctor to ask for his help as he senses an all-pervading evil connected to the family of Tremas (Anthony Ainley), the man who is named to become the next Keeper.

It is suspected that the source of evil is Melkur (which literally means "a fly caught in honey"), a name given to any evil creature that arrives on Traken, and like all others before it, it becomes calcified, taking on a statue-like appearance. But Melkur is more than he appears, being the Master's Tardis in disguise. He manipulates Tremas's wife, Kassia (Sheila Ruskin), into giving him access to the Source. With such power he can extend his lifespan by taking over the Doctor's body, but at the Doctor's behest, the Source has been tampered with, the feedback from which causes extensive damage to the Master's Tardis.

Thinking the Master dealt with, the Doctor leaves Traken, but his nemesis is not so easily disposed of. With what limited power he received from the Source, the Master paralyzes Tremas and takes over his body, escaping with the chilling words, "A new body, at last."

ANTHONY AINLEY

Ainley was a popular Master, and a worthy replacement for Roger Delgado, embodying a similar suave and villainous presence. Dressed in a black frock coat and gloves, his mannerisms and laugh projected a confidence and arrogance that had been sorely missing from the Master since Delgado's untimely death. This is also a Master who is demonstrably more ambitious in his desire for conquest and control, taking his time to conceive of and deploy all manner of elaborate traps and plans.

He confronts the Fourth Doctor (Tom Baker) in his final appearance (the 1981 story "Logopolis"), and then faces Peter Davison's Fifth Doctor throughout his run (the 1982 stories "Castrovalva," and "Time Flight," the 1983 stories "The King's Demons," and "The Five Doctors," and the 1984 story "Planet of Fire"). He continues playing the role when Colin Baker's Sixth Doctor appears on the scene (the 1985 stories "The Mark of the Rani" and "The Ultimate Foe") and then when Sylvester McCoy's Seventh Doctor takes over, appearing with him in the very last story of the classic series before its cancellation (the 1989 story "Survival"), making Ainley the longest-serving Master of all.

Ainley loved the role so much that he would keep up the Master's persona on set, even when the cameras had stopped filming. He reprised his role as the Master one last time in the 1997 computer game *Destiny of the Doctors*. A reclusive individual, he died, aged seventy-one, in May 2004.

One of the original concepts behind the Master is that he is the Doctor's brother, adding an element of sibling rivalry to their dynamic. While this was never officially established in the canon, hints were dropped that this might be the case. In the 1984 story "Planet of Fire," while experimenting on making a newer and even deadlier version of his TCE, the Master himself is shrunken and seeks to restore himself through the healing flames of a special chamber attached to a volcano. As the Master grows back to his original size, he threatens the Doctor. When the healing gases have dissipated, and conventional flames return, the Master begs the Doctor to stop it, but he doesn't. The Master then pleads, "Won't you show mercy to your own . . . ," before crying out, engulfed in fire, apparently immolated.[2]

ERIC ROBERTS

The Master returns in the 1996 *Doctor Who* television movie, this time played by American actor Eric Roberts. In a prologue scene, the Master (briefly portrayed by Canadian actor Gordon Tipple), is executed by the Daleks. As the Eighth Doctor (Paul McGann) himself explains in the opening monologue, "It was on the planet Skaro that my old enemy, the Master, was finally put on trial. They say he listened calmly as his list of evil crimes was read. Sentence passed. Then he made his last, and I thought somewhat curious, request. He demanded that I, the Doctor, a rival Time Lord, should take his remains back to our home planet, Gallifrey. It was a request they should never have granted."[3]

With Sylvester McCoy reprising his role as the Seventh Doctor, he takes the Master's remains on board the Tardis. The Master's essence has survived, appearing as a morphing, snakelike creature, which escapes containment and sabotages the Tardis console, causing it to be redirected from Gallifrey to an emergency landing on Earth. It lands in San Francisco's Chinatown and the Doctor emerges, only to be gunned down by violent gang members.

An ambulance is called, and the Doctor is rushed to hospital, but the Master's essence hitches a ride, hiding in the jacket of Bruce (Eric Roberts), the paramedic who is first on the scene. Once Bruce has returned home, and is lying asleep in bed, the Master's essence emerges and enters Bruce's body through his mouth, beginning a process of possession.

This version of the Master is a highly Americanized one—slicked-back hair, aviator sunglasses, and a long black leather coat—an appearance more commonly associated with a mobster from the silver screen than a Time Lord from Gallifrey. He has an air of menace, but it is remarkably overplayed by Roberts. Nevertheless, it still somehow works, invoking memories of cinematic malefactors from old black-and-white movies who were directed to dial up their wickedness as much as possible.

He wants to steal all the Doctor's remaining regenerations for himself, using the Eye of Harmony in the Tardis to drain them, before transferring them to himself.

With the combined efforts of the Doctor and Grace Holloway (Daphne Ashbrook), the Master's plan is halted, and he is pulled toward the entrance to the Eye of Harmony. Even now, after all he has done, the Doctor offers the Master his hand to save him, which he refuses, being drawn into his ostensible demise.

DEREK JACOBI

It is eleven years before we encounter the Master again in the 2007 episode "Utopia," the first in a three-part story along with "The Sound of Drums" and "Last of the Time Lords." The Tenth Doctor (David Tennant), Martha Jones (Freema Agyeman), and Captain Jack Harkness (John Barrowman) travel forward in time to a point where it is close to the end of the universe. On the planet Malcassairo they discover the last vestiges of humanity, struggling to survive against the Futurekind, a retrogressive form of humanoids who are primitive and savage, having sharpened teeth and cannibalistic tendencies.

Rescuing a young man from their clutches, the Doctor and his companions are taken to a missile silo where they meet Professor Yana (Derek Jacobi), an older man who, along with his insectoid assistant Chantho (Chipo Chung), is trying to use a rocket to transport the remnants of humanity to what they believe to be a place of safety—the titular "Utopia." However, the rocket will not work, and Professor Yana seeks the help of the Doctor to fix it.

Professor Yana has been plagued by something for as long as he can remember, the relentless sound of drums in his head. While the Doctor and Jack work on the rocket, Martha stays with Professor Yana and is taken aback when he produces a fob watch, like the one that the Doctor used to hide his real identity in the 2007 two-part story "Human Nature"/"The Family of Blood." She hurries to find the Doctor to tell him of this revelation.

While she is gone, Professor Yana opens the fob watch, having all his memories restored to him. When his assistant Chantho confronts him over his aberrant behavior in lowering the defenses and letting the Futurekind into the silo, the professor takes a live power cable and brandishes it before him. When she realizes that he is no longer the person she thought he was, she asks him who he is, to which he delivers the line, "I . . . am . . . the . . . Master," with a level of malevolence that chills the blood.[4]

He electrocutes Chantho, but she manages to get off a shot which mortally wounds the Master. The Doctor, Martha, and Captain Jack arrive, but not before the dying Master locks himself in the Doctor's Tardis. While there, he declares that if the Doctor can be young and strong, then so can he, and with that, he regenerates into a younger Master (John Simms). Although Derek Jacobi only got to play the Master for a very short period, his portrayal was one of the most menacing of all of them, utilizing his talent as an outstanding thespian to embody a character whose every line was delivered with utter contempt and evil.

JOHN SIMMS

The newly regenerated Master steals the Tardis and returns to Earth in 2007, where he takes up the mantle of John Saxon, who manipulates the public to win an election to become the prime minister. The Doctor, Martha, and Captain Jack manage to escape the Futurekind, with the Doctor having fixed Captain Jack's broken Time Agency Vortex Manipulator and using it to follow the Master.

The Master gives a public broadcast to tell the citizens of Great Britain that he has been contacted by an extraterrestrial race, the Toclafane, who proclaim that they have come in peace to share their technology and wisdom with the people of Earth.

The Doctor realizes that the Toclafane aren't what the Master claims they are. The name comes from Time Lord mythology. During a conversation with the Master, using Martha's phone, the Doctor reveals that Gallifrey and all the Time Lords are gone, having burned in the Time War. The Master, in turn, reveals that the Time Lords resurrected him because they thought he would be the perfect warrior for a Time War. He admits that when he saw the Dalek emperor in person, he was so scared that he ran, ran to the end of the universe where he made himself human in the hope the Daleks would never find him.

During "The Sound of Drums," when the Doctor is talking to both Martha and Captain Jack, she asks who the Master is to the Doctor. He admits that the Master was a friend. Martha admits she thought he was going to say that the Master is really his brother. The Doctor is scornful of this, declaring that she watches too much television, ending once and for all any ideas about the Master and the Doctor being closely related. He then tells them a story about when the young Master underwent the ritual of facing the Untempered Schism. He affirms that some Gallifreyan children are inspired by such an occasion, while some run away, and others go mad. It is heavily implied that the latter of these is what happened in the case of the Master. Indeed, John Simms's portrayal of the Master is one where the charming, charismatic, and coolheaded nature of the Master's past is replaced with a more frenetic, unhinged form of evil, something that heralds a striking disconnect from the way the Master has been depicted previously. Unfortunately, this makes the Master seem *less* malevolent, suggesting that his deviant behavior stems from a madness driving him to perform terrible deeds, rather than them being a cognizant choice, deliberately made by a rational, if evil, mind.

The American president (Colin Stinton) turns up, declaring that first contact is to be taken out of the prime minister's hands and that it is now a UNIT operation, taking place aboard UNIT's flying aircraft carrier, the *Valiant*. The Doctor, Martha, and Captain Jack sneak on board and discover the Tardis there, but it has been altered by the Master, having been converted into a Paradox Machine. When some of the Toclafane appear, they kill the president, and the Master reasserts control, activating the Paradox Machine and creating a rift in space-time through which six billion Toclafane descend. Following the Master's command, they begin to decimate the population of the Earth. The Doctor, having been artificially aged a hundred years by the Master, is helpless to stop him.

In the final part of the story "Last of the Time Lords," a year has passed, and Martha Jones has traveled the globe, looking to build up a resistance, and now she has returned home to Britain. She finds that the entire south coast of England has been converted into shipyards, one of many, building a fleet of two hundred thousand rockets from which the Master and the Toclafane will launch a war against the rest of the universe. Meanwhile, having survived a failed coup onboard the *Valiant*, the Master punishes the Doctor by suspending his ability to regenerate and aging him even further, until he is reduced to a smaller, wizened version of himself.

With the aid of Thomas Milligan (Tom Ellis) and Professor Docherty (Ellie Haddington), Martha captures one of the Toclafane. When the professor opens it up, they are horrified to discover that the Toclafane are actually the mutated evolution of the last vestiges of humanity. When the rocket ship bound for Utopia reached its destination, the humans found only darkness. They had to adapt, ridding themselves of their weak bodies and locking their heads away in floating metal spheres to survive. That is when the Master returned to find them, bending them to his will. He converted the Doctor's Tardis into a Paradox Machine so that the Toclafane could return to the past, attacking and killing humanity without canceling themselves out.

Martha reveals to Thomas and Professor Docherty that UNIT and Torchwood have been studying Time Lords in secret, and if it ever became necessary, they devised a weapon against them. It is an injector gun, one that uses a combination of four chemicals to kill a Time Lord while preventing them from regenerating. Thomas agrees to help Martha find the missing piece, but Professor Docherty betrays them, passing information to the Master in return for information about her missing son. However, it was all part of Martha's strategy. The gun was nothing more than a bluff. Her real reason for traveling around the world was to spread the word of the Doctor, coordinating people so that at the culmination of the Master's countdown, everybody would think one word, "Doctor," and the buildup of all that psychic energy would restore the Doctor once more. It is a highly contrived plot, paralleling the power of prayer and messianic resurrection. Regardless, the Master is overpowered and Captain Jack, using a machine gun, opens fire on the Paradox Machine, rendering it inert. Time is reversed by a whole year, so the space-time rift never opens and the Toclafane invasion force never appears.

With the Master captured, the Doctor says he will take him and look after him. Being the last two Time Lords, he feels a responsibility. Before he can act on this, however, Lucy Saxon, waking up to how much she has been manipulated, shoots the Master. The Doctor cradles him in his arms, begging him to regenerate, but the Master, in a final act of defiance, uses sheer willpower to suppress his ability to regenerate, and so he dies. The Doctor takes his body and burns it on a funeral pyre. In the end, a scene is shown, strongly mirroring a scene from the finale of the 1980 *Flash Gordon* movie, where a woman's hand picks up the Master's ring from the ashes next to the smoldering funeral pyre and the sound of the Master laughing can be heard.

The Master makes his foreseeable comeback in the two-part story "The End of Time," shown on Christmas Day 2009 and New Year's Day 2010. The Master's return is foreshadowed by people having bad dreams. Aliens from a race known as the Ood summon the Doctor, not only to warn him of the coming return of the Master but also to tell him that it is only part of a larger design.

In Broadfell Prison, where Lucy Saxon is being incarcerated, a group of disciples, utterly loyal to the Master, have been preparing the way for his return. They have concocted a series of potions that will restore him, but all that is needed is the biometric link that Lucy can provide. A ritual begins which sees the disciples sacrificing their own life energy to feed the Master's return. Before it is completed, Lucy, who herself predicted he would find a way to come back, throws a volatile potion of her own into the mix, creating an explosion, foreshortening the ritual, and causing the prison to burn to the ground.

The Master survives, but he is not entirely whole, being more irrational than ever, and is left with an insatiable hunger. He is burning up his life essence. When the Doctor finally finds the Master, the Master uses a telepathic link with him so that he too can hear the sound of drums inside his head. They both come to the realization that the sound is real and not just a product of the Master's madness.

The Master is then kidnapped by a force working for Joshua Naismith (David Harewood). He and his daughter, Abigail (Tracy Ifeachor), have been using a captured alien device they have dubbed the Immortality Gate which can initiate cellular regeneration and heal injuries. Naismith calculates that if the device is fully repaired, it could extend human life indefinitely, so that as a gift to her, his daughter need never die. The Master agrees to fix it, but he alters things so that it transfers his DNA template to every human on the earth, rewriting them to become copies of him, creating a master race.

We then see Rassilon (Timothy Dalton), now firmly cemented in lore as a villain, proclaiming the return of the Time Lords and the end of time itself!

Chapter 11

On the last day of the Time War, when the fall of Gallifrey is predicted, Rassilon concocts a plan to have a rhythm of four—the heartbeat of a Time Lord—broadcast back in time to the moment when the young Master looks into the Untempered Schism. What the Master interpreted as the sound of drums, which would torment him from that moment onward, was deliberately seeded into his mind so the Time Lords could use it as a beacon to find him, escaping from the time lock they are caught within, and their assured doom. Rassilon sends a white point star diamond to the location on Earth where the Master is and the Master, understanding the significance of this, uses it to amplify the signal.

When Rassilon and a small complement of Time Lords appear as a vanguard, the Master divulges that he only allowed them to return because he doesn't want to have his "master race" remain a mongrel species. No, he intends to use the Immortality Gate, and his own genetic template, to overwrite the Time Lords rather than the humans. He fails to take into account the power of Rassilon, who, in turn, reverses what the Master has done, returning the humans to their former selves. The Master's overconfidence made him overlook something else—the return of the Time Lords also means the return of Gallifrey, which will knock Earth out of its orbit, causing untold damage and rendering it uninhabitable.

Nevertheless, the Master assumes the restoration of the Time Lords is worth it, but the Doctor counters his viewpoint. "You weren't there in the final days of the war. You never saw what was born. But if the time lock's broken, then everything's coming through, not just the Daleks, but the Star of Degradations. The Hoard of Travesties. The Nightmare Child that could have been king with his army of meanwhiles and neverweres. The war turned into hell. And that's what you've opened, right above the Earth. Hell is descending."[5]

Rassilon announces his intention to escape such chaos by initiating what he calls the "final sanction." He will open a rupture, spilling the time vortex out into everything, ripping it apart, and bringing about the end of time and all creation. He, and his fellow Time Lords, plan to ascend to beings of pure consciousness to escape such devastation.

The Doctor, a man who has a distaste for guns, if forced to bear one, and to choose between shooing Rassilon, the architect of this folly, or the Master, within whom the beacon still resides, breaking the link and forcing the Time Lords back to whence they came. Never a man who chooses violence, he opts to shoot the white point star diamond, breaking the connection. As a fading Rassilon prepares to take vengeance on the Doctor, the Master steps forward, unleashing his fury upon Rassilon for using him as a pawn and making him think he was mad. This confrontation culminates in the Master seemingly being drawn back into the time lock along with the other Time Lords.

MICHELLE GOMEZ

It is another four years before the Master makes an appearance in the 2014 story "Deep Breath." However, this time it is with a more substantial change than ever before as *he* is now *she* (Michelle Gomez). She takes on the appearance of a malevolent Mary Poppins, complete with a hat and (sonic) umbrella. She has been using a device she calls the Neversphere, but which is really a Matrix data slice—a Gallifreyan hard drive—to upload the consciousness of the recently departed while their physical bodies are converted into Cybermen. Once she has edited out all the "boring" bits, like emotions, they are downloaded into their newly upgraded cyber bodies to create an army. It is not until the two-part season finale, "Dark Water"/"Death in Heaven," that her real identity is revealed to the Twelfth Doctor (Peter Capaldi), when she says, "I'm Missy. Short for Mistress. Well, couldn't really keep calling myself the Master, now could I?"[6]

When Cybermen take to the streets, the Doctor thinks that people will flee in fear, but in a telling critique of the technologically obsessed modern culture we live in, Missy throws down her hat and charges people money to take pictures with the metal men. People gather around, taking pictures with their smartphones, oblivious to the danger they are in.

Everywhere the dead are being converted into Cybermen, but not all conversions have gone to plan, such as Danny Pink (Samuel Anderson), the newly deceased boyfriend of Clara Oswald (Jenna Coleman), who still retains the memories of his former life. In a surprising move, Missy gives the control bracelet she uses to rule over the Cybermen to the Doctor, telling him that she is gifting him an army, one that he can use to do whatever he likes, even if that is saving people. The Doctor knows that nobody should have such power, and he throws the control bracelet to Danny Pink's Cyberman. He, in turn, uses it to order all the Cybermen, including himself, to fly into the sky and self-destruct, saving humanity.

Missy displays all the elements of madness that have become a signature of the modern-era Master's persona, but hers has a far more dangerous quality to it. She doesn't just enjoy her conquests; she *delights* in them, killing with both premeditated malice and casual callousness alike, and Michelle Gomez absolutely shines in the role.

Missy makes her return in the 2015 two-part story "The Magician's Apprentice"/"The Witch's Familiar," with the hilariously meta declaration, "Okay, cutting to the chase, not dead, back, big surprise, never mind."[7] She forms an unlikely alliance with Clara to save the Doctor from a perilous situation regarding the Daleks, but with an ally like that, who needs enemies? There are times when she coldheartedly endangers Clara's life to achieve her end goals, but at the same time, we get the impression that she doesn't really *want* Clara dead. Like the Doctor, this renegade Time Lord also enjoys someone to show off their brilliance to. In the end, surrounded by Daleks and a collapsing structure, Missy utters the line, "You know what? I've just had a very clever idea." Foreshadowing, once again, her escape and unavoidable return.

In the 2017 story "Extremis," the Doctor has been summoned to attend the execution of Missy. According to an ancient stipulation by something called the Fatality Index, when it comes to the execution of a Time Lord, another Time Lord must be the one to carry out the sentence. The execution device stops both hearts, and all three brain stems, and delivers a cellular shock wave that permanently disables regenerative ability. The body is then placed in a quantum fold chamber, which will be guarded for no less than a thousand years for, as Rafando (Ivanno Jeremiah), the chief executioner points out, "Life can be a cunning enemy."

When Missy begs the Doctor to spare her life, asking him to teach her how to be good, he alters the wiring of the machine to spare her, but he still locks her away in the quantum fold chamber and promises to guard over her. When he faces overwhelming odds in defeating an enemy that wants absolute control over the Earth, he needs her help, so he opens the vault to consult with her. In the 2017 story "Empress of Mars," the Doctor returns to the Tardis to find Missy out of her vault and at the Tardis console, but she has made no attempt to escape. Could her wish for redemption be real? In the following story "The Eaters of Light," the Doctor reveals that he has allowed Missy to leave the vault to conduct maintenance on the Tardis. It is all part of his test to see if he can trust her so they can become friends again.

In the two-part story "World Enough and Time"/"The Doctor Falls," the Doctor tests how Missy is doing on her path to redemption by sending her out to answer a distress signal. She introduces herself in the most meta way possible, "I am that mysterious adventurer in all of time and space, known only as *Doctor Who*, and these are my disposables, exposition and comic relief," referring to Bill Potts (Pearl Mackie) and Nardole (Matt Lucas) who accompany her.[8] The ship they are on is vast, with many levels and the front end is close to a black hole. It is a colony ship from Mondas, the twin planet of Earth and home of the Cybermen. Bill is mortally injured, and creatures with tight-fitting cloth hoods over their head, dressed in hospital gowns and carrying intravenous drip trolleys arrive, declaring that they will take her away for "repair."

Bill is taken to a hospital on the lowest level of the spaceship, where her destroyed heart is replaced with a mechanical one. She is told she is unable to leave the hospital, because her temporary heart will stop working if she does. While there she befriends Razor, a hospital employee. Because of the effect of time dilation caused by the black hole, ten years pass on the lowest level before the Doctor, Nardole, and Missy can get down there, by which time Razor betrays Bill, taking her for what is called "full conversion." She had now been turned into a Cyberman!

Razor appears to Missy and reveals that he is none other than John Simm's Master in disguise. That, and the traditional goatee he sports, is a nice nod back to Master's past. As an emerging Cyberman threat grows, it seems that Missy's good intentions have been swayed by her former self, falling under his influence. When the Doctor makes a last stand against the mechanical army, he asks the Master and Missy to stand with him. The Master laughs it off and leaves, and Missy follows. Whatever hope the Doctor had to reclaim his friend of old has seemingly been lost forever.

Just before the Master and Missy are about to escape via one of the lift shafts, Missy asks him to come closer, and as they embrace, she drives a blade into his side. When he asks why, she says it is because the Doctor is right, he needs a friend to stand with him, and she is prepared to do so. As she turns to leave, the Master uses his own weapon to shoot her in the back, and she falls. He tells her that she absorbed the full power of his weapon, so there is no hope of her regenerating. She dies as the dying Master descends it the lift to make his escape before he regenerates. Most heart-wrenching of all is that, in the end, Missy learned her lesson of redemption, willing to stand with the Doctor, but he will never get to know about it, always thinking that she abandoned him when he needed her the most.

SACHA DHAWAN

The Master makes his final run of television appearances (so far) with the 2020 two-part story "Spyfall." Someone is assassinating spies all over the world and the Doctor (Jodie Whittaker) is brought in by "C" (Stephen Fry) to investigate on behalf of MI6. An initial investigation points to an alien connection, leading the Thirteenth Doctor (Jodie Whittaker) to the outback of Australia, where MI6 analyst "O" (Sacha Dhawan) has been gathering information about extraterrestrial activity.

All the assassinated agents were investigating Daniel Barton (Lenny Henry), the CEO of the search engine company VOR. While VOR may have had its roots in search, it has grown to be much more than that, expanding to the web, apps, social, global mapping, advertising, scientific and medical research, robotics, data polling, and human analytics (a fictional equivalent to Google, in other words).

When the Doctor, Graham O'Brien (Bradley Walsh), Ryan Sinclair (Tosin Cole), Yasmin Khan (Mandip Gill), and "O" go in pursuit of Barton, they are led to an airfield where Barton is taking off in a plane. The Doctor uses her sonic screwdriver to open the rear hatch, and the group clambers aboard.

When "O" says something inconsistent with what the Doctor read in his file, he admits that he is not really "O," and that he killed and replaced him. He is, in fact, the Master! It transpires that Barton has already left the plane, and there is a bomb in the cockpit that will shortly detonate. Before the Master abandons them, teleporting to his own Tardis, he taunts the Doctor with the phrase, "Everything you think you know is a lie." It is the beginning of one of the most controversial storylines in the entire history of the show, one where writer and executive producer Chris Chibnall attempts to rewrite the origin story of the Doctor.

Having been transported to another dimension by the Kasaavin (the creatures in league with the Master and Barton), the Doctor meets Ada Lovelace (Sylvie Briggs) before being transported back to 1834. They are then propelled forward to Paris in 1943, where they meet SOE (Special Operations Executive) agent Noor Inayat Khan (Aurora Marion). Hotly pursued by the Master in both times, they get the better of him and steal his Tardis to get back to 2020, when Barton is at a press conference. The attendees think he is going to make another innovative announcement, but he tells them that he has been working with the Kasaavins to alter human DNA so that they can be used as DNA-based storage devices. Yes, he wants to turn humanity into hard drives.

The Doctor arrives and puts paid to their plans, driving the Kasaavins back to their own dimension, but not before revealing to them the Master's plan to use them and then discard them. As they disappear, as an act of revenge, they pull him into their own dimension as well. The Doctor then uses the Tardis to go back and create an escape strategy for her companions to ensure their survival from the plane, as well as returning Ada and Noor to their own times.

Sacha Dhawan's Master appears again in the 2020 two-part story "Ascension of the Cybermen"/"The Timeless Child," in which he takes the Doctor back to a destroyed Gallifrey, confessing that it was him who is responsible for the Time Lords' ultimate downfall, having learned of the supposed lies on which their society has been built. He lures a cyber army to Gallifrey and combines their technologies to create the Cyber Masters—Cybermen made out of the corpses of all the dead Time Lords that can regenerate after death, meaning they are a cyber army that is all but impossible to stop.

Dhawan's portrayal is extremely good, finding a balance between the charismatic nature of Masters of old, while retaining the hallmarks of madness that have consumed newer Masters.

The Master appears one last time in the finale, "Power of the Doctor," where he uses technology that he stole from the Time Lords to perpetrate a forced regeneration upon the Doctor, somehow transferring his own consciousness into her existing body (I am not even going to begin to touch upon how little sense this plot device makes). Her companions tap into the energy of regenerating Cyber Masters to expel the Master's consciousness from her, once more spoiling his plans.

WHAT BECAME OF THE MASTER?

Although he does not appear, there is mention of the Master made in the last of the three sixtieth-anniversary stories, "The Giggle," in which the Toymaker (Neil Patrick Harris) tells the Fourteenth Doctor (David Tennant) that a dying Master came to him, begging for his life with one final game, and when he lost, the Toymaker sealed him for all eternity inside his gold tooth. In the end, when the Toymaker is defeated, a woman's hand with red nail polish picks up the tooth to the sound of the Master laughing. Now, where have we seen something similar before . . . ?

It may seem ridiculous, almost pantomimesque, as to the number of times the Master is defeated, seemingly for good, yet he always manages to find a way to return, with little or no explanation. We may not call out, "He's behind you!" to our television screens each and every time he appears, but the sentiment remains. Everybody loves a good villain, and the Master is the archetypal one that we all want—and *need*—to see defeated for our peace of mind, yet somehow, we still root for in the hope that he survives to confront the Doctor another day.

The eternal battle between the Doctor and the Master is representative of one of the most classical elements of storytelling—light versus dark, good versus evil—and while good may prevail, evil is never truly conquered. The decision to create the Master as a polar opposite to the Doctor was probably one of the best decisions in the history of the series. While the Doctor will always be the central, and titular, character of the show, it would be greatly diminished without the threat of the Master lurking somewhere in the wings.

Chapter 12

His Own Worst Enemy

Figure 12 The War Doctor. BBC / Photofest © BBC

Steven Moffat, series showrunner from 2010 to 2017, attended a Q&A panel at the ExCel London in November 2013, celebrating the show's fiftieth anniversary. He said of the Doctor, "Heroes are important. Heroes tell us something about ourselves. History books tell us who we used to be. Documentaries tell us who we are now. But heroes tell us who we want to be. And a lot of our heroes depress me. But, you know, when they made this particular hero, they didn't give him a gun, they gave him a screwdriver to fix things.

They didn't give him a tank or a warship or an X-Wing fighter, they gave him a call box from which you can call for help, and they didn't give him a superpower or pointy ears a heat-ray, they gave him an extra heart. They gave him two hearts. And that's an extraordinary thing; There will *never* come a time when we don't need a hero like the Doctor."

There have been times when the Doctor has walked a fine line, fighting against his darker impulses. His integrity usually prevails, be that through his own resolve, or through the aid of friends and companions that remind him who he really is—the *Doctor*. He generally lives up to his self-appointed name, that which gives him his identity, but when he abandons it, and that identity, what then does he become?

THE VALEYARD

In the 1986 season-long story arc, "Trial of a Time Lord" (containing the individual stories "The Mysterious Planet," "Mindwarp," "Terror of the Vervoids," and "The Ultimate Foe"), the Sixth Doctor (Colin Baker) is abducted by the Time Lords and put on trial. The prosecutor in the case is known as the Valeyard (Michael Jayston). The Valeyard, however, is far more than he appears, being an amalgamation of the darker sides of the Doctor's nature, from somewhere between his twelfth and final incarnations, where all that was good within him has been lost, leaving him jaded, spiteful, and selfish.

He opens the case, stating, "By order of the High Council, this is an impartial inquiry into the behaviour of the accused person known as the Doctor, who is charged that he, on diverse occasions, has been guilty of conduct unbecoming a Time Lord. He is also charged with, on diverse occasions, transgressing the First Law."[1] Things go from bad to worse, for as the trial progresses, the Doctor is accused of nothing less than genocide.

To illustrate his case, the Valeyard uses examples of the Doctor's behavior, extracted from the Matrix, the repository of all Time Lord knowledge. It does not reflect well on the Doctor, who himself does not have a clear recollection of the events depicted. Nevertheless, any of his claims of evidence tampering within the Matrix are dismissed by the Keeper of the Matrix (James Bree), who asserts that only qualified persons bearing the Key of Rassilon can enter it.

In an unlikely turn of events, the Master (Anthony Ainley) appears on the courtroom screen, speaking from within the Matrix. He admits to having used a copy of the Key of Rassilon to achieve this, proving categorically that the Matrix can be accessed by unsanctioned means. He tells the court that he has been following the Doctor's trial with great interest and amusement, but he must intervene for the sake of justice. Regardless of his claims, it is quite clear that he is not doing this for the benefit of the Doctor, rather he is using this opportunity to air some of the Time Lords' dirty secrets, as well as not being prepared to countenance the defeat of the Doctor at the hands of a rival.

As the trial continues, the Master reveals two things. The first is that the Gallifreyan High Council has been working with the Valeyard to adjust evidence, using the Doctor as a scapegoat to shift the blame for some of their own reprehensible transgressions. The second is that the Master exposes the Valeyard. By condemning his earlier incarnation, the High Council has promised the Valeyard the remainder of the Doctor's regenerations.

With his plot uncovered, the Valeyard escapes into the Matrix, followed by the Doctor. Not for the first time, the Doctor is forced to face off against a foe within the virtual environment of the Matrix, only this time his enemy is his own darker nature. When the Doctor confronts him, asking why he is doing this, the Valeyard tells him, "How else can I obtain my freedom? Operate as a complete entity, unfettered by your side of my existence," and, "Only by releasing myself from the misguided maxims that you nurture, can I be free."

The Master and the Doctor meet within the Matrix. He tells the Doctor that he wants the Valeyard eliminated. He cites the very simple reason that with the Doctor as his enemy, he always has the advantage. The Valeyard, however—the distillation of all that is evil within the Doctor—is quite a different proposition altogether, his wicked machinations rivaling those of the Master's. Tricking the Doctor into a catatonic state, the Master uses the Doctor as bait to lure the Valeyard into showing himself, but the Valeyard is not taken in by such an obvious ploy, calling the Master a second-rate adversary for even attempting it.

The Valeyard's schemes extend beyond the destruction of his former self, with the Doctor uncovering a conspiracy to murder the entire Court of Appeal—the Supreme Guardians of Gallifreyan Law—using a particle disseminator, transmitted through the courtroom screen, killing everyone present at the trial. The Doctor sabotages the machine before this happens, causing massive feedback of energy within the Matrix, killing the Valeyard. Or, at least, that is how it appears. When the Doctor is cleared of all charges levied against him, and the courtroom is cleared, the Keeper of the Matrix, still in his ceremonial robes, turns around, revealing himself to be the Valeyard.

THE DREAM LORD

In the 2010 story "Amy's Choice," the Eleventh Doctor (Matt Smith) visits his former companions, Amy Pond (Karen Gillan) and her husband Rory Williams (Arthur Darvill), in the village of Leadworth. They soon find themselves involuntarily moving back and forth between what appears to be two different versions of "reality." Confused and trying to figure out what is going on, they are confronted by a stranger (Toby Jones). When the Doctor asks him who he is, he says, "What shall we call me? Well, if you're the Time Lord, let's call me the Dream Lord."[2] He proceeds to inform the group that only one of the realities they are experiencing is genuine, the other being nothing more than a dream state. As events progress, they realize that circumstances in both "realities" present a mortal danger to them, and the Dream Lord tasks them with discerning which is which to avoid the only threat that really matters.

The Dream Lord, as it turns out, is a twisted manifestation of the Doctor's psyche, brought into being by psychic pollen. The pollen itself is a kind of parasite, feeding off everything dark in the minds it possesses, giving it a voice and turning it against them. Being so very old, it had a lot to draw from within the Doctor, delivering some uncomfortable truths as just how much self-loathing he harbors. Not only that, the Dream Lord used the Doctor's memories and knowledge of Amy and Rory to play on their insecurities, trying to drive a wedge between them.

Given just how much delight the Dream Lord seems to derive from their predicament, it could be inferred that he stems from the Doctor's "id," a term coined by Austrian neurologist and the father of psychoanalysis, Sigmund Freud (1856–1939). The "id" represents the completely subconscious part of the mind that deals with primitive, almost animalistic, impulses and motivations to satiate desires. It is usually kept in check by the "ego" (the sense of self) and the "superego" (the sense of ethics) to ensure that it does not have free rein. Liberated from such control by the psychic pollen, the Dream Lord indulged in his cruel and self-satisfying games.

So, is the Dream Lord real or not? Not physically, but he remains a very real part of the Doctor, buried deep within his subconscious. Although the Doctor managed to figure out what was going on, defeating the Dream Lord's plans, he can never truly be rid of him, meaning there is always the chance that he may one day return.

THE WAR DOCTOR

In the 2013 mini-episode, "The Night of the Doctor"—tying into the show's fiftieth anniversary—the Time War rages on between the Daleks and the Time Lords, threatening all of reality. A dying Eighth Doctor (Paul McGann) accepts an offer from the Sisterhood of Karn to shape the outcome of his next regeneration, meeting the needs of what must be done. He wants no part in the war, having insisted on helping, not fighting, up until then, avoiding being drawn into the horror and violence of it all. But the Sisterhood insists that he is the only hope of putting an end to it, once and for all.

When the Doctor is confronted by the sheer scale of the devastation wrought by both sides, he acknowledges that there is no need for a Doctor anymore, accepting that the role of a warrior is what is required. With the words, "physician, heal thyself," he imbibes an elixir, regenerating into the fighter that he needs to be.[3]

Although this regeneration is commonly referred to as the War Doctor (John Hurt), he does not accept that name for himself. To him, a Doctor is one who helps, one who heals, and his newfound role is the very opposite, a soldier whose purpose is to destroy. In the 2013 story "The Name of the Doctor," the Eleventh Doctor (Matt Smith) tells Clara Oswald (Jenna Coleman) about this part of himself, "I said he was me. I never said he was the Doctor. Look, my name, my real name, that is not the point. The name I chose is the Doctor. The name you choose, it's like a promise you make. He's the one who broke the promise. He is my secret."[4]

In the 2013 fiftieth-anniversary story "The Day of the Doctor," the Doctor (Matt Smith) is taken by Kate Lethbridge-Stewart (Jemma Redgrave), the leader of UNIT, to a painting that does not belong on Earth. It is a piece of Time Lord art, an oil painting in three dimensions, depicting the fall of Arcadia, Gallifrey's second city. The title of the painting is *No More*, also known by the alternative title *Gallifrey Falls*.

Regarding the painting, the Doctor says to Clara, "He was there. The Other me. The one I don't talk about. I've had many faces, many lives. I don't admit to all of them. There's one life I've tried very hard to forget. He was the Doctor that fought in the Time War, and that was the day he did it. I did it. The day he killed them all. The last day of the Time War. The war to end all wars between my people and the Daleks. And in that battle, there was a man with more blood on his hands than any other. A man who would commit a crime that would silence the universe, and that man . . . was me."[5]

A flashback sequence shows the relentless Dalek war machine laying waste to Gallifrey, cutting down soldiers and civilians alike. Among the rubble, a lone combatant hides from the Daleks, and there he encounters the War Doctor, who asks him for his gun. Taking it, the War Doctor blasts the message "no more" into a nearby wall—a clear message of intent.

In the War Room, members of the Gallifreyan War Council are alerted to a breach of the Omega Arsenal in the Time Vaults, where they keep their forbidden weapons. Most of the weapons in there have been used at one time or another to defeat the Daleks, but one remains, the most devastating one of all—the Moment. The War Doctor steals it with the intent of activating it, knowing that the only way to take out the entire Dalek force that has amassed for this final battle is to sacrifice Gallifrey, removing both sides from the equation. He feels that both the Time Lords and the Daleks have forced his hand, leaving him no option but to end the war.

While trying to figure out how to operate the Moment, the War Doctor is confronted by a familiar figure, Rose Tyler (Billie Piper) in her Bad Wolf guise. She is not really Rose, but the sentient interface of the Moment, using her visage to communicate with the War Doctor.

When she asks the War Doctor why he parked so far away, having walked miles and miles to get to the place he intends to activate the Moment, she asks if he doesn't want Tardis to see what he is doing, acknowledging the shame that he feels. When he asks her to stop calling him "Doctor," she tells him that is the name he keeps inside his head. With great sadness he states that he has been fighting for a very long time and has lost the right to be the Doctor.

After he tells her that he has no desire to survive the war, she tells him that if he is to take such a drastic action then his punishment will be to survive. Daleks and Time Lords alike will die, but so will children. She tells the Doctor that on one terrible night he will count how many children died on Gallifrey as a result of what he is about to do.

She opens windows to his future to show him what the man he is today will make of him in the days to come. This leads to the Tenth Doctor (David Tennant) and the Eleventh Doctor (Matt Smith) meeting and joining forces with the War Doctor. Because both of them are from his future, he asks both of them if they ever did count the number of children on Gallifrey on the last day of the Time War. The Eleventh Doctor is evasive, claiming he doesn't remember, but the Tenth Doctor tells him that it is 2.47 billion. The moment appears, pointing out to the War Doctor that they are who he will become if he destroys Gallifrey—*the man who regrets, and the man who forgets.*

Having encountered two of his future selves, and seeing the burden or regret and guilt that they bear, it gives him pause. They tell him that they should not have buried his memory, pretending that he did not exist. They claim he is every bit as much the Doctor as they are, just that he was put in an impossible position where there was no right answer.

Putting their combined minds together, the Doctors conceive of a plan to utilize *all* of their regenerations, combining their efforts—and their Tardises—to try to phase shift Gallifrey into a pocket dimension, leaving the Daleks that have surrounded the planet firing on one another, wiping themselves out. They carry out this endeavor.

They are successful, knowing for sure that the Daleks are destroyed, but uncertain as to whether they saved Gallifrey or not. Because their time streams are out of sync, the War Doctor acknowledges that he will not remember trying to save Gallifrey, but at least he gets the chance to be the Doctor again.

The Eleventh Doctor returns to view the painting, and he is approached by the Curator (Tom Baker). When the Curator asks the Doctor what he thinks of the title of the painting, the Doctor asks which title he means, *No More* or *Gallifrey Falls*. The Curator corrects him, saying that is where everybody is wrong, it is all one title, *Gallifrey Falls No More*—proof positive that the Doctors were successful in their attempt to save their home.

PART III

CULTURAL IMPACT AND INFLUENCE

Chapter 13

Gender Identity and Awareness

Figure 13 Captain Jack Harkness. BBC America / Photofest © BBC America

If there is one thing that *Doctor Who* has always been very good at, it is reminding us that being different is quite an empowering thing. The Doctor is different, an outsider, even among his own people, but he never let that stop him being . . . well . . . *him*, even to the point of stealing a Tardis and running away so he could explore the universe, satisfying his burning curiosity.

For many people, change is scary. *Really* scary. But the thing about *Doctor Who* is that the show has always been about embracing change. When the Doctor is close to death, he regenerates, changing his face, his clothes, his mannerisms, and latterly, even his gender. Underneath all of that, though, he is still fundamentally the same person. Like the Doctor, the show itself changes over time, encompassing progressive views and values.

Our society has seen a significant increase in the acknowledgment and awareness of gender identity over the years, and while there is still a long way to go, it is no longer uncommon for characters who are on the nonbinary spectrum to be portrayed in mainstream media. *Doctor Who* has long been a show that has tried to incorporate shifts in cultural perception, but by no means has it got it right all of the time. In classic-era *Doctor Who*, casual sexism and racial bias reared their ugly heads both in front of and behind the camera. This was undeniably the result of outdated institutional prejudices, along with the inflexible attitudes of certain individuals behind the scenes. The industry should have evolved since then, but we should never be too complacent, always remembering that it takes a lot of people at all different levels to share in the responsibility of fair and unbiased representation.

I feel I should point out here that I am fully aware that there are a whole host of labels given to a wide range of people who fit on the LGBTQ+ spectrum. It is with the greatest of respect that I do not want anybody to feel excluded or marginalized, so it is with much consideration that I have chosen to use the catchall terminology of "nonbinary" when not directly relating to any specific gender or sexual designation.

FAILED ATTEMPTS

Even before open nonbinary depiction was generally acceptable on the show, there were attempts to introduce it. In the 1989 story "The Curse of Fenric," there is a character called Dr. Judson (Dinsdale Landen), who is a wheelchair user. Writer Ian Briggs based Dr. Judson on another wartime genius, Alan Turing. In an interview for the DVD release of this story Briggs recounts how Dr. Judson was originally intended to be homosexual, just like the real-life figure who inspired him, but it was not considered appropriate at the time to feature a character's struggle with his sexuality on a family-oriented show.

Judson's frustrations were therefore translated into his resentment at the limitations imposed upon him by his disability.

Writer Rona Munro, who created the 1989 story "Survival" (the last one shown in classic-era *Doctor Who*) intended to include a lesbian subtext between the characters of Ace (Sophie Aldred) and Karra (Lisa Bowerman) of the Cheetah people. She had envisaged the Cheetah people to look relatively human, just with catlike eyes, sharp canine teeth, and a faint pigmentation of the skin. By the time they made it to screen, they were given far more pantomime-like costumes, with headpieces that concealed all expressiveness, nuanced or otherwise, so any suggestion of a deeper connection between Ace and Karra was lost.

Another instance of nonbinary representation almost making it to screen was in the 2008 two-part story "Silence in the Library"/"Forest of the Dead." Donna Noble (Catherine Tate) is uploaded into a computer simulation, and having no recollection of her life beforehand, meets a nice man called Lee (Jason Pitt) and marries him. The original draft of the story had Lee as having been assigned the birth gender of a woman in the real world, with their simulated representation aligning with how they saw themselves. It was decided that it was too confusing to attempt to convey this narrative twist in the short time given, so it was dropped.

The Sarah Jane Adventures nearly had nonbinary representation as well, with the character of Luke Smith (Tommy Knight), planning to come out as gay and have a relationship with his university dorm mate, Sanjay. The death of Elisabeth Sladen, and the subsequent decision not to continue the series without her, meant this never came to fruition. In the 2020 webcast, written by Russell T. Davies and intended to be a wrap-up of the show on the anniversary of Sladen's passing, Luke relates how it was Sarah Jane who first noticed that Sanjay looked at him in "that way," and that Luke should talk to him.[1] He then goes on to say that he and Sanjay have been married for five years.

How canonical the contents of this webcast are is uncertain. Although Luke's homosexuality was something planned in canon, it also mentions "a nice couple from Australia, Tegan and Nyssa," suggesting a romantic pairing between the two. To be honest, this comes across as pure fan service appeasement and is negated by the events that happen in the 2022 *Doctor Who* story "The Power of the Doctor," in which Tegan (Jane Fielding) says, "I have spent the past 30 years living like a nomad. I have done land mines, coups, I have been hijacked, and I've nearly drowned trying to help people. I've seen off two husbands, and somewhere out there is an adopted son who hasn't called me for six weeks."[2]

In the 2023 "Tales of the Tardis" special episode, titled "Earthshock" (written by Russell T. Davies), Tegan and the Fifth Doctor (Peter Davison) are reunited. At first, she is confused, saying, "I was fast asleep, in bed. I said goodbye to Nyssa, and . . ." she never completes the sentence, distracted by telling the Doctor how good it is to see him again.[3] Whether her statement is meant to be a recollection from the distant past, or something that happened just before she arrived, is never made clear, so make of that what you will.

CAPTAIN JACK HARKNESS

Doctor Who's first openly nonbinary character came along in the 2005 story "The Empty Child," as Captain Jack Harkness (John Barrowman), a former Time Agent from the fifty-first century. Within *Doctor Who*, Harkness's sexuality is never officially labeled, and although the character is often described as being bisexual in other media, during an interview with the *Chicago Tribune*, Barrowman said that he believes the term "omnisexual" is far more fitting. Labels aside, he quickly became a heroic figure for a generation of young nonbinary men.

Harkness is a dashing figure in his military greatcoat. In combination with his disarming smile and smooth talking, he seems like the kind of character that could charm his way out of the trickiest of situations. As beloved as he is, in *Doctor Who*, his character does come across as emotionally shallow. The fact that he flirts with just about everybody he encounters, male, female, human, and alien, is referenced on multiple occasions, as a sort of in-joke, but not once does any suggestion of him having deeper, more tangible emotions, or a desire to be anything other than a serial seducer, enter the picture.

His character is explored in much greater depth in the adult-themed spin-off show *Torchwood*, in which, over time, he is given a more fleshed-out and much more sympathetic portrayal. He, like the rest of the central characters on the show, is damaged in one way or another, but he alone has a far more complex and darker past, having left the Time Agency that he once worked for when he woke up to discover that they had stolen two years of his memories.

In the 2007 *Torchwood* episode "Captain Jack Harness," when transported back in time to 1941 after passing through a rift in a dancehall, Harkness gets to meet his namesake—the young man whose identity he assumes after he dies (Matt Rippy). There is a clear attraction between the two men, and in an emotive scene, they dance together, much to the confusion and consternation of the other dancers present, culminating in a kiss before they part. It is a highly romanticized scene, and one that ignores the harsh realities of the period. Given that homosexuality in Britain was illegal at the time, and seen as deviant behavior, it is highly unlikely that the other men there would remain passive and allow such a scene to be conducted in front of their female partners.

It raises a question that springs up when it comes to stories about time travel. Is it ethical to retroactively impose modern-day values on stories set in the past, making them not only historically inaccurate but portraying a false view of the hardships that people of the time endured? This is not limited to nonbinary people either. It has become more common in period dramas to portray ethnic minorities in positions of wealth and power, which could leave young audiences with a very distorted opinion of how prevalent racial prejudice really was.

Harkness has a complicated relationship with fellow Torchwood colleague, Ianto Jones (Gareth David-Lloyd). Despite Harkness being responsible for the death of the self-proclaimed love of Ianto's life—a young woman called Lisa (Caroline Chikezie) who had become a partially converted Cyberman in the 2006 story "Cyberwoman"—Ianto finds himself falling in love with him. It is a rocky road, as Harkness seems emotionally distant a lot of the time, but the true extent of Harkness's feelings is finally revealed when Ianto dies, leaving him utterly devastated.

MADAME VASTRA AND JENNY FLINT

Victorian London of 1888 seems an unlikely place to find a pair of sword-wielding warriors and their Sontaran butler, but this group, known collectively as the Paternoster Gang, was introduced in the 2014 *Doctor Who* story "A Good Man Goes to War." A Silurian, Madame Vastra (Neve McIntosh), and a human, Jenny Flint (Catrin Stewart), are a married couple, posing as mistress and maid. Madame Vastra, having been roused from her hibernation by construction work on the London Underground, usually dresses in black, with a black veil over her face, appearing as though she is in mourning, but she is really hiding her features from society. She met Jenny after she was ostracised by her family for her "preferences in companionship."

CHARLIE SMITH

The 2016 spin-off series *Class* featured a central character, Charlie Smith (Greg Austin), an alien posing as a human student at Coal Hill Academy, and who has a same-sex relationship with another character, Matteusz Andrzejewski (Jordan Reno).

BILL POTTS

Back with *Doctor Who*, the 2017 story "The Pilot" introduced us to another prominent nonbinary character, Bill Potts (Pearl Mackie). In this story the Doctor (Peter Capaldi) and Nardole (Matt Lucas) have been posing as a university professor and his assistant for somewhere between fifty and seventy years (the actual length of time is not determined). The Doctor summons Bill to his office. He is curious as to why she has been attending his lectures when she is not even registered as a student. Bill, as it turns out, works in the university canteen, but she is smart, very smart, and when the Doctor realizes this, he offers to be her personal tutor.

Bill is also a lesbian, and it is something that is cleverly highlighted when she recounts the story of seeing a beautiful student come into the canteen every day, where Bill would give her extra chips. It is a casual, matter-of-fact revelation that really works, informing viewers of her sexuality without making too big a deal of it, and showing sensitivity toward the importance of normalization.

Bill meets a young woman by the name of Heather (Stephanie Hyam) who has a starlike pattern in the iris of her left eye. Bill is enamored with Heather and inquisitive about her interest in a strange puddle. The puddle, it turns out, is intelligent material, left behind from a spacecraft. It absorbs Heather and begins chasing Bill. The Doctor, Nardole, and Bill use the Tardis to try and evade it, but no matter how far they go, it follows. But it is not a threat, it is an invitation by the transformed Heather, holding on to a lingering memory of her attraction toward Bill. Bill tells her she cannot go with her, and Heather departs, but not before leaving Bill with tears that were not her own.

In the 2017 two-part story "Extremis"/"The Pyramid at the End of the World," Bill has brought a girl, Penny (Ronke Adekolejo), back to her apartment for a date night, but is interrupted when she hears the arrival of the Tardis in another room. When Penny asks what the noise is, Bill tries to deflect, saying that it is the plumbing. Penny seems nervous, saying she is not used to any of this, perhaps because she has not long been "out," but Bill assuages her, telling her she has absolutely nothing to feel guilty about. Suddenly, the Pope (Joseph Long) bursts out of Bill's bedroom, acting excitable and speaking in Latin, before rushing back in again. When Bill follows, so does Penny, only to find a group of cardinals gathered in there too. It is enough to scare Penny off, and Bill tells them they are all going to Hell, before admonishing the Doctor, "Here's a tip. When I'm on a date, when that rare and special thing happens in my real life, do not . . . do not under any circumstances, put the Pope in my bedroom!"[4]

In the 2017 two-part season finale, "World Enough and Time"/"The Doctor Falls," Bill, along with Nardole, is taken to a massive colony ship on the edge of a black hole as part of Doctor's attempts to reform Missy (Michelle Gomez). There, Bill is shot through the heart and taken to the lowest deck to be "fixed." She is given an artificial heart assembly, not realizing that this is the first step toward conversion into a Cyberman. Eventually, the conversion process is completed, but she doggedly holds onto the last vestiges of her humanity, determined not to succumb. She kneels beside a mortally injured Doctor but suddenly finds herself standing outside of her cyber body, appearing as her human self once more. Heather materializes, having found Bill through the tears she left, and she tells Bill that she is just like her now, saying it is a different kind of living. They take the dying Doctor back to the Tardis and, not being able to do anything more for him, they depart together.

ROSE NOBLE

The first of the sixtieth-anniversary specials, "The Star Beast," in November 2023, saw the return of Donna Noble (Catherine Tate) and introduced audiences to her daughter, Rose Noble (Yasmin Finney). Rose is transgender and has had to overcome a lot of obstacles to be the person she is now. We even witness some boys on bikes that she knew from school, from before her transition, and who are cruelly deadnaming her, calling her Jason. Donna is incensed, and hugely protective of Rose, telling her, "I would burn down the world for you darling. Anyone has a go, I will be there, and I will descend."[5]

The portrayal of Rose is a thoughtful one. Someone who just wants to be left alone to be who she is, without having to put up with the prejudices of others. While gay, lesbian, bisexual, and queer representation on-screen has grown steadily, transgender depiction is still trailing. Transphobia is an especially relevant issue these days, with public figures still criticizing attempts made to accommodate transgender people in society. The BBC received 144 messages of complaint after the episode aired, many of which claimed it featured the inappropriate inclusion of a transgender character.[6] Hopefully, more instances of transgender people like Rose on prime-time television shows will diminish the voices of those who try to use fearmongering to create divisions.

A BRIGHT OUTLOOK

Great strides have been made since the days when the BBC balked at the suggestion of any kind of nonbinary representation in a show such as *Doctor Who*, and most real fans are happy with that. With Russell T. Davis returning to take up the mantle of showrunner once more, himself being an openly homosexual male, we can expect to see more LGBTQ+ representation integrated into the show going forward, and *Doctor Who* will continue to be inclusive, welcoming new fans, regardless of gender, sexuality, skin pigmentation, or planet of origin.

Chapter 14

Changes in Pronouns and Ethnicity

Figure 14 The Thirteenth Doctor. BBC / Photofest © BBC

In 2017 it was announced that Peter Capaldi was retiring from the role of the Doctor and that Jodie Whittaker would be replacing him as the show's first female Doctor. While this was initially hailed as a progressive move and had the potential to be a paradigm shift for the series, the way it was handled, and the subsequent backlash, meant that a lot of the positivity surrounding the change was washed away in a storm of polemic opinions. Yes, it broadened the show's scope of inclusivity, but it could have—it *should* have—been so much more.

THE INTRODUCTION OF GENDER CHANGE

Now, let us be very clear, it was not as if such a move was unforeseen. It has long been an established story device in the history of the show that Time Lords can regenerate into new bodies. However, the fact that Time Lords can also change gender during the process of regeneration is something that was only introduced into canon in the modern-era series. This was first mentioned in the 2011 Neil Gaiman story "The Doctor's Wife," with the Eleventh Doctor (Matt Smith) sharing a recollection about another Time Lord, the Corsair, who not only liked to have a snake tattoo in every different regeneration but who had changed gender a few times too.

In the fiftieth-anniversary mini-episode "The Night of the Doctor," featuring a welcome—if an all too brief—return of Paul McGann's Eighth Doctor, the Sisterhood of Karn (first seen in the 1976 story "The Brain of Morbius") offers the Doctor an elixir that would force trigger a regeneration, stating that such a change wouldn't have to be random as Time Lord science has been elevated on Karn. The Doctor could choose to be fat or thin, young or old, man or *woman*.

By far, the most overt gender change of the series came along in 2014 with Missy, portrayed by the ever-wonderful Michelle Gomez. In the two-part finale, "Dark Water"/"Death in Heaven," she is revealed to be the first female regeneration of the Doctor's old nemesis, the Master. In the 2015 episode "Hell Bent," the Time Lord known as the General (last seen in the 2013 fiftieth-anniversary story "The Day of the Doctor"), having been shot, regenerates from a white man, played by Ken Bones, into a black woman, played by T'Nia Miller (cleverly establishing changes of skin color into the canon at the same time).

With all of this being brought to the fore, the writing was clearly on the wall that a gender change for the Doctor was inevitable, not so much an *if* but rather a *when*. The big question was how such a change would be implemented, given that audiences had been used to having male Doctors for well over half a century. For a transformation of such magnitude to occur, and to be widely accepted by viewers, it had to be handled thoughtfully, providing a plausible narrative reason as to why, after thirteen male regenerations, *now* was the time for our central protagonist to become a woman. In the end, what reason was conveyed to audiences to account for the change? Frustratingly, the answer is none whatsoever.

In January 2016, the BBC announced that Chris Chibnall (1970–) would be taking over the role of showrunner for *Doctor Who* from Steven Moffat. When answering questions from the understandably curious news media about what he wanted to do with *Doctor Who*, he asserted that nothing was ruled out, but that he did not want any casting choices to be seen as a gimmick. If a statement like that was not already enough of a clue as to what was coming, once the official announcement was made that Jodie Whittaker (1982–) would be the next Doctor, executive producer Matt Strevens revealed that Chibnall took on the role on the proviso that the next Doctor would be cast as a woman.

REACTIONS

Whittaker's debut story the 2018 episode "The Woman Who Fell to Earth," aired, and almost immediately there was a reaction. Echoing the fractured nature of modern-day politics, it created deep divisions within the fanbase. It wasn't long before misogynistic trolls appeared on the internet, decrying the change as being an exercise in *wokeness* and *virtue signaling*, and designed to appeal to the *politically correct brigade*.[1] Even the British gutter press indulged in vulgar anti-Whittaker trolling, shamefully publishing nude pictures of her from roles that she had previously undertaken.[2]

Reactions from actors who had previously played the Doctor were mixed. Notably, Colin Baker, who portrayed the Sixth Doctor, took to social media, saying, "Change my dears, and not a moment too soon—she IS the Doctor, whether you like it or not."[3] Peter Davison, who portrayed the Fifth Doctor, indicated that he was saddened by the thought that a female Doctor might not be considered "a role model for boys." His comment was criticized by several people, including Baker, who called Davison's opinion, "rubbish."[4] To be fair, though, boys do tend to gravitate to other male figures as role models, and any male role model that does not promote the views and values of toxic masculinity *is* important. In no way does mean we could not, or should not have a female Doctor, but I feel that Davison's thoughts were branded as being misogynist, whereas I think he was expressing a genuine concern, albeit a badly phrased one.

Of course, there were a great many people who praised the move as being an important blow struck for equality and female empowerment. Rather famously, author Jenny Trout posted her young daughter's reaction to the announcement on Twitter, her face lighting up and excitedly shouting, "The new Doctor is a girl!" a sentiment I am sure was echoed among many of her peers.[5] *Doctor Who* has always had a large LGBTQ+ community, and they were quick to support the move too, hailing the Doctor as being gender-fluid.

EQUALITY OR HYPOCRISY?

There were quite a few indicators in the show that gender was a big part of the Thirteenth Doctor's identity. The show's logo had been redesigned with the "H" and "O" of WHO combining to form the traditional female symbol of Venus, laid on its side. The rainbow decal on the Thirteenth Doctor's T-shirt is a popular symbol for the LGBTQ+ community, representing the spectrum and diversity of gender and sexuality.

However, such raw excitement and enthusiasm tended to overlook some of the negative aspects inherent in such a change. When introducing a woman into a role that has habitually been male, especially one that has been so for a *very* long time, it invariably invites comparison to all her male predecessors, no matter how unintentional or unfair that might be. Could the first female Doctor *ever* be judged on her own merits, or would she simply be destined to remain in the shadow of all the male counterparts that had come before?

It can also be perceived as a lazy thing to do, taking a traditionally male character and gender flipping them to a female version, paying lip service to equality without really going the extra mile to make such a change count. To avoid this happening, questions need to be asked:

- Does a change in gender develop the character in any meaningful way?
- What impact does this have on other characters?
- Do the stories alter to reflect this?

Essentially, we are asking if a woman needs to stand in a man's shoes to be regarded as an equal. The world could certainly do with newly created intelligent, dynamic, and powerful female characters, ones who are iconic in their own right, and not just a rehash of an already male-dominated legacy.

But even among genuine fans, those who did not recoil at the gender change, there was still a feeling of confusion. Some wrote to the BBC, looking for an explanation as to why, after fifty-plus years, the Doctor had suddenly become a woman. The BBC responded by issuing a statement, saying, "Since the Doctor regenerated back in 1966, the concept of the Doctor as a constantly evolving being has been central to the programme. The continual input of fresh ideas and new voices across the cast and the writing and production teams has been key to the longevity of the series. The Doctor is an alien from the planet Gallifrey and it has been established in the show that Time Lords can change gender."[6] It is rather quite a dismissive statement, merely asserting a fact and not really addressing the puzzlement of fans.

REWRITING HISTORY

Still, if Chris Chibnall was determined to hit home the point that the Doctor could also be female, he did so, not once, not twice, but thrice! In a move that could be interpreted as overcompensating for there being so many male Doctors in the past (and ripping off a story device used by Steven Moffat to introduce the War Doctor) he unveiled the Fugitive Doctor (Jo Martin), in the 2020 episode "Fugitive of the Judoon." She is meant to be a hidden regeneration of the Doctor, from some undisclosed point in the past, one that Jodie Whittaker's Thirteenth Doctor had no recollection of. To bastardize a quote from Oscar Wilde, *to have one hidden regeneration may be considered a misfortune, to have two looks like carelessness.*

In a move that was far more controversial than having a female Doctor, Chibnall decided to retcon the Doctor's past, making it so that they aren't even a native of Gallifrey! In his rewriting of the show's core history—seen in the 2020 episode "The Timeless Children"—the Master reveals to the Doctor that a woman from a pre-Gallifreyan society, known as the Shobogan, discovers a female child beneath a wormhole that leads to an entirely different universe. The woman is Tecteun (Barbara Flynn) and she adopts this mysterious child, only discovering the girl's ability to regenerate when she has a fatal fall. Tectuen experiments on the child to unlock the secrets of regeneration, so she can bestow it upon her own kind. If you have not already guessed by now, this girl child is destined to be the person known as the Doctor, who has all memories of their past erased to cover up the truth.

Take a moment to process this. Rather than come up with a clever and credible reason for the Doctor's gender change, one that could have been powerful and insightful, the entire history of the series was adulterated to incorporate *forgotten* female regenerations, something that only *diminishes* the impact and importance of Whittaker being the first female Doctor. What is the point of making a big deal about casting the *first* female regeneration, when the very same people who did so then change the narrative to state that she is *not* the first female regeneration? It teases a level of newfound transformation and empowerment, only then to strip it all away, marginalizing Whittaker's relevance. The mind boggles!

It seems that Chibnall's validation for the First Doctor (William Harnell) not actually being the first comes from a throwaway scene from the 1976 story "The Brain of Morbius." In it, the Doctor (Tom Baker) and Morbius (Michael Spice/Stuart Fell) engage in a mind-bending contest—a sort of mental wrestling challenge. During this exchange, the faces of previous regenerations of both the Doctor and Morbius are shown. Chibnall has interpreted that some unknown faces seen here belong to the Doctor and not Morbius. However, if, according the Chibnall, the Time Lords altered the Doctor's mind so that he is unable to recall any regenerations before the one he believes is his first, how did these appear during the mind-bending contest? It is a plot hole that is not addressed and flies in the face of all other stories that reinforce the notion that William Hartnell's Doctor was indeed the first. Look at Moffat's Impossible Girl story arc, where Clara (Jenna Coleman) enters the Doctor's personal timestream and encounters all the Doctor's previous regenerations, leading to her discovering the aberration that is the War Doctor (John Hurt).

If the whole debate over gender was not already enough for Whittaker to contend with, it is widely acknowledged among *Doctor Who* fandom that the stories provided for her were weak, often resorting to storytelling tropes such as imperialism, climate change, and automation as being bad (the 2018 stories "Demons of the Punjab," "Orphan 55," and "Kerblam!" respectively) although, somewhat curiously, the negatives surrounding rampant consumerism were somewhat glossed over in the latter of these stories, with the namesake company, Kerblam!, being a thinly veiled substitute for Amazon.

Whittaker is an accomplished actor in her own right and has played outstanding roles, such as Beth Latimer in ITV's *Broadchurch* (2013–2017) and Cath Hardacre in BBC's *Trust Me* (2017–2019). In *Doctor Who*, a combination of questionable direction and writing for the Thirteenth Doctor left her prone to making long, rambling, fast-paced, jargon-filled, overtly moralistic speeches, even when she is talking to herself (which she does a *lot* as an overused means of exposition). Whittaker brought boundless energy and enthusiasm to the part, something she absolutely cannot be faulted for, but there really wasn't an awful lot to distinguish the character of the Thirteenth Doctor, certainly not enough to warrant the occasion of her being the first woman to take on the role.

FLUX

The final nail in the coffin for Chibnall and Whittaker's tenure was the 2021 story "Flux," which spanned an entire season (albeit a shortened one due to the COVID-19 pandemic). Here was a sprawling, multi-threaded, convoluted plot about the Doctor trying to uncover lost truths from her past, and those who sought to stop her. The Flux (from the story title) was a devastating wave of energy unleashed by Tectuan and the Division, intended to kill the Doctor and destroy everything she cared about. By the end of the story half the universe is wiped out by the Flux. It is a lamentably unimaginative scenario that clearly takes inspiration from Marvel's Thanos, snapping his fingers while wearing the Infinity Gauntlet, and wiping out half of all life.

The BBC subsequently released a fifteen-minute video, featuring Chibnall and Whittaker, explaining what happened during the Flux storyline. In December 2021, Niall Gray, writing for ScreenRant, opined that such a video was tantamount to an admission by the BBC that Flux was a failure that left viewers utterly baffled by the events of the story necessitating the release of an explainer video.[7] It's hard to disagree.

The failure of "Flux" as a storyline had nothing whatsoever to do with having a female Doctor, but it came on the back of Whittaker's prior two seasons, both of which were criticized for poor writing and direction. If anything, Whittaker is a victim here, not being given adequate material to truly make her Doctor shine.

LOST OPPORTUNITIES

In July 2021 the BBC announced that both Chibnall and Whittaker were giving up their roles on *Doctor Who*. Chibnall commented, "Jodie and I made a 'three series and out' pact with each other at the start of this one-in-a-lifetime blast. So now our shift is done, and we're handing back the Tardis keys."[8] Whether or not they ever contemplated extending this, we will never know, but bowing out at that point made sense. Under Chibnall's tenure, viewing figures plummeted, going from a respectable 8.5 million average viewers at the Thirteenth Doctor's premiere story down to 3.7 million average viewers when Whittaker's series finale, "The Power of the Doctor," aired in October 2022.[9]

Perhaps if the change of gender had occurred at some point earlier in the show's history it might have been less confusing and generally easier for people to accept. Back in 1980, when Tom Baker spoke to a gathering of the press to announce his impending departure from the role, he said, "I certainly wish my successor luck whoever he—or she—might be." The producer of the show then, John Nathan-Turner, later admitted that Baker's statement was a bit of a joke, intended to grab headlines.

However, the man credited as being the creator of *Doctor Who*, Sydney Newman, was one of the people who seriously considered just such a change. In 1986 he met with Michael Grade, who had put *Doctor Who* on an eighteen-month hiatus, to discuss his concerns regarding the direction the show had taken, branding it *largely socially valueless, escapist schlock*. Grade invited Newman to submit some ideas for the show, and in a subsequent memo, dated

October 6, 1986, Newman suggested, "at a later stage Doctor Who should be metamorphosed into a woman," adding, "this requires some considerable thought—mainly because I want to avoid a flashy Hollywood Wonder Woman because this kind of heroine with no flaws is a bore. Given more time than I have now, I can create such a character." Newman even recommended he be appointed the show's executive director to *ensure the concept is properly executed*. Even if Grade had been willing to entertain the idea, Jonathan Powell, then head of drama at the BBC, was not.[10]

UNOFFICIAL FEMALE DOCTORS

While Jodie Whittaker's Doctor is the first canon one, there have been unofficial female Doctors in the past. In 1999, as part of the BBC's Red Nose Day charity broadcast, a spoof *Doctor Who* story "The Curse of Fatal Death," was aired (which, incidentally, was penned by Steven Moffat, who would eventually become executive producer and head writer for the series from 2010 to 2017). In it, the Doctor is played by comedic actor Rowan Atkinson, and after suffering a succession of fatalities, and regenerating multiple times (featuring Richard E. Grant, Jim Broadbent, and Hugh Grant) the Doctor regenerates once more, this time into a woman (Joanna Lumley).

In 2003, Big Finish, producers of *Doctor Who* audio dramas, commissioned Doctor Who Unbound, a series of tales that were alternative takes on the conventional *Doctor Who* universe. The sixth story in the series featured comedic actor Arabella Weir as an alcoholic Doctor, attempting to avoid the scrutiny of the Time Lords by living the most mundane and unexciting life possible.

PUBLICITY STUNT?

Looking back at the questions I asked earlier, it does not appear that the Doctor's change in gender developed the character in any meaningful way. Aside from a radically different external appearance, the Doctor does not gain any new perspectives or insights that might have come about as a result, which is a real shame. Nor does the change seem to have any notable impact on other characters, although the Doctor starts referring to her companions as her "Fam," suggesting that she has adopted a matriarchal role, signifying a certain amount of gendered stereotyping creeping in. As for the stories themselves, there is virtually nothing about them that accommodates the relevancy of having a female Doctor.

So, was the gender change just a publicity stunt to garner attention and drive up viewing figures? No, I do not think so, although I can see how some people may have been left with that impression. I believe there was a genuine motivation to do something positive, both for the series and for the fans. Sadly, whatever that vision was, it was not carried out with conviction, failing to give any tangible meaning to the Doctor's gender change. In the end, it turned out to be more performative than progressive. The fact that the change happened at a time when there are aggressive culture wars going on, exacerbated by extreme political views, certainly did not help.

Will we see more female Doctors in the future? Most certainly. The genie is out of the bottle and having had one female regeneration of the Doctor brought into the canon (or more, if the revised Doctor's past is to be believed), there is simply no reason not to have more. I only hope that next time round it will be an easier ride for whoever takes up the mantle, and that she will not have to bear the same pressures and prejudices that Whittaker had as the first on-screen female Doctor.

In the future, when more female Doctors arrive, it would be nice to see both the showrunner and the writers leaning into such a change, embracing it and all the potential therein, and having fun with all the experiences and circumstances that could arise. That way, it will feel a lot less awkward than what we got with the arrival of Jodie Whittaker's Doctor—a gender change that was heavily hyped but also largely overlooked.

RACE

As a long-standing television program, *Doctor Who* has a complicated relationship to race and racial depiction. In 1963, when the show first started, it was only five years after the release of the seminal kitchen-sink drama *A Taste of Honey*, written by Shelagh Delaney. Not only did the play examine working-class struggles in postwar Britain, but it delved into taboo topics such as homosexuality, teenage pregnancy, and interracial relationships, as well as resulting prejudices. Its undaunted look at such controversial subject matters was an open challenge to the prevailing attitudes of the British public at the time.

To get an idea of such prevailing attitudes, we need only look at some of the popular British television shows of the 1960s and 1970s. *Till Death Us Do Part* (BBC) was a comedy about an East End London family, ruled over by a patriarchal figure, Alf Garnett, played by Warren Mitchell (1926–2015). Garnet was famous for going off on long verbal rants, much of which were racist in nature. The program was defended, claiming viewers were meant to laugh *at*, not *with*, Garnett's outdated values, but not everybody saw it that way. *Love Thy Neighbour* (ITV) was a comedy that focused on the tensions between a Black couple and a white couple living next door to one another. While the wives generally got along just fine, it was the husbands who would frequently trade racist insults. This too was defended, claiming it took a lighthearted look at the prejudices that arose from mass immigration, but it only really served to set a bad example. Then there was *Mind Your Language* (ITV), another comedy about a group of racially diverse students trying to improve their English at an adult education college. While its comedy was gentler, and far less abrasive, the students themselves were nothing more than cardboard cutout racial stereotypes, largely playing into a negative depiction of immigrants.

CULTURAL STEREOTYPING

Doctor Who may have made some blunders in the past regarding racial portrayals, such as characters in blackface in the early years (i.e., "Marco Polo," 1964; "The Aztecs," 1964; "The Crusade," 1965; and "The Savages," 1966). However, it must be pointed out that in 1965, noted English thespian Laurence Olivier (1907–1989), appeared in the lead role of a film adaptation of Shakespeare's *Othello*, and he was in blackface. Praise was certainly not universal, with columnist Inez Robb (1900–1979) likening Olivier's camp portrayal as being akin to Al Jolson[11] (1886–1950), a prolific blackface performer, but that did not stop the film from gathering Oscar nominations. At the time, many simply did not see the potential for offense.

Asian depictions have also been problematic. Western audiences had become used to "Yellow Peril" stereotypes, such as the villain Fu Manchu, created by novelist Arthur Henry Ward, better known as Sax Rohmer (1883–1959), and who featured in multiple books and films. A *Doctor Who* story from 1977, "The Talons of Weng-Chiang," is frequently cited as one that people take issue with.[12] This is down to its stereotypical representation of Chinese characters, for the villain, Li H'sen Chang, being played by English actor John Bennett (1928–2005) in yellowface, and for the occasional use of sinophobia-related terminology, even if such use would have been historically and contextually accurate for the period in which the story is set.

It could also be interpreted that the attire of the original Celestial Toymaker (Michael Gough), in his Chinese silk robes, was chosen because they were indicative of his malevolent nature, further playing into the stereotyping of Asian villainy. There is also the unfortunate fact that the term "celestial" used to be used as a racial slur against Chinese people, since they hailed from the "Celestial Empire," or "Heavenly Dynasty" (both older terms for China, referencing the status of their Emperor as being the "Son of Heaven").

It would be wrong to touch upon the subject of race without mentioning slavery. Humans have had a long and horrific inclination toward the subjugation of other humans because of ethnic, cultural, or geographical differences. *Doctor Who* has actively explored this, not only by looking backward (i.e., "The Romans," 1965, and "The Highlanders," 1966–1967), but by looking forward, and projecting the worst conduct to emerge from eras of imperialism and colonialism, having humans engaged in the enslavement of alien races as they expand their frontiers out into the universe (i.e., the Tharils from "Warriors' Gate," 1981, and the Ood, who first appeared in "The Impossible Planet," 2006). This has not always been handled with the greatest of sensitivity though, with the 1966 story "The Ark" having a servile race of alien refugees, the Monoids, performing laborious work for humans in return for sanctuary on a generational colony ship. When the opportunity arises, the seemingly peaceful Monoids overthrow the humans and enslave them, but so devious are they that they end up resorting to infighting, undermining their own efforts for emancipation. All in all, it comes across as quite xenophobic, playing into bigoted narratives of immigrants and refugees seeking to undermine the societies that give them asylum.

DIVERSITY IN CASTING

Shockingly, it wasn't until the modern era that *Doctor Who* started to have a truly racially diverse cast, and this began with companions, tentatively with Mickey Smith (Noel Clarke), and then properly with Martha Jones (Freema Agyeman). Under Chris Chibnall's tenure, we got Yasmin Khan (Mandip Gill) and Ryan Sinclair (Tosin Cole). He also gave us the Fugitive Doctor (Jo Martin) and the first nonwhite Master (Sacha Dhawan).

One misstep that has come about through having a more racially diverse cast, albeit one where I do not believe there is any intentional prejudice at play, lies in how the show signals a confusing message about the likely success of mixed-race relationships. The romance between Rose Tyler (Billie Piper) and Mickey Smith (Noel Clarke) fizzles out when the Tenth Doctor (David Tennant) arrives on the scene. That same Doctor then spurns any romantic advances made by Martha Jones (Freema Agyeman). The burgeoning romance between Clara Oswald (Jenna Coleman) and Danny Pink (Samuel Anderson) comes to naught when he is killed by a car when crossing the road. Lastly, the apparent attraction between the Thirteenth Doctor (Jodie Whittaker) and Yasmin Khan (Mandip Gill) never really goes anywhere. Accordingly, showrunners need to be more aware of how mixed-race relations are portrayed in *Doctor Who*, because as it stands, they never appear to work out, and so might be perceived as supporting the skewed ideologies of those who believe that interracial relationships are wrong.

By far, though, the biggest and most progressive leap in racially diverse casting in *Doctor Who* has been with the introduction of the immensely talented Ncuti Gatwa in the lead role of the Fifteenth Doctor. Along with Jodie Whittaker being cast as the first female lead, this should be celebrated as a historic milestone for ongoing inclusivity in the series. The show has come a long way, both in terms of casting and representation of race, but there is still much work to be done to truly reflect the breadth and depth of multiculturalism found in contemporary society.

Science-fiction has always been a fantastic genre for addressing issues of race. The sheer diversity of life that has evolved here on Earth is remarkable, but no doubt pales in comparison to what might exist elsewhere in the universe. When humanity as a whole truly grasps that fact, perhaps then we will finally understand that for the people of our little planet, regardless of skin color or country of origin, there is so much more that unites us than divides us.

Chapter 15

Impact on Popular Media

Figure 15 *Community's* Troy and Abed cosplaying. NBC / Photofest © NBC

A show as innovative and as long-lasting as *Doctor Who* cannot exist without having a cultural impact on popular media during its lifetime. There can be few places left on Earth where the sight of a police box or a Dalek is not instantly recognizable, the former invoking the unmistakable sound of a Tardis materializing or dematerializing, and the latter summoning a harsh metallic shriek of *"EXTERMINATE!"* bringing back memories of young children diving behind sofas the world over.

In 1965, in an endeavor to seize on the popularity of the television series—particularly Terry Nation's iconic Daleks—a separate and quiet stand-alone movie was created, titled *Dr. Who and the Daleks*. Written by Milton Subotsky and directed by Gordon Flemyng, it was filmed in widescreen Technicolor format. It was, essentially, a retelling of the "*Doctor Who* and the Daleks" story from the television series, albeit with significant changes.

In the film, the central character is *literally* called Dr. Who (played by Peter Cushing). He is a human inventor who has created a space-time machine that he calls Tardis. Just like its television counterpart, it is bigger on the inside, but the sleek and glossy high-tech interiors are gone, replaced by a jumble of laboratory equipment and a jungle of wires and cables (I mean, who needs the Daleks when you have a health-and-safety death trap like that to contend with?). Along with his granddaughters, Susan (Roberta Tovey) and Barbara (Jennie Linden) and Barbara's boyfriend, Ian Chesterton (Roy Castle), they are accidentally transported to a strange planet where they encounter the Daleks. Even they did not escape design changes, with their bases and dome lights being much bigger and more pronounced, and rather than death rays (or flamethrowers, as was originally envisaged) they emitted jets of gas that would stun and paralyze their targets.

It was largely derided by critics and fans alike, but that did not prevent them from making a sequel, *Daleks' Invasion of Earth 2150 A.D.* Now joined by actual *Doctor Who* screenwriter David Whitaker (who also wrote a Dalek comic strip in the weekly children's magazine *TV Century 21*), Subotsky and Flemyng unleashed this reimagining of the television series story "The Dalek Invasion of Earth." Peter Cushing returns as Dr. Who, as does Roberta Tovey as Susan, but they are joined by two new characters, Louise (Jill Curzon) and Tom Campbell (Bernard Cribbins). When Special Constable Tom Campbell stumbles into a police box after a jewelry shop burglary, he encounters Dr. Who and his companions, and is whisked off into the future, where the Daleks have invaded the Earth, and have converted some humans into brainwashed slaves they call "Robomen." It underperformed at the box office, and a third planned film was canceled as a result.

Because of their popularity, the mid-1960s experienced a new craze, a phenomenon known as Dalekmania, where manufacturers scrambled to acquire licenses to manufacture Dalek-themed toys, board games, jigsaws, collector's cards, sticker sets, and even PVC playsuits.[1] You name it, if you could slap an image of a Dalek on it, it was fair game. By the time the 1970s came around, Dalekmania was past its peak, although Dalek merchandise could still be found.

While talking about Daleks in a historical context, here is an interesting fact. Although Terry Nation (1930–1997) created the Daleks, describing them in his script, the visual design was to be undertaken by one of the BBC

Impact on Popular Media 167

designers. Originally this was going to be a young man by the name of Ridley Scott. Yes, *that* Ridley Scott, later to become a renowned film director, famous for films such as *Alien* (1979), *Blade Runner* (1982), and *Gladiator* (2000). He was unavailable at the time, so the task fell to Raymond Cusick (1928–2013). According to him, as recounted in a video from 1992 titled, *Daleks: The Early Years*, the Dalek look was conceived on a Saturday night and designed on a Sunday afternoon.[2]

In America in the late 1970s and early 1980s, limited runs of *Doctor Who* could be found showing on affiliates of Public Broadcasting Service (PBS), which gave rise to the advent of stateside fandom. Longtime series producer John Nathan-Turner (1947–2002), was heavily motivated to get the show to expand out into international markets, and he became known for making appearances at PBS fundraising drives which were held to finance the acquisition of more episodes of *Doctor Who* to be broadcast in the United States. Nathan-Turner's approach to increasing international appeal was sometimes controversial, deliberately casting Brisbane-born Janet Fielding as Tegan Jovanka to pull in Australian viewers, and wanting an American companion for Peter Davison's Doctor, ending up with Perpugilliam "Peri" Brown (played by British actor, Nicola Bryant, using an American accent).

In 1996, seven years after the series had been canceled, hope sprang anew with the *Doctor Who* television movie. Philip Segal, a British-American television producer, had been trying, and failing, for some time to revive the show, but while working for Universal Studios, he managed to garner interest from the Fox Network, who commissioned a one-off television movie that could act as a possible backdoor pilot for a new series. It was originally intended to be a completely American reboot, with no ties whatsoever to the defunct BBC show. When scriptwriter Matthew Jacobs was brought on board, he persuaded Segal that it *should* be a direct continuation of what had come before, as well as giving the newly regenerated Doctor amnesia, so his process of self-discovery would also help new audiences learn who the Doctor is.

With a brief appearance by the outgoing Doctor of the classic-era series, Sylvester McCoy, and the introduction of a new Doctor, the vastly underrated Paul McGann, the stage was set for *Doctor Who* to make a monumental comeback. Sadly, that did not happen. In the 2022 American documentary film *Doctor Who Am I*, scriptwriter Matthew Jacobs reflects on two decisions that he feels were misjudged.[3] The first of these was making the Doctor half-human, and the second, and arguably the most contentious, was having the Doctor kiss the female lead.

With regard to the Doctor's lineage, fans on both sides of the Atlantic took exception to this. As far as they were concerned, the Doctor is 100 percent Gallifreyan, always has been, always will be (and this was *long* before much bigger controversies surrounding the Doctor's lineage would emerge under the auspices of Chris Chibnall). But if that was what lit the fuse, the kiss(es) between the Doctor (Paul McGann) and Grace Holloway (Daphne Ashbrook) caused the explosion. It was shocking, even to American fans of the show, who had seen enough of the British series to know the Doctor and his quirks, and to know that the Doctor does *not* go around kissing people. To British audiences, it was even more outrageous. For thirty-three years we had seen this television character grace our screens and never—not once—kiss a companion. It even prompted a feature cover on *Doctor Who Magazine* (no. 268) proclaiming, *NO SEX PLEASE . . . he's British!* Traditionally, the Doctor showed no romantic interest in any of his companions because that could be seen as an abuse of his position of power and authority (not to mention that it could be considered creepy, given that he was many hundreds of years older than they were).

It all seems quite tame these days, given that modern-era *Doctor Who* has seen him flirting, even with companions, and exchanging the odd kiss now again with characters like River Song. It is not as if any of us were under the illusion that he is part of some kind of intergalactic monastic order that has dedicated his life (lives?) to the observance of celibacy. He had a granddaughter, which means he had a child of his own, which means . . . well . . . *you get the point.*

With the return of *Doctor Who* in 2005, and easier access to the show than ever before in the United States, via BBC America, stateside fandom really took off, with conventions of dedicated and passionate followers coming together to share their love of it, and their love of a character for whom hatred and violence is never an acceptable solution. Whatever cultural differences we may have on either side of the Atlantic, it is heartening to know that we will always have that in common.

Outside of *Doctor Who* itself, and all of its direct influences, there have been many other parts of popular media culture, especially in America, that have taken inspiration from it. Let us take a look at some of the most well-known.

In 1989, an American science-fiction comedy film called *Bill and Ted's Excellent Adventure* burst onto the scene. The premise is that Ted "Theodore" Logan (Keanu Reeves) and William "Bill" S. Preston (Alex Winter), two dim-witted high-school students, are struggling to pass their history class. If they fail, they will not graduate, and Ted's father has threatened to send him to a military school in Alaska. There are much bigger implications of this, as a utopian society of the future has drawn inspiration from the music and philosophy of Bill and Ted, and their band, Wyld Stallyns. If they fail, the very future of mankind could be in jeopardy!

Enter Rufus (George Carlin), who is tasked with traveling back in time—in a time machine cunningly disguised as a telephone booth (now where could *that* idea have come from?)—to aid Bill and Ted. Using the time machine, they travel to various points in the past to meet and learn about historic characters and events, even bringing some of them back to the present to participate in Bill and Ted's assignment presentation. They pass the course, and the future is saved.

This goofy comedy received mixed reviews, but did reasonably well at the box office, grossing over $40 million on a budget of $10 million. It spawned two sequels, 1991's *Bill and Ted's Bogus Journey* and 2020's *Bill and Ted Face the Music*.

Dan Harmon's *Community* is a beloved American sitcom, set in a struggling community college and revolving around the lives of a group of students who come together to form a study group—Jeff Winger (Joel McHale), a lawyer who is disbarred when it is discovered that he lied about his qualifications; Britta Perry (Gillian Jacobs), a would-be activist who wants to make a difference; Shirley Bennett (Yvette Nicole Brown), a deeply religious single mother of two boys; Pierce Hawthorn (Chevy Chase), a racist, sexist, homophobic elderly millionaire; Annie Edison (Alison Brie), an inexperienced overachiever; Troy Barnes (Donald Glover), a former high-school star quarterback and best friend of Abed Nadir (Danny Pudi), a socially awkward fantasist. Together with the dean, Craig Peldon (Jim Rash), and psychotic staff member Ben Chang (Ken Jeong), they navigate the highs and lows of community college life.

Best friends Troy and Abed love immersing themselves in geek culture, hanging out, and enjoying sci-fi fare, such as *Kickpuncher* (a film about a cybernetically enhanced cop whose punches are as strong as kicks). In the 2011 episode "Biology 101," Abed is introduced to a long-running British sci-fi show called *Inspector Spacetime* (an obvious *Doctor Who* parody), and he is hooked. It details the adventures of Inspector Spacetime, a character who is portrayed by different actors over the length of its run, although they all wear the familiar costume of a trench coat and bowler hat. He is accompanied by a partner who is a constable, and he is equipped with his trusty Quantum Spanner. They travel through time and space in an X-7 Dimensionizer, which has the appearance of a traditional British red telephone box, facing off against deadly foes, not least of which is the cybernetic race known as the "Blorgons."

It is astutely observational humor, taking a lighthearted swipe at *Doctor Who* and its legion of die-hard fans. It is even quite prescient, predicting the outcry that would ensue with the arrival of a female Doctor. When Britta accompanies Abed to an Inspector Spacetime convention, she sees a poster indicating that there was once a female lead called Inspector Minerva. When she asks Abed about this, he replies, "Yes, and everyone hates her. Not because they're sexist. Because she sucks."[4] Britta then proceeds to wind Abed up by wearing an Inspector Minerva T-shirt for the remainder of their time at the convention.

Incidentally, that very same episode, 2013's "Conventions of Space and Time," guest-starred British comedian Matt Lucas as Toby, another convention attendee. Matt Lucas would later go on to appear in *Doctor Who* as a character called Nardole. The episode ends with the group watching an unwelcome American adaptation of Inspector Spacetime, with the Inspector (Luke Perry) emerging from a generic telephone booth, wearing a pristine white naval-style uniform, and saying, "Here we are, the 1960s, the greatest, grooviest period in the entire history of the entire universe. I'm lucky. I get to visit places like this because I can travel through time. And space. But not both at once. Do you know why that is, Ensign?" His attractive ensign (Jennie Garth) appears, also wearing white and wielding a tennis racket, saying to him, "Because, Inspector Spacetime, our minds would be blown into space-time confusion."

Another show, both inspired by and which makes references to *Doctor Who*, is DC's *Legends of Tomorrow*, a show set in the "Arrowverse." A Time Master called Rip Hunter (Arthur Darvill) goes rogue from the agency he works for to hunt down the tyrant Vandal Savage (Casper Crump) who, in the future, has conquered Earth and killed Hunter's family. Using his stolen time ship, the *Waverider*, Hunter recruits a group of misfits (including superheroes and villains) to aid him in his task. The agency disapproves of Hunter's actions and seeks to stop him.

Aside from obvious high-concept similarities, the ties to *Doctor Who* are numerous, not least in the casting department. Rip Hunter is played by Arthur Darvill, who also played Rory Williams in *Doctor Who* (and who wears a long brown coat, reminiscent of the one worn by the Tenth Doctor). Another character, Malcolm Merlyn, is played by John Barrowman, who was Captain Jack Harkness in *Doctor Who* (and who also has an uncanny ability to come back from the dead). And Dinah Lance, the mother of Sara Lance (Caity Lotz) who takes command of the Waverider, is none other than Alex Kingston, who played River Song in *Doctor Who*.

In the 2018 Episode "Necromancing the Stone,"[5] Ava Sharpe (Jes Macallan) criticizes John Constantine (Matt Ryan) for not doing enough to locate a spaceship floating through a temporal stream. He states, "My business card says Master of the Dark Arts, not ruddy Doctor Whats-his-face," to which Sharpe replies, "Who?" and Constantine says, "Exactly!"

Legend of Tomorrow's progenitor series, *Arrow*, has itself seeded many *Doctor Who* references throughout its time, clearly hailing it as a benchmark of geek culture.

Incidentally, while much of *Legends of Tomorrow* may have been inspired by *Doctor Who*, the character of Rip Hunter actually precedes it. First appearing in DC's Showcase comic anthology series in May 1959, Hunter then went on to feature in his own comic, *Rip Hunter . . . Time Master*, which ran for twenty-nine issues, from 1961 to 1965.

Curiously, animation is one of the mediums that has really celebrated *Doctor Who*, with a great many references being made to it in popular shows such as *Archer*, *Family Guy*, *Futurama*, *Phineas and Ferb*, *Regular Show*, *Rick and Morty*, *Rugrats*, *The Simpsons*, and *South Park*.

Such is the reach of *Doctor Who* that its influence has touched a myriad of films (*The Lego Movie 2*; *The Forgiven*; *Big Hero 6*; *Bumblebee*; *Looney Tunes: Back in Action*; *Iron Sky*; *The Lego Batman Movie*), television shows (*CSI: NY*; *NCIS*; *Supernatural*; *The Orville*; *Sesame Street*), books (*The Condition of Muzak*, by Michael Moorcock; *Later*, by Stephen King; *Outlander*, by Diana Gabaldon; *High Wizardry*, by Diane Duane), computer games (*Life Is Strange*; *RuneScape*; *Beneath a Steel Sky*; *Fallout*; *Fallout 2*; *EverQuest*; *Borderlands 2*; *Watch Dogs: Legion*), and music (*I'm Gonna Spend My Christmas with a Dalek* by the Go-Go's; *Doctorin' the Tardis* by KLF; *Remote Control* by the Clash; *Exterminate Annihilate Destroy* by Rotersand; *Smile* by the Supernaturals). All of these (and more—much, much more) have featured imagery associated with—or verbal references made to—*Doctor Who*. Can you spot them all?

There have been many other successful science-fiction television shows that have really cemented themselves in popular culture. *Lost in Space* ("Danger Will Robinson"), the *X-Files* ("The truth is out there"), *Star Trek*—in all its guises ("I'm a doctor, not an engineer"), *Agents of SHIELD* ("Tahiti, it's a magical place"), and *Red Dwarf* ("Smoke me a kipper, I'll be back for breakfast"). The thing to remember is that *Doctor Who* preceded *all* of these, and it is as much a part of British culture as tea, fish-and-chips, freezing days at the beach, and black taxicabs. Regardless of that, it has grown to become a shared cultural experience of global proportions, reminding all of us that sometimes it takes an alien to see the very best of humanity.

Chapter 16

Spin-Offs

Figure 16 Sarah Jane Smith and K9. BBC / Photofest © BBC

In what has become known as the "Whoniverse," there have been multiple Doctor Who spin-offs over the years, featuring characters familiar and new. Truthfully, few of these have stood the test of time. Nevertheless, they help build up a view of the universe that the Doctor lives in. There have been a great many spin-offs, spanning comics, books, and audiobooks (such as the award-winning audio dramas from *Big Finish*), but, like the rest of this book, I will be focusing on those that are considered canon within the context of the lore of *Doctor Who*.

K-9 AND COMPANY

The very first spin-off was *K-9 and Company*, an idea touted by John Nathan-Turner. While the robot dog K9 (first introduced in the 1977 *Doctor Who* story "The Invisible Enemy") turned out to be popular, especially with child viewers, the radio-controlled prop was beset with all manner of technical problems, and it could only really travel on even surfaces. In an interview with *Radio Times* in 2014, Tom Baker admitted that he did not enjoy working with the K9, "I didn't like it at all. Every time we had a shot, it meant that I had to get on my knees, which reminded me of the days when I was a Catholic."[1]

A pilot episode was commissioned, featuring the welcome return of Sarah Jane Smith (Elisabeth Sladen) and, of course, K-9 (voiced by John Leeson). Subtitled "A Girl's Best Friend," this tale of Sarah Jane Smith and K-9 becoming embroiled in the sinister witchcraft practices of a rural coven was broadcast in December 1981 and was met with respectable viewing ratings of 8.4 million viewers. Despite this, it did not go forward into production, with senior staffing changes at the BBC often believed to have been behind the series not getting picked up.

TORCHWOOD

Fresh from his bringing back *Doctor Who* to mainstream television, Russell T. Davies was presented with the opportunity to develop a post-watershed series (i.e., something to be viewed after nine o'clock at night—the BBC's cutoff for family viewing and entering adult viewing). He had already been developing a science-fiction series for a more mature audience under the working title "Excalibur." When working on the return of *Doctor Who*, the codeword "Torchwood' (an anagram of Doctor Who) had been used during production to divert attention and to avoid unnecessary leaks. Davies took his Excalibur concept, applied the *Torchwood* title to it, and reworked it into an official *Doctor Who* spin-off.

Torchwood featured an ensemble cast, led by the irrepressible Captain Jack Harkness (John Barrowman). He was joined by Gwen Cooper (Eva Miles) as a police officer who is recruited, Owen Harper (Burn Gorman) as their medical officer, Toshiko Sato (Naoko Mori) as their computer specialist, and Ianto Jones (Gareth David-Lloyd) who, in effect, is there to perform all the other functions that nobody else wants to do. It aired in October 2006 to a mixed reception.

The biggest problem with *Torchwood* is that many of the principal characters are unlikable, repeatedly making poor choices, both personally and professionally. We are introduced to one of them using confiscated alien technology as a date-rape-drug substitute. There is no shortage of swearing and plenty of references to sex and sexuality. In the 2006 story "Cyberwoman," someone ends up sexually fetishizing a partially converted Cyberman. It all comes across as trying far too hard to live up to its mature audience status, relying on tropes rather than clever storytelling to achieve this. The BBC parody show *Dead Ringers* did a comedy skit about it, joking that an assessment of an alien life-form revealed it to be "Horny, horny, horny," asserting that "Temporal disruptions in the timeline and fissures in space create enormous plot holes," and of *Torchwood* itself being "The most secret organisation in the world, so secret we don't even know our own character's motivations."[2]

Regardless, *Torchwood* gave the BBC Three digital channel its highest-ever viewing figures to date and it was not long before a second series was commissioned. Moving to the far more established BBC Two channel, the opening episode of the second season, broadcast in January 2008, attracted a healthy 4.22 million viewers.[3] The scripts become tighter and the characters less reprehensible, but this did not stop it from losing viewers throughout its run. Two of the principal characters, Owen and Toshiko, are killed off in the final episode, "Exit Wounds."

Torchwood returned in 2009, this time to BBC One, with a five-episode story arc titled "Children of Earth," broadcast over consecutive nights. As part of a secret agreement, twelve human children were handed over to an alien race in 1965 in return for a cure to a deadly virus. Those same aliens return some forty years later, demanding 10 percent of Earth's children be given over to them or they will destroy humanity. It is a dark and compelling story with John Frobisher (Peter Capaldi), a civil servant, being ordered by the prime minister to hand over his own daughters. He kills them to spare them this fate, before killing his wife and then turning the gun on himself. It is an emotionally charged scene and probably one of the best in all of *Torchwood*. In the end, Harkness drives the aliens away from Earth, but only at the cost of sacrificing his grandson. This third season received critical acclaim and achieved peak ratings of 6.76 million viewers, much higher than expected.[4]

Torchwood returned for a fourth and final season in July 2011 with a ten-episode story arc titled, "Miracle Day." This was part of a British-American collaboration between BBC Worldwide and the Starz network. The premise of the story is that one day—dubbed "Miracle Day"—people all over Earth stop dying. Initially heralded as a religious event, it quickly becomes apparent how much trouble this will cause. Governments around the world estimate that faced with only a growing population, the world's resources will be unable to sustain everybody within months. People who are in bad shape and who would have otherwise died under normal circumstances are relocated to camps where they are incinerated as part of covert population control measures.

Conversely, at the same time that everybody on Earth gains immortality, Harkness loses his, indicating a connection. Thus, a convoluted plot involves a powerful group of families, an incident from Harkness's past, and the effect that his blood has on a mysterious subterranean fissure, one that is somehow alive, known as the "Blessing." It stretches through the Earth, from Shanghai to Buenos Aires, and it emits a morphic field, one that is altered through the introduction of Harkness's blood, transferring his immortality to everyone else. The process is reversed by presenting some of his now mortal blood on both sides, nullifying the previous effect.

"Miracle Day" attempted to replicate the success of the newer format of "Children of Earth," along with another uncompromising story arc, but it was not quite as favorably met by critics. Many felt that it would have been better off as another five-part story with there being far too much repetition throughout its ten-part run. The biggest and most valid criticism, however, stems from the fact that *Torchwood* is a spin-off of *Doctor Who*, and as such, an impactful global event like "Miracle Day" is wholly incompatible with happenings that occur around the same time in the parent show. It is almost as though *Torchwood*, as a show, got too big for its boots and forgot about its humble origins, trying to overtake *Doctor Who* in high-stakes storytelling, and compromising its integrity as a result.

Outside of television, *Torchwood* had minor success after branching out into other media. A web series titled, *Torchwood: Web of Lies*, was released in 2011, and several *Torchwood* BBC radio dramas have been released (2008's "Lost Souls"; 2009's "Asylum," "Golden Age," and "The Dead Line"; and 2011's "The Devil and Miss Carew," "Submission," and "House of the Dead").

THE SARAH JANE ADVENTURES

Sarah Jane Smith (Elisabeth Sladen) may not have had her day in the sun with *K-9 and Company*, but that was to change in January 2007 when another Russell T. Davies creation, *The Sarah Jane Adventures*, was broadcast with a special episode, "Invasion of the Bane." This followed the continuing adventures of Sarah Jane Smith as she investigated extraterrestrial activities on Earth. Aimed at a younger audience, it was a big hit and was quickly commissioned as an ongoing series.

In the stories, Sarah Jane Smith is joined by her adopted son, Luke (Tommy Knight), her thirteen-year-old neighbor, Maria Jackson (Yasmin

Paige), and Clyde Langer (Daniel Anthony), a classmate of Maria's, and a budding coming book writer and illustrator. K-9 makes some cameo appearances (still voiced by John Leeson) and Sarah Jane has the help of a sentient supercomputer in her attic, dubbed "Mr. Smith" (voiced by Alexander Armstrong). As Maria leaves the regular cast, she is replaced by a new character, Rani Chandra (Anjli Mohindra), a new neighbor.

The show went from strength to strength, featuring cameos from Nicholas Courtney (Brigadier Alistair Gordon Lethbridge-Stewart), the Tenth and Eleventh Doctors (David Tennant and Matt Smith), and even Jo Grant (Katy Manning), appearing under her married guise of Jo Jones. The series only ended after the tragic death of Elisabeth Sladen to cancer in April 2011. The series was fully wrapped in the form of a tribute webcast, titled, "Farewell, Sarah Jane," scripted by Russell T. Davies and narrated by Jacob Dudman, and released in 2020 on the anniversary of Sladen's death. In it, it is implied that Sarah Jane Smith had been killed while preventing an alien invasion, and all her friends gather at her funeral to wish her a fond farewell.

CLASS

In October 2016, a new spin-off called *Class* was broadcast on BBC Three. Set in Coal Hill Academy, the same—albeit slightly rebranded—school that Susan Foreman (Carole Ann Ford), Barbara Wright (Jaqueline Hill), and Ian Chesterton (William Russell) went to in the original series of Doctor Who (and Clara Oswald in latter series). Written and conceived by Patrick Ness, it focuses on the lives of a group of students who attend an educational establishment where the fabric of space and time has been stretched far too thin, and creatures from elsewhere seek to break through.

It is another ensemble cast, featuring Charlie Smith (Greg Austin), an alien prince of the Rhodian people (not to be confused with the green-skinned aliens from the *Star Wars* franchise whose species have the same name), who is posing as a human student. He is the last of his kind after a species called the Shadow Kin wiped out the rest of his people. There is Ram Singh (Fady Elsayed), a hard-nosed, football-loving student, who loses part of his leg when he is attacked by the Shadow Kin (it is replaced with a prosthetic, given to him by the Doctor). There is April MacLean, an everyday student whose life is changed when she ends up sharing a heart with Corakinus (Paul Marc Davis), the king of the Shadow Kin. There is also Tanya Adola (Vivian Oparah), a prodigy of Nigerian descent whose remarkable intellect has seen her move up several years in school. Lastly, there is Miss Andrea Quill (Katherine Kelly), an alien of the Quill species, long-standing enemies of the Rhodians, and who, in retribution for her leadership in a war against the Rhodians, is psychically linked to Charlie—the aggressor being forced to take on the role of a protector.

Right from the trippy title sequence and associated upbeat music, it is very clear that the target audience for *Class* is older than younger children, but younger than mature audiences. The idea of older students having to balance fighting monsters, managing their love lives, and doing their homework is an interesting one (albeit not very original, having been done by *Buffy the Vampire Slayer* decades before), but its uneven pacing and inability to strike the right balance between lightheartedness and the darker issues presented meant that it created too much of a niche for itself, potentially failing to attract wider audience interest. In many ways, and quite opposed to the science-fiction show that it was, it was at its most engaging when dealing with the far more relatable and down-to-earth issues.

While it scored poorly in terms of viewership, critics were quick to praise the talented cast, clearly giving it their all.[5] Most reviewers were right to single out Katherine Kelly's Miss Quill, who is simply outstanding in her role, combining the best lines with an effortlessly acerbic wit and sarcasm.

TIME LORD VICTORIOUS

In 2020, the BBC launched a cohesive multiplatform *Doctor Who* story spanning audio, novels, comics, vinyl, digital, immersive theater, escape rooms, and games. They all fell under the banner of *Time Lord Victorious* and featured stories involving the Fourth, Eighth, Ninth, and Tenth Doctors, as well as classic enemies such as the Daleks (appearing in their own animated series on the Official Doctor Who YouTube Channel).

TALES OF THE TARDIS

November 2023 saw the release of the first original "Whonivese" series, titled *Tales of the Tardis*. This was a six-part collection of short episodes, featuring Doctors and/or companions of old brought together to share recollections of their days together in the Tardis. Not only did it serve as a pleasant nostalgia trip but had the capacity to familiarize new followers of the *Doctor Who* franchise with figures from the classic-era series, hopefully prompting them to take a chance and dive further into the wealth of stories from the series' long history.

BBC IPLAYER

The BBC iPlayer, its digital streaming service, now has a dedicated "Whoniverse" section, and as well as featuring the show and its many spin-offs, it is known that more are in the works and will find a home here. After sixty long years, the show, and all its associated spin-offs, are at the peak of their potential and, just like the Doctor, show no sign of slowing down.

DOCTOR WHO IN PROSE

Up until the point when the videocassette recorder (VCR) medium started to become commonplace in homes in the late 1970s and early 1980s, missing an episode of *Doctor Who* on television meant that it was effectively lost to you. Once a story had aired, it was consigned to history never to be repeated (at least, not in the United Kingdom). There were few exceptions to this, such as the *Five Faces of Doctor Who*, a one-off season of repeats shown on BBC 2 in late 1981. Timed to celebrate the arrival of the Fifth Doctor, Peter Davison (and to fill a scheduling gap, with his debut season having been pushed back from August 1981 to January 1982), it featured one story from each previous Doctor.

Such limitations meant that for fans of *Doctor Who*, the scheduled airtime for each episode was sacrosanct, never to be missed. As a collective, we gathered in front of our respective television screens at the appointed hour, our faces, bathed in the glow of the light from the cathode ray tube, filled with excitement and wonder. Still, we would think about the stories that had aired before our time and wish that we could have enjoyed them too.

The closest we ever came to doing so back then was through Target Books. An imprint rather than an independent publishing house, Target has changed owners several times over the decades (Universal-Tandem Publishing Co. Ltd., W.H. Allen & Co., Virgin Books, and Ebury Publishing, the latter of which continues to publish *Doctor Who* books under the Target imprint to this day), and they became famous for releasing novelizations of televised *Doctor Who* stories. They started in 1973 with the novelization of a few William Hartnell stories ("The Daleks," "The Zarbi"—a renaming of the television story "The Web Planet"—and "The Crusaders"). All these books had previously been released in the 1960s under different publishers, but Target acquired the rights and rereleased them under their colorful brand. The popularity of these led to Target striking a deal with Barry Letts and the BBC for options on *Doctor Who* scripts for novelization.

Most excitingly for fans of the series, the novelizations have been written by people who were heavily involved in the television series itself. Names like David Whitaker, Malcolm Hulke, Terrance Dicks, Barry Letts, Philip Hinchcliffe, Gerry Davis, and even Ian Marter, graced the covers. They were the perfect way for fans to revel in stores they had never seen, or even if they had, they wanted to enjoy again.

In 1991, Virgin Books, which had also purchased the Target imprint, began publishing independent *Doctor Who* stories under the "New Adventures" subheading. These continued the adventures of the Seventh Doctor (Sylvester McCoy) beyond the cancellation of the television series. A few of the books loosely followed the direction of where Andrew Cartmel (the television series story editor before it was canceled) indicated he had wanted to go in terms of the Doctor's backstory. Some of the writers of these books, such as Paul Cornell and Mark Gatiss, would go on to write for the television series when it was rebooted in 2005, and, in the case of Russell T. Davies, become an instrumental figure in bringing it back. Incidentally, Paul Cornell is one of several writers who cut his teeth having fan fiction produced in *Doctor Who* fanzines.

The late 1970s saw the rise of *Doctor Who* fan fiction. Fanzines such as *TARDIS* and *The Celestial Toyroom* appeared (the latter of which was a monthly publication released by the Doctor Who Appreciation Society [DWAS] before merging with TARDIS, and which has become the longest-running *Doctor Who* fanzine in the world). The DWAS also produced another fanzine, *Cosmic Masque*, which started in 1977 and was tailored more toward the publishing of fan fiction. In the 1990s, *Doctor Who* fan fiction moved online with stories appearing in Usenet newsrooms, becoming even more prevalent on fan fiction sites that sprang up, and on *Doctor Who* fan fiction sites specifically.

Throughout the sixteen years that *Doctor Who* was off the air, fanzines and books were among the biggest and most popular ways of indulging in fandom for a show that was gone but which simply refused to die.

Chapter 17

The Eternal Optimist

Figure 17 The Twelfth Doctor and Bill Potts. BBC / Photofest © BBC

In chapter 12, I quoted Steven Moffat, who referred to the Doctor as a hero, ending with the line, "There will *never* come a time when we don't need a hero like the Doctor." It is a good quote, but it may not be entirely accurate. Moffat has also likened *Doctor Who* to a modern fairy tale, and that is interesting because fairy tales tend to view things in extremes—good or evil, hero or villain.

While the Doctor may perform heroic deeds, he does not fit the classical attributes necessary for the archetype of *hero*. He is not strong, at least not in a physical sense, he does not wield a weapon with which to slay monsters, and he does not go on epic quests with the objective of overcoming great evils, he sort of stumbles upon them and makes things up as he goes along.

No, the Doctor more closely fits the archetype of *antihero*. His morality has often been called into question, putting those he travels with in danger, either to satisfy his curiosity or to achieve his end goals. He harbors the best of intentions, but he is not constrained by them, and he will take up a noble cause, although he is unorthodox and sometimes wins the day by questionable means.

It is interesting to raise the subject of *morality* in relation to the Doctor. We may question where he falls on the moral spectrum, but all we can do is look at an alien being and try to decide where he fits into the scope of *human* ethics. In truth, we would be just as effective in trying to assign him an *alignment*, as used in role-playing games such as *Dungeons & Dragons*, which was created by Gary Gygax (1938–2008) and Dave Arneson (1947–2009) in the 1970s.

Even doing that is difficult, as the Doctor is a complex character and ends up having many personalities, but I would argue that throughout his immense lifespan, his different regenerations have displayed characteristics that generally fit the attributes of the following alignment categories:

Neutral Good

- likely to act altruistically but will sometimes give in to selfish impulses
- is not beholden to traditional laws, content to break rules whenever they believe it to be necessary

Chaotic Good

- challenges authority
- acts as their conscience guides them, caring little about what others think or expect in the process
- places great importance on freedom and individuality
- is not compelled to adhere to laws or rules that they think are likely to impede them

Chaotic Neutral

- free-spirited and highly individualistic
- shuns traditions and authority
- often impulsive and unpredictable
- not limited by dichotomous thinking, viewing things simply as either good or evil

The Eternal Optimist

Certainly, on a *human* scale of *good* and *evil*, the Doctor is neither wholly one nor the other, existing somewhere in the liminal space between, and as we have explored in this book, while he is far more likely to inhabit the more positive end, this has not always been the case.

Let us not forget that at the heart of the mythos of *Doctor Who*, he is a rebel and a thief. He turned his back on the authority figures of his own society, and he stole a Tardis so he could escape from what he saw as a passive and restrictive culture. He is not reliable, often failing to take companions where and when he promised, or omitting to do something that he said he was going to. The Doctor also lies, as attested by River Song, suggesting that he follows a consequentialist system of morality (i.e., lying, generally perceived to be a wrong or morally ambiguous act, can be seen as good if it leads to the saving of lives). There are no two ways about it, as characters go, the Doctor is deeply and profoundly flawed.

Despite all this, the Doctor still tries to do the right thing, even when the odds are stacked against him, and failure seems all but assured. Why?

Just before the Twelfth Doctor (Peter Capaldi) is about to regenerate in the 2017 episode "Twice Upon a Time," he verbally reminds himself about the things that matter, and which he wants to hold on to, regardless of who he is about to become. He encapsulates this with, "Never be cruel, never be cowardly . . . Remember, hate is always foolish, and love is always wise. Always try to be nice, but never fail to be kind."[1]

This is coming from someone who spent most of his regeneration looking for the answer to a deceptively simple question that he asks his companion, Clara Oswald (Jenna Coleman), "Am I a good man?" She takes some time to think about it and responds, "You asked me if you're a good man and the answer is . . . I don't know. But I think you try to be, and I think that's probably the point." The Eleventh Doctor (Matt Smith) said that he chose the name "Doctor" as a promise. One who saves lives. It stands as a reminder of the man he wishes to be.[2]

The Doctor's unconventional ethical stance—even toward his enemies—is best illustrated in the 1975 story "Genesis of the Daleks." The Fourth Doctor (Tom Baker) has placed explosives in the incubation room that houses the mutations that are to be transferred into the Dalek machines, which is to be the beginning of the Dalek race. As he holds the ends of the wire that is connected to the explosives, he asks himself if he has the right to wipe them out. When his self-doubt is questioned by his companions, he adds, "If someone who knew the future pointed out a child to you and told you that child would grow up totally evil, to be a ruthless dictator who would destroy millions of lives, could you then kill that child?"[3]

The Twelfth Doctor (Peter Capaldi) finds himself faced with that very same dilemma when he travels to the past and ends up on the war-torn Skaro (homeworld of the Daleks), in the 2015 episode "The Magician's Apprentice." He finds a young boy trapped in the middle of a minefield. The Doctor has every intention of saving the boy but hesitates when he learns that he is none other than Davros, the person who will go on to create the Daleks in the future. At first, it appears that the Doctor's compassion has abandoned him, but being true to himself, he cannot leave a young boy to die, no matter who he will become. The Doctor clears a path through the mines, takes the boy's hand, and leads him to safety, hoping against hope that this act of mercy might leave a lasting impression on him.

In the 2014 story "Flatline," the Twelfth Doctor (Peter Capaldi) discovers that there is an incursion of two-dimensional beings in our three-dimensional universe. In the end, when confronting the creatures (which he dubs the "Boneless"), he says to them, "I tried to talk. I want you to remember that. I tried to reach out, I tried to understand you, but I think that you understand us perfectly. And I think that you just don't care. And I don't know if you are here to invade, infiltrate or just replace us. I don't suppose it really matters now. You are monsters. That is the role you seem determined to play. So it seems I must play mine. The man that stops the monsters."[4]

The Twelfth Doctor's moralistic introspection stems from the face he subconsciously chose to adopt during his last regeneration. It is the face of a man he met before. In the 2008 episode "The Fires of Pompeii," the Tenth Doctor (David Tennant) and Donna Noble (Catherine Tate) travel back to Pompeii in 79 AD, just before the eruption of Mount Vesuvius, something that history records as being cataclysmic for the population. The Doctor and Donna meet Lobus Caecilius (Peter Capaldi), a merchant of marble, and his family.

The Doctor discovers that the survivors of an alien race, the Pyroviles (humanoid rock-based life-forms), have created a base underneath Mount Vesuvius. They are using energy converters to siphon off power from the volcano so they can convert humans into Pyroviles with a view to eventually taking over the planet. The Doctor's first ethical dilemma arises when he realizes that by siphoning off power from Mount Vesuvius, the Pyroviles have been reducing the likelihood of it erupting. However, the eruption and the resulting devastation for the citizens of Pompeii is a historical fact, so the event is a fixed point in time and *must* happen. Donna tries to convince the Doctor that they should start an evacuation, but the Doctor is adamant that he cannot save all the people. The event happened and not even a Time Lord can change that. He tells her, "Some things are fixed, some things are in flux. Pompeii is fixed." When she asks how he knows that, he replies, "Because that's how I see the universe. Every waking second, I can see what is, what was, what could be, what must not. That's the burden of a Time Lord."[5]

The only way to save the human race, and stop the plans of the Pyroviles, is to disrupt the power siphoning process, triggering the very eruption that will destroy Pompeii. Donna concedes that as terrible as this is, it is the lesser of two evils. As fire and ash and rock rain down on Pompeii, the Doctor and Donna head back to Caecilius's house, where the Tardis is located. As Caecilius and his family huddle in fear, the Doctor walks right past them into the Tardis. Donna implores him to stop, but he does not, and when she enters, he makes the Tardis dematerialize, leaving them. She pleads with him to do something, anything. Not to save the whole town, but to save *somebody*. Her human compassion reaches him and pulls him from the depths of the nihilistic frame of mind into which he has retreated, and he returns to save Caecilius and his family. It is a stark reminder that as much as humanity needs the Doctor, the Doctor needs humanity.

When the Eleventh Doctor (Matt Smith) regenerates into the Twelfth Doctor (Peter Capaldi), he takes the face of Caecilius. In the 2015 episode "The Girl Who Died," Clara (Jenna Coleman), tells the Doctor that he is always talking about what they can and cannot do, but he never tells her the rules. He replies that it is all right to make ripples, just not tidal waves. In the same episode, a girl, Ashildr (Maisie Williams), helps the Doctor to save her village, but at the cost of her own life. The Doctor feels responsible. Fearful of losing Clara too, he tells her that he is sick of losing people and that one day the memory of her, when she is gone, will be too much and he will climb into the Tardis and run away to escape the pain. Clara reassures the Doctor that he did his best, and that there is nothing he can do. He is not satisfied with this, bemoaning the fact that he can pretty much do anything, but there are certain things he is not *supposed* to.

At that moment he has a realization. The answer to one of the questions he had been asking himself, namely, why *this* face? He tells Clara, "I know where I got this face, and I know what it's for. To remind me. To hold me to the mark. I'm the Doctor, and I save people."[6]

He recovers a small battle medical kit from one of the armored suits the enemy that attacked the village was wearing. He reprograms it for human use and places it on the forehead of the lifeless Ashildr. It is quickly absorbed into her body and begins the work of repairing her, restoring her to life. The Doctor leaves another reprogrammed kit, for Ashildr to give to someone else, as he puts it, once she *understands*. The Doctor tells Clara that there is every chance that the modified medical kit will never stop working, never stop repairing Ashildr. He says that the reason he left a spare medical kit is because immortality is not about living forever, it is about losing everybody else, and that one day she might meet somebody she cannot bear to lose. Although he had done a good thing, on some level he knows that he did it for all the wrong reasons. He acknowledges that he was angry and emotional and that he may have made a terrible mistake, and that time will tell.

In the next episode, "The Woman Who Lived," the Doctor has traveled eight hundred years into the future, to 1651. He meets Ashildr again, who is now posting as a highwayman. The medical kit has indeed kept her alive all this time, but her human brain is not designed to retain all the memories of such an extraordinarily long lifespan. She does not remember most of it. She cannot even clearly recall her own name, Ashildr. As she tells the Doctor, "I don't even remember that name . . . I call myself *Me*. All the other names I chose died with whoever knew me. *Me* is who I am now. No-one's mother, daughter, wife. My own companion. Singular. Unattached. Alone."[7] She invites the Doctor to look through her journals, and as he does, he realizes just how much loss and suffering she has endured, which has resulted in her becoming cold and desensitized. When the Doctor asks her what happened to the other medical kit he left for her, she shows it to him, saying that nobody has ever been good enough to warrant it.

The Doctor learns that she has been deceiving him, that she wants to use an alien artifact to open a portal to get off Earth. But it needs a life taken to make it work and she is fully prepared to undertake such a venture. The reality of what she has become hits the Doctor hard, with him telling her that he wanted to save a scared young woman's life, not realizing that her compassion would eventually run out.

But she has been tricked, and in the process of taking a life, a portal opens to reveal an alien invasion fleet waiting to come through. This shocks her into understanding just how selfish and uncaring she has become, putting the entire world at risk to satisfy her own needs. She uses the remaining medical kit to restore life to the man she was taking it from, closing the portal in the process. With things set right, the Doctor addresses her newfound epiphany, telling her that people like them go on for far too long, and that they need mortal humans, because only they know how precious and fleeting life is.

In the 2015 episode "Face the Raven," the Doctor encounters Ashildr once more when she becomes part of an elaborate trap set for him. She fakes the death of a resident of a hidden sanctuary street in London, a place where alien species can find refuge, and frames Rigsy (Jovian Wade), a young man that the Doctor and Clara met on a previous occasion. The Doctor slowly pieces the mystery together, but Clara, who has spent so much time with the Doctor that she has become quite blasé about danger, tries to help and takes the death sentence upon herself. In doing so it means that it can no longer be revoked, and Clara is fated to die. The Doctor unleashes a torrent of threats upon Ashildr and Clara begs him to stop. She does not want the Doctor to lose himself, to become vengeful and wrathful, over a mistake that she made. Once Clara has died, the Doctor tells Ashildr that he will do his best to honor Clara's wish not to enact revenge on her, but he tells her to avoid him, saying, "You'll find it's a very small universe when I'm angry with you."[8]

Consequences. This is one of the things that the Doctor struggles with. He can see the past and he can view the future, but he can be blind to the consequences of his own actions. He broke a fundamental rule in his desire to save an innocent life, but it could be argued that what he was really doing was consigning Ashildr to endless lifetimes of suffering to make himself feel better in the moment. Regardless, it is a decision that costs him dearly.

Therein lies the paradox of the Doctor saving lives. He cannot save everybody, for despite him having been alluded to as *the lonely god* (the 2006 episode "New Earth"), he is just a man and bound by his limitations. When he does save people, that does not necessarily mean they go on to live full and long lives, as sometimes he only ends up buying them a little bit more time. In the instance of Ashildr and Clara, he saves one life only to discover that it leads to the death of another.

Some have tried to liken the mythos of the Doctor to that of Christianity. On some levels there might appear to be parallels—the Doctor being a messianic figure with a savior complex who gathers followers around him and who undergoes a resurrection after death. However, given the Doctor's control over space and time, and his power to determine the fate of the people he meets, in terms of representation, he could be seen as being closer to God than Christ. Ultimately, though, he is neither. While humanity may put its faith in God, the Doctor puts his faith in humanity.

While the Doctor himself may be no god, he has no qualms about confronting those who would claim to be. In the 2013 episode "The Rings of Akhaten," the Doctor visits the episode's namesake, a series of planetoids forming a ring system around a much larger planet. Here currency is not based on monetary value, but sentimental worth. The more treasured something is, the more value it holds. Their culture has a figure, a young girl known as the Queen of Years. She becomes the vessel of their history learning every chronicle, every poem, every legend, every song. At a determined point, the Queen of Years must sing a song, a lullaby without end, to the Old God of Akhaten, to feed it. But this is no metaphor. The Old God is nothing more than a planet-sized parasite that feeds off memories and stories, and it will consume her in the process.

The Doctor is not about to let a young girl get sacrificed to feed this monster, so he takes her place, telling it, "You like to think you're a God. But you're not a God. You're just a parasite eaten out with jealousy and envy and longing for the lives of others. You feed on them. On the memory of love and loss and birth and death and joy and sorrow. So . . . come on them. Take mine."[9] The parasite gorges itself on his vast collection of memories, and when Clara, the impossible girl, offers up her own, that is the tipping point, it simply cannot take anymore and is itself consumed.

Clearly, it is a mistake to underestimate the wealth of experience and knowledge that the Doctor holds. To the Doctor, knowledge and intelligence are powerful things. In the 2006 episode "Tooth and Claw," when the Doctor (David Tennant) and a group of people, including Queen Victoria (Pauline Collins), are faced with what appears to be a werewolf, one of the party laments that they are not in possession of any weapons. The Doctor says, "You want weapons? We're in a library. Books! Best weapons in the world. This room's the greatest arsenal we could have. Arm yourself!"[10] In the 1977 story "The Face of Evil," the Doctor (Tom Baker) tells Leela (Louise Jameson), "You know, the very powerful and the very stupid have one thing in common. They don't alter their views to fit the facts. They alter the facts to fit their views."[11] A phrase that is just as relevant today as when it was first spoken.

The 2017 episode "Twice Upon a Time" sees Bill Potts (Pearl Mackie) ask the First Doctor (David Bradley), not what he was running away from when he left Gallifrey, but what he was running to. He thinks it is a very good question, and after a moment of pondering, he says, "There is good and there is evil. I left Gallifrey to answer a question of my own. By any analysis, evil should always win. Good is not a practical survival strategy—it requires loyalty, self-sacrifice and love. So, why does good prevail? What keeps the balance between good and evil in this appalling universe? Is there some kind of logic? Some mysterious force?"[12]

This harks back to one of the original concepts that was devised when the series was being created. It ties perfectly into the notion that the Doctor was *searching for something, as well as running away from something*, and it credibly answers the question as to why the Doctor is motivated to do what he does. He may never find the answer, but he has hope, and sometimes that is enough. In our world, hope is a powerful commodity. Unlike other commodities, it cannot be traded on the stock market, yet its value is *priceless*.

Hope has always been a core theme that runs through *Doctor Who*. In the classic-era series, the Doctor used the phrase, *while there's life, there's hope*, on multiple occasions. In the 2018 episode "The Tsuranga Conundrum," when someone asks the Thirteenth Doctor (Jodie Whittaker) what exactly she is a doctor of, she rattles off a list of things, concluding with, "Hope. Mostly hope," adding, "It doesn't just offer itself up. You have to use your imagination. Imagine the solution and work to make it a reality. Whole worlds pivot on acts of imagination."[13]

The Eleventh Doctor (Matt Smith) sums this up well in the 2011 two-part story "The Rebel Flesh"/"The Almost People," telling Amy Pond (Karen Gillan), "I am and always will be the optimist, the hoper of far-flung hopes and the dreamer of improbable dreams.[14]

Chapter 18

From Then, to Now, and Beyond

Figure 18 The Eleventh Doctor. BBC / Photofest © BBC

There is a delicious irony in the fact that a television series that deals with time travel as a central concept has, itself, become a fascinating record of cultural and societal change over its sixty-year lifespan. It is quite different from the kitchen sink dramas and soap operas that have emerged during this time, which also end up chronicling the periods in which they exist. However, while they directly tackle gritty down-to-earth issues, or take a lighthearted look at everyday slices of life, *Doctor Who* is not limited by the boundaries of realism—or even the Earth—having all of space and time to explore. Nevertheless, it has reflected on many cultural and societal issues, past and present, while anticipating others.

At its heart, science-fiction can be a subversive genre. In a BBC Culture article by Tom Cassauwers in December 2018, Mingwei Song, associate professor at Wellesley College, when talking about the emergence of Chinese science-fiction such as *The Three-Body Problem* by Cixin Liu, says, "This new wave of science-fiction has a dark and subversive side that speaks either to the invisible dimensions of reality, or simply the impossibility of representing a reality dictated by the discourse of a national dream."[1] She adds, "I'm always amazed by the continued prosperity of the genre. Some of it is very subversive and provocative. But so far they haven't been censored. My theory for why it continues to grow is that it isn't protest literature. It's a literary genre that uses the imagination to explore unseen realities. But it doesn't directly challenge the Chinese government."

Believe it or not, *Doctor Who* has played a subversive role too, but this is nothing new, with its subtle and not-so-subtle embedding of political messaging into its storytelling over the decades, particularly in the 1970s and 1980s.

Rightly or wrongly, the 1970 story "The Silurians" (and, effectively, all subsequent stories featuring them) has been seen by some as an allegory for the rights of indigenous peoples who have found themselves displaced by colonial expansionism. To my knowledge, it was never the express intention of writer Malcolm Hulke (1924–1979) for this to be the case. An ardent socialist who held strong left-wing views, and whose works explore antiauthoritarian and antiestablishment themes, there is every possibility there were subconscious influences at play.

The 1970 story "Inferno" sees the Third Doctor (Jon Pertwee) transported to a parallel world where Britain is on the brink of an environmental catastrophe. This is because the fascist government that is in charge has ignored scientific warnings by drilling deep through the Earth's crust to exploit the untapped energies within. The 1973 story "The Green Death" is also widely regarded as an attempt to highlight the importance of environmentalism, long before such issues became commonplace. Producer Barry Letts and script editor Terrance Dicks were both increasingly taking an interest in environmental issues. In 1972 a special edition of *The Ecologist*, titled *A Blueprint for Survival* caught their attention.² It focused on the ways that post–World War II industries had become unsustainable and proposed a more stable society with minimal ecological destruction. *Doctor Who* was seen as a platform from which to promote a message of caution through storytelling.

This sentiment was echoed a decade later in the landmark 1983 essay, "Television as a Cultural Forum,"³ by Horace Newcomb and Paul M. Hirsch and reiterated by Heather Hendershot in the book *How to Watch Television*.⁴ Both argue that television provides a space to express collective cultural concerns.

The 1972 story "The Curse of Peladon" finds the Doctor (Jon Pertwee) visiting the planet Peladon, which is attempting to join a Galactic Federation, with opposing sides strongly arguing for and against such a move. It is no coincidence that this story went out at a time when Britain was undertaking negotiations to join the European Economic Community. Its sequel, the 1974 story "The Monster of Peladon," has the Doctor caught in the middle of a power struggle between the ruling elite and striking miners who are calling for improved working conditions, a clear allusion to the strikes implemented by miners in the United Kingdom the same year, which saw them get a pay deal from Harold Wilson's newly appointed Labour government, more than double what they were offered under Edward Heath's Conservative government that had been voted out of power.

The 1984 story "Warriors of the Deep" conveys powerful antiwar and anti–nuclear proliferation messages, seeing unnamed superpowers on the brink of all-out war having their paranoia exploited to benefit a combined force of Silurians and Sea Devils that hope to reclaim the Earth by having humanity wipe itself out. It ends on a depressing note, with all characters, save for the Fifth Doctor (Peter Davison) and his companions, dying in the conflict—a small-scale representation of what would likely happen if war had indeed broken out.

That same year, the story "The Caves of Androzani" revolves around a war being fought over a life-prolonging substance called Spectrox. Written by Robert Holmes, his first *Doctor Who* story since 1978, it is a bleak tale of greed and power and is regarded as an indictment of the pernicious influence of Big Pharma and corporate greed.

In an article in *The Telegraph* written by Stephen Adams in February 2010, Sylvester McCoy indicates that during his time on the show (from 1987 to 1989), stories were quietly but deliberately seeded with anti-Thatcher rhetoric (Margaret Thatcher being the prime minister of the United Kingdom's Conservative government at the time, and a much revered or reviled character, depending on which side of the political spectrum you found yourself on).⁵ "Our feeling was that Margaret Thatcher was far more terrifying than any monster the Doctor had encountered," said McCoy.

Script editor Andrew Cartmel, when asked by producer John Nathan-Turner what he would like to achieve, said, "I'd like to overthrow the government," adding, "I was a young firebrand and I wanted to answer honestly. I was very angry at the social injustice in Britain under Thatcher and I'm delighted that came into the show."

The 1988 story "The Happiness Patrol" features a character called Helen A (Sheila Hancock), a barely concealed caricature of Thatcher (1925–2013) and the head of a tyrannical regime who wants to do away with anybody who appears to be unhappy living under her rule.

The 1989 story "Battlefield" sees a continuation of Britain's Arthurian legend, with the sorceress Morgaine (Jean Marsh) taking control of a nuclear missile and preparing to use it. The Seventh Doctor (Sylvester McCoy) gives her an impassioned speech on the futility of nuclear weapons, "If this missile explodes, millions will die, you will die. All over the world, fools are poised, ready to let death fly. Machines of death, Morgaine, screaming from above, of light, brighter than the sun. Not a war between armies, nor a war between nations, but just death, death gone mad. A child looks up into the sky, his eyes turn to cinders. No more tears, only ashes. Is this honour? Is this war? Are these the weapons you would use?"[6] No subtlety here, just a brutal tub-thumping reminder that when it comes to nuclear weapons, there are no winners, only losers. It is what Cartmel has described as the CND (Campaign for Nuclear Disarmament) speech.

Moving into the modern era, the 2005 two-part story "The Aliens of London"/"World War Three" has the British prime minister and key government and military figures replaced by alien creatures who wish to start a nuclear war, reducing the planet to radioactive slag which they will then sell off to power starships on tight budgets. To set this in motion, the faux prime minister gives a press conference where he claims that an alien enemy is poised above the Earth with massive weapons of destruction, capable of being deployed within forty-five seconds. He does so in the hopes of getting the United Nations to release nuclear access codes, claiming extinction for humanity unless they strike first. The term *massive weapons of destruction* is deliberately similar to that of *weapons of mass destruction*, the claimed presence of which was used by Labour prime minister Tony Blair (1953–) to have Britain deploy troops in Iraq in 2003, leading to mass protests in the United Kingdom. The subsequent investigation led to the Chilcot Report, named after its author, Sir John Chilcot (1939–2021), who, among his conclusions, found that "Military action at the time was not a last resort" and that "The judgements about the severity of the threat posed by Iraq's weapons of mass destruction—WMD—were presented with a certainty that was not justified."[7]

The 2005 episode "The Long Game" sees the Ninth Doctor (Christopher Eccleston) arrive on Satellite 5, a huge space station that broadcasts news across the human empire in the year 200,000. Journalist Cathica (Christine Adams) states that the process of gathering news should be open, honest, and beyond bias. A nice sentiment, although not one shared by the Editor (Simon Pegg) who, along with an alien creature—the Jagrafess—runs the station, manipulating humanity through news media. The Editor tells the Doctor about the power they wield, "Create a climate of fear, and it's easy to keep the borders closed. It's just a matter of emphasis. The right word in the right broadcast repeated often enough can destabilise an economy. Invent an enemy. Change a vote."[8] A disconcerting notion, and one that would become even more meaningful over a decade later, with allegations of voter manipulation by foreign-backed entities through fabricated news and social media plaguing Donald Trump's presidency in America from 2017 to 2021, and accusations of right-wing media spin influencing the outcome of Britain's Brexit referendum, which ultimately saw it leave the European Union in 2020.

The 2008 episode "Turn Left" sees Donna Noble (Catherine Tate) manipulated into creating an alternative reality where the Tenth Doctor (David Tennant) has died. Many of the disasters that the Doctor would have averted have now happened—including central London being destroyed. An emergency government is established, Britain is put under martial law, and Noble's family is relocated to Leeds to share accommodation with other families, feeling as powerless as refugees. People of foreign origin are moved to labor camps under a new law, which one character describes as "England for the English." This deeply affects Noble's grandfather, Wilf (Bernard Cribbins) who sees Britain becoming everything he fought against in World War II. It has been widely praised for both Tate's performance and for raising the chilling possibility of a Britain that succumbs to rampant xenophobia—something that is not inconceivable given the inflammatory rhetoric of the conservative government of the United Kingdom, with former home secretary Suella Braverman likening the number of migrants crossing the Channel to an "invasion."

The 2017 story "Oxygen" takes the Twelfth Doctor (Peter Capaldi) to a space station where all the workers wear smart AI-driven spacesuits that regulate oxygen flow and can operate independently (the mining company not being willing to provide a breathable atmosphere *inside* the station as doing so is not considered profitable, with personal oxygen supplies offered at "competitive prices"). When all but four of the crew are killed, starved of oxygen, the race is on to find out why before everybody dies. A ship is on the way, believed to be a rescue ship, but the Doctor learns otherwise. It is not filled with rescuers, but replacement workers. As oxygen in the suits is regulated to limit wasteful consumption, inefficient workers are deliberately terminated. As the Doctor puts it, "The end point of capitalism. A bottom line where human life has no value at all. We're fighting an algorithm. A spreadsheet. Like every worker, everywhere—we're fighting the suits."[9] Again, subtlety takes a back seat to this raw admonition of unchecked capitalism, where corporations constantly push to maximize profit margins at the expense of the safety and welfare of people.

Doctor Who could never be regarded merely as a *passive* observer of the culture and society that it exists in. It may seem obvious to say, but it is necessary given that a core component of science-fiction is . . . well . . . *science*, and in science, the *observer effect* is the disturbance of an observed system through the act of observation. As a television program, and a slice of shared media in the public consciousness, *Doctor Who* not only acts as a record of the times in which it exists but also can influence them.

Lindy Orthia, senior lecturer in science communication, conducted a fascinating study into how *Doctor Who* shapes public attitudes to science.[10] Although it is a limited study, she indicates it demonstrates the potential importance of fiction as a science communication medium.

As the twenty-first century has progressed, there has been a disturbing increase in indifference or intolerance to science. A 2022 article in the *Proceedings of the National Academy of Sciences Journal*, titled "Why Are People Antiscience, and What Can We Do about It?"[11] indicates the difficulty for people in the scientific community to gain and keep public trust and to impart information in way that is both understood and accepted.

Doctor Who as having a positive and inspiring effect on attitudes toward science can be seen in real-world examples. In November 2013, Professor Brian Cox (1968–), a physicist in the School of Physics and Astronomy at the University of Manchester, England, gave a televised lecture titled "The Science of *Doctor Who*" at the Royal Institution's lecture hall. Between May 2022 and October 2024, the *Doctor Who Worlds of Wonder: Where Science Meets Fiction* exhibition toured (I visited it several times when it appeared at the National Museum of Scotland), exploring the science behind the show. On their publicity material, they state, "The eight zones set within this educational exhibition explore a diverse selection of exciting scientific topics and feature a wealth of iconic props and sets, and a unique collection of behind-the-scenes resource materials from the world's longest-running science-fiction show. Created in close collaboration with the team at BBC Studios along with advisors specialising in a broad range of scientific topics. This inspiring, interactive and all-encompassing exhibition has been designed for science centres, natural science museums and attractions. It is a must-see for families, school groups, *Doctor Who* fans, curious minds and future scientists, whether or not they have seen the TV show."[12]

Doctor Who is also quite different from other mainstream science-fiction television shows. The *Star Trek* franchise has been wildly popular, spanning no less than eleven official spin-off shows from *The Original Series* (1967–1969), namely *The Animated Series* (1974), *The Next Generation* (1988–1994), *Deep Space Nine* (1993–1999), *Voyager* (1995–2001), *Enterprise* (2002–2005), *Discovery* (2018–2024), *Picard* (2020–2023), *Lower Decks* (2020–2023), *Prodigy* (2022–), *Strange New Worlds* (2022–), and *Starfleet Academy* (forthcoming).

Star Wars too has expanded far beyond its cinematic origins to many television shows, namely *Droids* (1985–1986), *Ewoks* (1985–1985), *The Clone Wars* (2008–2020), *Rebels* (2014–2018), *Resistance* (2018–2020), *The Bad Batch* (2021–2024), *Visions* (2021–2023), *Tales* (2022–2024), and *Young Jedi Adventures* (2023–2024).

So, what sets *Doctor Who* apart from *Star Trek* and *Star Wars*? *Star Trek* largely focuses on the future of humanity. It examines new and unusual problems that we might face as we explore the final frontier of space, as well as looking at those problems that might stay the same (after all, as humans, we tend to take our baggage with us). It attempts to maintain a positive attitude on how humanity will evolve to meet the challenges of the future, but that is just it—it is all about the future—from the mid-twenty-second century to the thirty-second century.

Star Wars, conversely, is set—as they put it—*A long time ago in a galaxy far, far away*. There are *no* humans in the *Star Wars* universe, not even one, and while a great many of the characters may look and act like us, they are *all* aliens (and long-dead ones, from our perspective—remember the timeframe in which it is all set), so there is not much to directly relate to there.

Doctor Who, on the other hand, examines humanity in the here and now, as seen through the eyes of an alien, very much drawing on the old notion that sometimes we see ourselves most clearly through the eyes of a stranger. Time travel is often involved, but even when it is, humanity is still central. We can look at it thus.

1. In looking at the past it forces us to ask how far we have come, what progress we have made, and what opportunities we may have squandered.
2. In looking at the present it makes us consider how we are coping in what seems like increasingly difficult and/or challenging times.
3. In looking at the future uses informed deductions based on what we have learned from 1 and 2, to extrapolate where we might end up.

For a show that appears to be about an alien and his space-time machine, it is a celebration of humanity and human nature, unafraid to expose the very worst of it, but unashamed to embrace the very best of it. And because *Doctor Who* has the ability to tell stories set in the past, present, and future, as well as here on Earth and far out into the realms of space, it is in the enviable position of having nearly infinite narrative possibilities.

What does all of this bode for the future of *Doctor Who*? Like the Doctor himself, the show can regenerate, reinventing itself for each subsequent generation of fans. The trick here is to keep it feeling fresh and vibrant, drawing upon its rich heritage, but not to become immured by it, nor jettison it entirely so that it feels unrecognizable. Finding the right balance to attract and hold new audiences while remaining faithful and respectful to the existing ones has to be one of the hardest things that any *Doctor Who* production team can face.

Something that used to loom over *Doctor Who* was the limitation of only twelve regenerations in a Time Lord's life. Back when the creators came up with an arbitrary number of times the Doctor could regenerate, twelve might have seemed like a lot. But it set the clock ticking, an inevitable countdown to the potential demise of the Doctor and of the show. Modern-era producers have found ways around that limitation. Moffat allowed the Time Lords to give the Doctor a whole new regeneration cycle. Chibnall did away with the limitation altogether, suggesting that the Doctor had an infinite number of regenerations. Either way, I think it is safe to say that we no longer need to concern ourselves about the longevity of the Doctor.

Now that modern-era *Doctor Who* has shaken things up with the introduction of both a female Doctor (Jodie Whittaker) and a Black Doctor (Ncuti Gatwa), this only serves to broaden its appeal. We have already established in this book that *Doctor Who* is not just for children, it is for adults too, but it goes beyond that. It is for *everyone*, and every person, regardless of age, gender, sexuality, or race, should not only have the opportunity to enjoy it but to find their connection to it.

Back in the classic era, one of the things that *Doctor Who* was (reluctantly) famous for was wobbly sets and dodgy special effects. Budgets were tight and effects (both practical and digital) were limited by the technologies of the time. To be honest, much of what they did, given the restrictions they faced, was quite remarkable, and it gave the series a quaint kind of charm. However, television audiences these days are far more sophisticated and, dare I say it, spoiled by the myriad of generously budgeted and slickly produced shows that are broadcast in all their 4K HDR glory. Since its revival in 2005, *Doctor Who* has seen a notable jump in quality, with great sets, props, and costumes, and it is only going to get better. A brand-new partnership deal between the BBC and Disney+ has seen a significant cash injection into the series, and a new home for *Doctor Who* outside of the United Kingdom, allowing for much wider global reach.

As *Doctor Who* is a franchise that has lasted a very long time (and will hopefully continue for a long time yet to come), those who produce it must remember that they are only a small part of an ongoing legacy. Think of it as being like the responsibility that befalls those who purchase a very old property. There will be a desire to retain details and features that give the property its distinctive characteristics, but also a need to adapt it to the requirements of modern-day living. Even so, that property will eventually pass onto someone else, and any changes made will end up affecting them too (especially the bad ones). It should, therefore, be the charge of every *Doctor Who* producer not only to take on this cultural phenomenon but to see themselves as its guardians, preserving a legacy that owes much to the past but helping it to evolve, keeping it relevant as it moves into the future.

As the Eleventh Doctor (Matt Smith) says to a sleeping young Amy Pond (Caitlin Blackwood) in the 2010 episode "The Big Bang," "You won't even remember me. Well, you'll remember me a little. I'll be a story in your head. But that's OK. We're all stories in the end. Just make it a good one, eh? Cos it was you know. It was the best. A daft old man who stole a magic box and ran away."[13]

Appendix
Essential Episodes

For a show that has spanned sixty-plus years, there are a great many episodes to choose from in terms of essential viewing. The following is a list of must-see stories, giving a reason as to why they are so important.

1. "An Unearthly Child" (November 23, 1963)

    This is possibly the most important episode ever because it introduces viewers to the Doctor, his original companions, and the Tardis. The following episodes in this story (from an era when *Doctor Who* episodes were individually titled) are "The Cave of Skulls," "The Forest of Fear," and "The Firemaker." While interesting, they are not nearly as engaging or as well structured as the very first episode that sets out the foundations for everything that is to follow.

2. "The Daleks" (December 21, 1963, to February 1, 1964)

    Made up of the individual episodes, "The Dead Planet," "The Survivors," "The Escape," "The Ambush," "The Expedition," "The Ordeal," and "The Rescue" (now referred to collectively as "The Daleks"), this story was when *Doctor Who* truly entered the public consciousness. Terry Nation's Daleks grabbed the attention of viewers and set up one of the Doctor's oldest and deadliest enemies.

3. "The Tenth Planet" (October 8–29, 1966)

    This story introduces another of the Doctor's greatest foes, the Cybermen. As William Hartnell's final story, it also introduces viewers to the Doctor's ability to regenerate—the capacity to heal oneself in times of dire need, but at the cost of enduring complete physical transformation, as well as unpredictable changes in temperament.

4. "The Tomb of the Cybermen" (September 2–23, 1967)

   This story contains all the elements that make up a great *Doctor Who* story: fantastic sets, engaging characters, clever pacing, sublime cinematography, and the return of an established adversary. The scene of the Cybermen breaking out of their "tomb" is truly iconic and nightmare fuel for those of a nervous disposition.

5. "The Three Doctors" (December 30, 1972, to January 20, 1973)

   A story that stands out because we get to witness several regenerations of the Doctor interacting with one another for the first time. This circumstance is brought about by the Time Lords, who are forced to break the fundamental laws of time when they face annihilation at the hands of one of their own.

6. "Genesis of the Daleks" (March 8 to April 12, 1975)

   This story is notable in that we go back in time to see the very origins of the Daleks. It also sees the Time Lords trying to manipulate the Doctor into averting their creation, a seemingly minor plot point that is picked up again and used as the catalyst for the Time War in modern-era *Doctor Who*.

7. "The Deadly Assassin" (October 30 to November 20, 1976)

   When the Doctor returns home to Gallifrey after having a premonition about an assassination, he is caught up in a web of deceit and intrigue. This story takes a far deeper dive into Time Lord society than ever before, as well as bringing back the Doctor's archenemy, the Master.

8. "Horror of Fang Rock" (September 3–24, 1977)

   This collaboration between writer Terrance Dicks and script editor Robert Holmes is a tense period drama about a shape-shifting alien that slowly picks off and mimics the inhabitants of a remote lighthouse. It may follow some well-worn sci-fi tropes about isolation and paranoia, but it does so far better than most.

9. "The Caves of Androzani" (March 8–16, 1984)

   Doctor Who veteran Robert Holmes returns after a long absence with this compelling story of power, greed, and betrayal. It is Peter Davison's last story as the Doctor, and his own personal favorite from his time in the role. In 2009, *Doctor Who Monthly* magazine ran a poll for the top 200 *Doctor Who* stories and fans ranked this story in the number one slot.

10. "Rose" (March 25, 2005)

    Making a bold return after the show's cancellation sixteen years previously, this story sets the benchmark for modern-era *Doctor Who*. It may not be groundbreaking from a narrative perspective, but it serves as a welcome return for long-term fans who missed the show, as well as a great introduction for new fans.

Bibliography

Adams, Stephen. "Doctor Who 'Had Anti-Thatcher Agenda'." *The Telegraph.* February 14, 2010. www.telegraph.co.uk/culture/tvandradio/doctor-who/7235547/Doctor-Who-had-anti-Thatcher-agenda.html.

Ahmed, Tufayel. "Peter Capaldi on Diversity and 'Doctor Who': 'It Should Reflect the Times'." *Newsweek.* March 10, 2016. www.newsweek.com/peter-capaldi-diversity-doctor-who-needs-reflect-times-435048#:~:text=%22He's%20an%20astonishing%20talent%2C%20but,to%20an%20individual%20is%20immense.

Barnes, Alan. "The Brain of Morbius." *Doctor Who Magazine.* #508. Panini. February 2017.

BBC. "Dalekmania." November 1, 2023. https://www.bbc.co.uk/articles/cev7zy0grrlo.

BBC Media Centre. "Chris Chibnall and Jodie Whittaker to Leave Doctor Who in a Trio of Specials." July 19, 2021. www.bbc.co.uk/mediacentre/2021-doctor-who-jodie-whittaker-chris-chibnall.

BBC News. "BBC Wins Police Tardis Case." BBC. October 23, 2002. http://news.bbc.co.uk/1/hi/entertainment/tv_and_radio/2352743.stm.

BBC News. "Doctor Who Is a Saturday Night Hit." March 27, 2005. http://news.bbc.co.uk/1/hi/entertainment/4385801.stm.

BBC News. "Under-12 Ban on Dalek Torture DVD." BBC. May 16, 2005. http://news.bbc.co.uk/1/hi/entertainment/tv_and_radio/4550967.stm

BBC News. "Plymouth Shooting: Who Can Own a Firearm or Shotgun in the UK?" BBC. August 24, 2021. www.bbc.co.uk/news/uk-58198857.

Bone, Christian. "Former Doctor Who Showrunner Responds to Christopher Eccleston's Criticisms." *We Got This Covered.* April 29, 2018. https://wegotthiscovered.com/tv/doctor-who-showrunner-forgives-eccleston-criticisms/.

Burk, Graeme, and Robert Smith. *Who's 50: The 50 Doctor Who Stories to Watch before You Die—An Unofficial Companion.* Toronto: ECW Press, 2013.

Cassauwers, Tom. "What Our Science Fiction Says about Us." BBC Culture. December 3, 2018. www.bbc.com/culture/article/20181203-what-our-science-fiction-says-about-us.

Cultbox. "'Class' Ratings: 'Doctor Who' Spin-off Loses Half Its Audience on BBC One." January 11, 2017. https://cultbox.co.uk/news/headlines/class-ratings-doctor-who-spin-off-loses-half-its-audience-on-bbc-one.

Davies, Heather Greenwood. "Scary Good: Why It's OK for Kids to Feel Frightened Sometimes." *National Geographic*. October 21, 2021. www.nationalgeographic.com/family/article/scary-good-why-its-ok-for-kids-to-feel-frightened-sometimes.

Gov.UK. *The Report on the Iraq Inquiry*, July 6, 2016. www.gov.uk/government/publications/the-report-of-the-iraq-inquiry.

Gray, Niall. "The BBC Just Admitted That Doctor Who: Flux Was a Total Failure." December 10, 2021. https://screenrant.com/doctor-who-flux-bbc-story-explained-video-chibnall-failed/.

Greene, Sir Hugh. "The Third Floor Front: A View of Broadcasting in the Sixties." London: Bodley Head, 1969.

Harrison, Ian. "Doctor Who Writers Neil Gaiman and Terrance Dicks Talk to The Reg." *The Register*. November 22, 2013. www.theregister.com/2013/11/22/doctor_who_gaiman_dicks/?page=2.

Hayward, Anthony. "David Maloney." *Independent*. August 10, 2006. www.independent.co.uk/news/obituaries/david-maloney-411226.html.

Hearn, Marcus. *The Dawn of Knowledge*. Doctor Who Magazine. #207. Marvel UK. 8-18. December 22, 1993.

Hendershot, Heather. "24. Parks and Recreation: The Cultural Forum." In *How to Watch Television, Second Edition*, edited by Ethan Thompson and Jason Mittell, pp. 230–38. New York: New York University Press, 2020.

Holden, Michael. "Actor David Tennant to Leave 'Doctor Who.'" Reuters. October 30, 2008. www.reuters.com/article/idUSTRE49T8VB/.

Hubbard, Bethany. "The Ecologist January 1972: A Blueprint for Survival." January 27, 2012. https://theecologist.org/2012/jan/27/ecologist-january-1972-blueprint-survival.

Hussein, Waris. "How Doctor Who Was Nearly Exterminated at Birth." *MailOnline*. November 14, 2013.

Jeffery, Morgan. "Doctor Who's Ex-Script Editor Says the BBC 'Ghosted' the Show in 1989: 'We Weren't Really Cancelled'." *Radio Times*. December 3, 2019. https://www.radiotimes.com/tv/sci-fi/doctor-who-cancellation/.

Jeffries, Stuart. "'There Is a Clue Everybody's Missed': Sherlock Writer Steven Moffat Interviewed." *The Guardian*. January 20, 2012. www.theguardian.com/tv-and-radio/2012/jan/20/steven-moffat-sherlock-doctor-who.

Joest, Mick. "Former Doctor Who Star Tom Baker Reflects on Why He Quit the Show." Cinemablend. July 3, 2018. www.cinemablend.com/television/2444570/former-doctor-who-star-tom-baker-reflects-on-why-he-quit-the-show#.

Jones, Paul. "Tom Baker: 'I didn't like K9 at all.'" Radio Times. April 19, 2014. www.radiotimes.com/tv/sci-fi/tom-baker-i-didnt-like-k-9-at-all/.

Langley, William. "He Eats, Sleeps and Breathes Television—and at Last He's Got Around to Watching Some." *The Telegraph*. January 3, 2009. www.telegraph.co.uk/comment/personal-view/3638380/He-eats-sleeps-and-breathes-television-and-at-last-hes-got-round-to-watching-some.html.

Lewis, Paul. "Crusader Was Dubbed Britain's 'Queen of Clean'." *New York Times*. December 20, 2001.

Marson, Richard. *The Life and Scandalous Times of John Nathan-Turner*. Miwk Publishing, 2013.

Martin, Dan. "The Deadly Assassin: Doctor Who Classic Episode #8." *The Guardian*, June 14, 2013. www.theguardian.com/tv-and-radio/tvandradioblog/2013/jun/14/deadly-assassin-doctor-who-classic-episode#:~:text=Armchair%20censor%20Mary%20Whitehouse%20was,episode%20was%20Doctor%20Who%20drowning.

McIntosh, Steven. "Doctor Who: Critics Praise Jodie Whittaker's Swansong." BBC News. October 24, 2022. www.bbc.co.uk/news/entertainment-arts-63346244.

Midgley, Simon. "So Has the Mary Whitehouse Experience Been Worth It?" *Independent*. May 21, 1994. www.independent.co.uk/news/uk/home-news/so-has-the-mary-whitehouse-experience-been-worth-it-simon-midgley-explores-the-legacy-of-the-campaigner-who-is-retiring-at-the-age-of-83-1437749.html.

Miles, Lawrence. "The Unquiet Dead." Mileswatch. April 9, 2005. http://lawrencemiles.blogspot.com/2005/04/unquiet-dead.html

Molina-Whyte, Lidia. "Christopher Eccleston Says It's 'Very Doubtful' He'll Return to Doctor Who on TV." *Radio Times*. September 8, 2021. www.radiotimes.com/tv/sci-fi/christopher-eccleston-not-returning-doctor-who-60th-anniversary-newsupdate/.

National Geographic. "Plastic Bag Found at the Bottom of World's Deepest Ocean Trench." https://education.nationalgeographic.org/resource/plastic-bag-found-bottom-worlds-deepest-ocean-trench/.

Newcomb, Horace M., and Paul M. Hirsch. "Television as a Cultural Forum: Implications for Research." *Quarterly Review of Film Studies* 8, no. 3 (1983): 45–55. Doi:10.1080/10509208309361170.

Orthia, L. A. "How Does Science Fiction Television Shape Fans' Relationships to Science? Results from a Survey of 575 'Doctor Who' Viewers." *Journal of Science Communication* 18(04), A08 (2019). https://doi.org/10.22323/2.18040208.

Philipp-Muller, Aviva, Spike Lee, and Richard Petty. "Why Are People Antiscience, and What Can We Do about It?" *Proceedings of the National Academy of Sciences* 119 (2022). 10.1073/pnas.2120755119. 2022.

Sandilands, John. "Behind Every Dalek There's This Woman." *Daily Mail*, November 28, 1964.

Saward, Eric. "The Revelations of a Script Editor." *Starburst*, no. 97, September 1986.

Schmidt, Gavin A., and Adam Frank. "The Silurian Hypothesis: Would It Be Possible to Detect an Industrial Civilization in the Geological Record?" *International Journal of Astrobiology* 18, no. 2 (2019): 142–50. https://doi.org/10.1017/S1473550418000095.

Science History Institute, History and Future of Plastics. www.sciencehistory.org/education/classroom-activities/role-playing-games/case-of-plastics/history-and-future-of-plastics/.

Shapland, Mark. "Business Interview: Michael Grade Talks Glory Days, Brexit and Fiddler on the Roof." *The Standard*, July 2, 2020. www.standard.co.uk/business/business-interview-michael-grade-talks-glory-days-brexit-and-fiddler-on-the-roof-a4248781.html.

Stubbs, David. "The Moral Minority." *The Guardian*, May 24, 2008, www.theguardian.com/culture/2008/may/24/features16.theguide12.

Taylor, Kelly-Anne. "David Tennant on His Life-Long Doctor Who Fandom and Good Omens Backlash." *Radio Times*, August 10, 2023, www.radiotimes.com/tv/fantasy/david-tennant-good-omens-interview/.

Notes

CHAPTER 1

1. "An Unearthly Series—The Origins of a TV Legend," *Doctor Who News*, July 25, 2012, https://www.doctorwhonews.net/2012/07/an-unearthly-series-origins-of-tv-legend.html.
2. Marc Saul, "Doctor Who: Genesis," *Television Heaven*, January 21, 2022, https://televisionheaven.co.uk/articles/doctor-who-genesis.
3. Elliot Ball, "Doctor Who: BBC Nearly Gave Time Lord the Surname 'Who'," *Plymouth Herald*, January 31, 2022, https://www.plymouthherald.co.uk/news/celebs-tv/doctor-who-bbc-nearly-gave-6579790#.
4. "Doctor Who: General Notes on Background and Approach," October 11, 2010, https://doctorwhoconcordance.fandom.com/wiki/Dr._Who:_General_Notes_on_Background_and_Approach.
5. Fatemeh Mirjalili, "Doctor Who Could Have Been a Much Darker Sci-Fi Show," Slashfilm. April 10, 2022. https://www.slashfilm.com/827811/doctor-who-could-have-been-a-much-darker-sci-fi-show/
6. Richard Molesworth, writer. *Doctor Who—Origins*. Roberts, Steve, executive producer. BBC Worldwide. 2006. (From *Doctor Who: The Beginning DVD* boxset.)
7. Marcus Hearn, "The Dawn of Knowledge," *Doctor Who Magazine*, #207, Marvel UK, 8–18, December 22, 1993.
8. John Sandilands, "Behind Every Dalek There's This Woman," *Daily Mail*, November 28, 1964.
9. Waris Hussein, "How Doctor Who Was Nearly Exterminated at Birth," *MailOnline*, November 14, 2013.

CHAPTER 2

1. Russell T. Davies, writer. *Doctor Who*. Season 1. "Rose." Keith Boak, director. Phil Collinson, producer. March 26, 2005. BBC One.
2. Paul Cornell, writer. *Doctor Who*. Season 3. "Human Nature"/"The Family of Blood." Charles Palmer, director. Susie Liggat, producer. May 26–June 2, 2007. BBC One.
3. Russell T. Davies, writer. *Doctor Who*. Season 4. "The Stolen Earth"/"Journey's End." Graeme Harper, director. Phil Collinson, producer. June 28–July 5, 2008. BBC One.

CHAPTER 3

1. Steven Moffat, writer. *Doctor Who*. "The Snowmen." Saul Metzstein, director. Marcus Wilson, producer. December 25, 2012. BBC One.
2. Wayback Machine, "In the matter of application no. 2104259 by the British Broadcasting Corporation to register a series of three marks in classes 9, 16, 25 and 41 and in the matter of opposition thereto under no. 48452 by the Metropolitan Police Authority." https://web.archive.org/web/20041022182733/http://www.patent.gov.uk/tm/legal/decisions/2002/o33602.pdf.
3. "BBC Wins Police Tardis Case." BBC News, October 23, 2002. http://news.bbc.co.uk/1/hi/entertainment/tv_and_radio/2352743.stm.
4. Neil Gaiman, writer. *Doctor Who*. Season 6. "The Doctor's Wife." Richard Clark, director. Sanne Wohlenberg, producer. May 14, 2011. BBC One.

CHAPTER 4

1. Heather Greenwood Davies, "Scary Good: Why It's OK for Kids to Feel Frightened Sometimes," *National Geographic*, October 21, 2021, www.nationalgeographic.com/family/article/scary-good-why-its-ok-for-kids-to-feel-frightened-sometimes.
2. Paul Lewis, "Crusader Was Dubbed Britain's 'Queen of Clean'," *New York Times*, December 20, 2001.
3. David Stubbs, "The Moral Minority," *The Guardian*, May 24, 2008, www.theguardian.com/culture/2008/may/24/features16.theguide12.
4. Sir Hugh Greene, *The Third Floor Front: A View of Broadcasting in the Sixties* (London: The Bodley Head, 1969), pp. 100–101.
5. Anthony Hayward, "David Maloney," *Independent*, August 10, 2006, www.independent.co.uk/news/obituaries/david-maloney-411226.html.
6. Alan Barnes, "The Brain of Morbius," *Doctor Who Magazine*, #508, Panini, February 2017.

7. Dan Martin, "The Deadly Assassin: *Doctor Who* Classic Episode #8," *The Guardian*, June 14, 2013, www.theguardian.com/tv-and-radio/tvandradioblog/2013/jun/14/deadly-assassin-doctor-who-classic-episode#:~:text=Armchair%20censor%20Mary%20Whitehouse%20was,episode%20was%20Doctor%20Who%20drowning.

8. Graeme Burk and Robert Smith, *Who's 50: The 50* Doctor Who *Stories to Watch before You Die—An Unofficial Companion* (Toronto: ECW Press, 2013), pp. 148–49.

9. David Stubbs, "The Moral Minority," *The Guardian*, May 24, 2008, www.theguardian.com/culture/2008/may/24/features16.theguide12.

10. Simon Midgley, "So Has the Mary Whitehouse Experience Been Worth It?" *Independent*, May 21, 1994, www.independent.co.uk/news/uk/home-news/so-has-the-mary-whitehouse-experience-been-worth-it-simon-midgley-explores-the-legacy-of-the-campaigner-who-is-retiring-at-the-age-of-83-1437749.html.

11. Martin, Philip, writer. *Doctor Who*. Season 22. *Vengeance of Varos*. Ron Jones, director. John Nathan-Turner, producer. January 19–26, 1985. BBC One.

12. "Plymouth Shooting: Who Can Own a Firearm or Shotgun in the UK?" BBC News, August 24, 2021, www.bbc.co.uk/news/uk-58198857.

13. "Under-12 Ban on Dalek Torture DVD," BBC News, May 16, 2005, http://news.bbc.co.uk/1/hi/entertainment/tv_and_radio/4550967.stm.

14. Lawrence Miles, "The Unquiet Dead," Mileswatch, April 9, 2005, http://lawrencemiles.blogspot.com/2005/04/unquiet-dead.html.

CHAPTER 5

1. Mick Joest, "Former *Doctor Who* Star Tom Baker Reflects on Why He Quit the Show," Cinemablend, July 3, 2018, www.cinemablend.com/television/2444570/former-doctor-who-star-tom-baker-reflects-on-why-he-quit-the-show#.

2. Eric Saward, "The Revelations of a Script Editor," *Starburst Magazine*, #97, September 1986.

3. Voiceover commentary on the DVD release of *Doctor Who: Revenge of the Cybermen*, 2010, BBC.

4. Ian Harrison, "*Doctor Who* Writers Neil Gaiman and Terrance Dicks Talk to The Reg," *The Register*, November 22, 2013, www.theregister.com/2013/11/22/doctor_who_gaiman_dicks/?page=2.

5. Mark Shapland, "Business Interview: Michael Grade Talks Glory Days, Brexit and Fiddler on the Roof," *The Standard*, July 2, 2020, www.standard.co.uk/business/business-interview-michael-grade-talks-glory-days-brexit-and-fiddler-on-the-roof-a4248781.html.

6. Ratings guide. Doctor Who News. https://guide.doctorwhonews.net/info.php?detail=ratings&type=date.

7. William Langley, "He Eats, Sleeps and Breathes Television—and at Last He's Got around to Watching Some," *The Telegraph*, January 3, 2009, www.telegraph.co.uk/comment/personal-view/3638380/He-eats-sleeps-and-breathes-television-and-at-last-hes-got-round-to-watching-some.html.

8. Doctor Who Interview Archive, https://drwhointerviews.wordpress.com/2009/09/17/colin-baker-1987/.

9. Doctor Who Interview Archive, https://drwhointerviews.wordpress.com/2009/11/02/john-nathan-turner-1987/.

10. Morgan Jeffery, "*Doctor Who*'s Ex-Script Editor Says the BBC 'Ghosted' the Show in 1989: 'We Weren't Really Cancelled'," *Radio Times*, December 3, 2019, https://www.radiotimes.com/tv/sci-fi/doctor-who-cancellation/.

11. Richard Marson, *The Life and Scandalous Times of John Nathan-Turner* (Miwk Publishing, 2013).

CHAPTER 6

1. BBC News, "*Doctor Who* Is a Saturday Night Hit," March 27, 2005, http://news.bbc.co.uk/1/hi/entertainment/4385801.stm.

2. Lidia Molina-Whyte, "Christopher Eccleston Says It's 'Very Doubtful' He'll Return to *Doctor Who* on TV," *Radio Times*, September 8, 2021, www.radiotimes.com/tv/sci-fi/christopher-eccleston-not-returning-doctor-who-60th-anniversary-newsupdate/.

3. Christian Bone, "Former *Doctor Who* Showrunner Responds to Christopher Eccleston's Criticisms," *We Got This Covered*, April 29, 2018, https://wegotthiscovered.com/tv/doctor-who-showrunner-forgives-eccleston-criticisms/.

4. Kelly-Anne Taylor, "David Tennant on His Life-Long *Doctor Who* Fandom and Good Omens Backlash," *Radio Times*, August 10, 2023, www.radiotimes.com/tv/fantasy/david-tennant-good-omens-interview/.

5. Michael Holden, "Actor David Tennant to Leave 'Doctor Who,'" Reuters, October 30, 2008, www.reuters.com/article/idUSTRE49T8VB/.

6. Stuart Jeffries, "'There Is a Clue Everybody's Missed': Sherlock Writer Steven Moffat Interviewed," *The Guardian*, January 20, 2012, www.theguardian.com/tv-and-radio/2012/jan/20/steven-moffat-sherlock-doctor-who.

7. Tufayel Ahmed, "Peter Capaldi on Diversity and 'Doctor Who': 'It Should Reflect the Times,'" *Newsweek*, March 10, 2016, www.newsweek.com/peter-capaldi-diversity-doctor-who-needs-reflect-times-435048#:~:text=%22He's%20an%20astonishing%20talent%2C%20but,to%20an%20individual%20is%20immense.

CHAPTER 7

1. Robert Sloman, writer. *Doctor Who*. Season 9. "The Time Monster." Paul Bernard, director. Barry Lets, producer. May 20–June 24, 1972. BBC1.

2. Russell T. Davies, writer. *Doctor Who*. Season 3. "Gridlock." Richard Clark, director. Phil Collinson, producer. April 14, 2007. BBC One.

3. Russell T. Davies, writer. *Doctor Who*. Season 3. "The Sound of Drums"/"Last of the Time Lords." Colin Teague, director. Phil Collinson, producer. June 23–30, 2007. BBC One.

4. Robin Bland, writer. *Doctor Who*. Season 13. "The Brain of Morbius." Christopher Barry, director. Philip Hinchcliffe, producer. January 3, 1976. BBC1.

CHAPTER 9

1. Robert Sloman, writer. *Doctor Who*. Season 11. "Planet of the Spiders." Barry Letts, director. Bary Letts, producer. May 4-June 8, 1974. BBC1.
2. Steven Moffat, writer. *Doctor Who*. "Twice Upon a Time." Rachel Talalay, director. Peter Bennett, producer. December 25, 2017. BBC One.
3. Steven Moffat, writer. *Doctor Who*. Series 4. "Silence in the Library"/"Forest of the Dead." Euros Lyn, director. Phil Collinson, producer. May 31–June 7, 2008. BBC One.
4. Steven Moffat, writer. *Doctor Who*. Season 5. "The Time of Angels"/"Flesh and Stone." Adam Smith, director. Tracie Simpson, producer. April 24–May 1, 2010. BBC One.
5. Steven Moffat, writer. *Doctor Who*. Season 6. "A Good Man Goes to War." Peter Hoar, director. Marcus Wilson, producer. June 4, 2011. BBC One.
6. Steven Moffat, writer. *Doctor Who*. Season 6. "Let's Kill Hitler." Richard Senior, director). Marcus Wilson, producer. August 27, 2011. BBC One.
7. Steven Moffat, writer. *Doctor Who*. Season 6. "The Wedding of River Song." Jeremy Webb, director. Marcus Wilson, producer. October 1, 2011. BBC One.

CHAPTER 10

1. Science History Institute, History and Future of Plastics. www.sciencehistory.org/education/classroom-activities/role-playing-games/case-of-plastics/history-and-future-of-plastics/.
2. *National Geographic*, "Plastic Bag Found at the Bottom of World's Deepest Ocean Trench," https://education.nationalgeographic.org/resource/plastic-bag-found-bottom-worlds-deepest-ocean-trench/.
3. Gavin A. Schmidt and Adam Frank, "The Silurian Hypothesis: Would It Be Possible to Detect an Industrial Civilization in the Geological Record?" *International Journal of Astrobiology* 18, no. 2 (2019): 142–50. https://doi.org/10.1017/S1473550418000095.

CHAPTER 11

1. Johnny Byrne, writer. *Doctor Who*. Season 18. "The Keeper of Traken." John Black, director. John Nathan-Turner, producer. January 31–February 21, 1981. BBC1.
2. Peter Grimwade, writer. *Doctor Who*. Season 21. "Planet of Fire." Fiona Cumming, director. John Nathan-Turner, producer. February 23–March 2, 1984. BBC1.

210   Notes

3. Matthew Jacobs, writer. *Doctor Who*. Geoffrey Sax, director. Peter V. Ware and Matthew Jacobs, producers. May 1996. Universal Studios and BBC Worldwide.

4. Russell T. Davies, writer. *Doctor Who*. Season 3. "Utopia." Graeme Harper, director. Phil Collinson, producer. June 16, 2007. BBC One.

5. Russell T. Davies, writer. *Doctor Who*. "The End of Time." Euros Lyn, director. Tracie Simpson, producer. December 25, 2009–January 1, 2010. BBC One.

6. Steven Moffat, writer. *Doctor Who*. Season 8. "Dark Water"/"Death in Heaven." Rachel Talalay, director. Peter Bennett, producer. November 1–8, 2014. BBC One.

7. Steven Moffat, writer. *Doctor Who*. Season 9. "The Magician's Apprentice"/"The Witch's Familiar." Hettie MacDonald, director. Peter Bennett, producer. September 19–26, 2015. BBC One.

8. Steven Moffat, writer. *Doctor Who*. Season 10. "World Enough and Time"/"The Doctor Falls." Rachel Talalay, director. Peter Bennett, producer. June 24–July 1, 2017. BBC One.

CHAPTER 12

1. Robert Holmes, writer. *Doctor Who*. Season 23. "The Mysterious Planet." Nicholas Mallett, director. John Nathan-Turner, producer. September 6–27, 1986. BBC1.

2. Simon Nye, writer. *Doctor Who*. Season 5. "Amy's Choice." Catherine Morshead, director. Tracie Simpson, producer. May 15, 2010. BBC One.

3. Steven Moffat, writer. *Doctor Who*. "The Night of the Doctor." John Hayes, director. Denise Paul, producer. November 14, 1013. BBC One.

4. Steven Moffat, writer. *Doctor Who*. Season 7. "The Name of the Doctor." Saul Metzstein, director. Denise Paul and Marcus Wilson, producers. May 18, 2013. BBC One.

5. Steven Moffat, writer. *Doctor Who*. "The Day of the Doctor." Nick Hurran, director. Marcus Wilson, producer. November 23, 2013. BBC One.

CHAPTER 13

1. Doctor Who Channel. "Farewell, Sarah Jane." YouTube. April 19, 2020. www.youtube.com/watch?v=F8sU45ax2Hs

2. Chris Chibnall, writer. *Doctor Who*. "The Power of the Doctor." Jamie Magnus Stone, director. Nikki Wilson, producer. October 23, 2023. BBC One.

3. Russell T. Davies, writer. *Doctor Who. Tales of the Tardis:* "Earthshock." Joshua M. G. Thomas, director. November 1, 2023. BBC One.

4. Steven Moffat, writer. *Doctor Who*. Season 10. "Extremis"/"The Pyramid at the End of the World." Daniel Nettheim, director. Peter Bennett, producer. May 20–27, 2017. BBC One.

5. Russell T. Davies, writer. *Doctor Who.* "The Star Beast." Rachel Talalay, director. Vicki Delow, producer. November 25, 2023. BBC One.

6. James Whitbrook, "BBC Responds to Anti-Trans *Doctor Who* Complaints," Gizmodo. January 3, 2024, https://gizmodo.com/bbc-doctor-who-transgender-complaints-response-disney-1851136244#:~:text=It%20was%20reported%20last%20month,character%20in%20the%20story%3A%20Rose.

CHAPTER 14

1. Lucy Jones, "*Doctor Who* Backlash Shows Why It's Time to Bin the Phrase 'Politically Correct,'" *The Independent*, https://www.independent.co.uk/arts-entertainment/tv/features/doctor-who-politically-correct-backlash-bbc-jodie-whittaker-mandip-gill-tosin-cole-a8669156.html.

2. Maya Oppenheim, "Sun and Mail Online under Fire for Publishing Nude Photos of New Female *Doctor Who* Jodie Whittaker," *The Independent*, https://www.independent.co.uk/arts-entertainment/tv/news/sun-mail-online-jodie-whittaker-nude-photos-doctor-who-published-under-fire-images-pictures-printed-a7846956.html.

3. https://x.com/SawbonesHex/status/886613052447129601

4. https://www.bbc.co.uk/news/entertainment-arts-40679134#:~:text=Peter%20Davison%2C%20who%20played%20the,by%20his%20successor%20Colin%20Baker.

5. https://x.com/Jenny_Trout/status/886615696062459908

6. Jacob Stolworthy, "*Doctor Who*: BBC Responds to Complaints Made about Jodie Whittaker's Casting," *The Independent*, https://www.independent.co.uk/arts-entertainment/tv/news/doctor-who-new-jodie-whittaker-female-bbc-complaints-response-woman-time-lord-peter-capaldi-a7849391.html.

7. Niall Gray, "The BBC Just Admitted That *Doctor Who*: Flux Was a Total Failure," December 10, 2021, https://screenrant.com/doctor-who-flux-bbc-story-explained-video-chibnall-failed/.

8. BBC Media Centre, "Chris Chibnal and Jodie Whittaker to Leave *Doctor Who* in a Trio of Specials," July 19, 2021, www.bbc.co.uk/mediacentre/2021-doctor-who-jodie-whittaker-chris-chibnall.

9. Steven McIntosh, "*Doctor Who*: Critics Praise Jodie Whittaker's Swansong," BBC News, October 24, 2022, www.bbc.co.uk/news/entertainment-arts-63346244.

10. Barry McCann, "*Doctor Who* and the 1986 Memo That Recommended a Female Doctor," Cultbox, https://cultbox.co.uk/features/doctor-who-and-the-1986-memo-that-recommended-a-female-doctor.

11. Mason Wiley and Damien Bona, *Inside Oscar: The Unofficial History of the Academy Awards* (New York: Ballantine Books, 1986), p. 383.

12. Kate Orman, "*One of Us Is Yellow*": Doctor Fu Manchu and The Talons of Weng Chiang, Eruditorum Press, August 23, 2018.

CHAPTER 15

1. BBC, "Dalekmania," November 1, 2023, https://www.bbc.co.uk/articles/cev7zy0grrlo.
2. John Nathan-Turner, writer. "*Doctor Who*: Daleks—The Early Years," 1992, BBC. https://www.imdb.com/title/tt0387182/.
3. Matthew Jacobs and Vanessa Yuille, directors. "*Doctor Who* Am I," 2022, https://www.imdb.com/title/tt12029866/.
4. Maggie Bandur, writer. *Community*. Season 4. Episode 3. "Conventions of Space and Time." Jann, Michael Patrick, director. February 21, 2013. NBC.
5. Greg Berlanti, Marc Guggenheim, and Andrew Kreisberg, writers. *Legends of Tomorrow*. Season 3. Episode 15. "Necromancing the Stone." Mullen, April, director. April 4, 2018.

CHAPTER 16

1. Paul Jones, "Tom Baker: 'I Didn't Like K9 at All'," *Radio Times*, April 19, 2014, www.radiotimes.com/tv/sci-fi/tom-baker-i-didnt-like-k-9-at-all/.
2. BBC Studios channel. *Torchwood Special*. June 16, 2008. https://www.youtube.com/watch?v=zqFFFgdo1Zc.
3. Doctor Who News. *Kiss Kiss, Bang Bang*. August 30, 2015. https://guide.doctorwhonews.net/story.php?story=KissKissBangBang.
4. Doctor Who News. *Torchwood—UK Final Viewing Figures*. https://www.doctorwhonews.net/2009/07/torchwood-final-viewing-figures.html?m=0.
5. Cultbox, "'Class' Ratings: 'Doctor Who' Spin-Off Loses Half Its Audience on BBC One," January 11, 2017, https://cultbox.co.uk/news/headlines/class-ratings-doctor-who-spin-off-loses-half-its-audience-on-bbc-one.

CHAPTER 17

1. Steven Moffat, writer. *Doctor Who*. "Twice Upon a Time." Rachel Talalay, director. Peter Bennett, producer. December 25, 2017. BBC One.
2. Steven Moffat, writer. *Doctor Who*. Series 8. "Into the Dalek." Ben Wheatley, director. Nikki Wilson, producer. August 30, 2014. BBC One.
3. Terry Nation, writer. *Doctor Who*. Season 12. "Genesis of the Daleks." David Maloney, director. Philip Hinchcliffe, producer. March 8–April 12, 1975. BBC1.
4. Jamie Mathieson, writer. *Doctor Who*. Series 8. "Flatline." Douglas Mackinnon, director. Nikki Wilson, producer. October 18, 2014. BBC One.
5. James Moran, writer. *Doctor Who*. Season 4. "The Fires of Pompeii." Colin Teague, director. Phil Collinson, producer. April 12, 2008. BBC One.

6. Jamie Mathieson and Steven Moffat, writers. *Doctor Who*. Season 9. "The Girl Who Died." Ed Bazalgette, director. Derek Ritchie, producer. October 17, 2015. BBC. BBC One.

7. Catherine Tregenna, writer. *Doctor Who*. Season 9. "The Woman Who Lived." Ed Bazalgette, director. Derek Ritchie, producer. October 24, 2015. BBC One.

8. Sarah Dollard, writer. *Doctor Who*. Season 9. "Face the Raven." Justin Molotnikov, director. Nikki Wilson, producer. November 21, 2015. BBC One.

9. Neil Cross, writer. *Doctor Who*. Season 7. "The Rings of Akhaten." Farren Blackburn, director. Denise Paul and Marcus Wilson, producers. April 6, 2013. BBC One.

10. Russell T. Davies, writer. *Doctor Who*. Season 2. "Tooth and Claw." Euros Lyn, director. Phil Collinson, producer. April 22, 2006. BBC One.

11. Chris Boucher, writer. *Doctor Who*. Season 14. "The Face of Evil." Pennant Roberts, director. Philip Hinchcliffe, producer. January 1–22, 1977. BBC1.

12. Steven Moffat, writer. *Doctor Who*. "Twice Upon a Time." Rachel Talalay, director. Peter Bennett, producer. December 25, 2017. BBC One.

13. Chris Chibnall, writer. *Doctor Who*. Season 11. "The Tsuranga Conundrum." Jennifer Perrott, director. Nikki Wilson, producer. November 4, 2018. BBC One.

14. Matthew Graham, writer. *Doctor Who*. Season 6. "The Rebel Flesh"/"The Almost People." Julian Simpson, director. Marcus Wilson, producer. May 21–28, 2011. BBC One.

CHAPTER 18

1. Tom Cassauwers, "What Our Science Fiction Says about Us," BBC Culture, December 3, 2018, www.bbc.com/culture/article/20181203-what-our-science-fiction-says-about-us.

2. Bethany Hubbard, "The Ecologist January 1972: A Blueprint for Survival," January 27, 2012, https://theecologist.org/2012/jan/27/ecologist-january-1972-blueprint-survival.

3. Horace M. Newcomb and Paul M. Hirsch, "Television as a Cultural Forum: Implications for Research," *Quarterly Review of Film Studies* 8, no. 3 (1983): 45–55. Doi:10.1080/10509208309361170.

4. Heather Hendershot, "24. Parks and Recreation: The Cultural Forum," in *How to Watch Television, Second Edition*, edited by Ethan Thompson and Jason Mittell (New York: New York University Press, 2020), pp. 230–38.

5. Stephen Adams, "*Doctor Who* 'Had Anti-Thatcher Agenda,'" *The Telegraph*, February 14, 2010, www.telegraph.co.uk/culture/tvandradio/doctor-who/7235547/Doctor-Who-had-anti-Thatcher-agenda.html.

6. Ben Aaronovitch, writer. *Doctor Who*. Season 26. "Battlefield." Michael Kerrigan, director. John Nathan-Turner, producer. September 6–27, 1989. BBC1.

7. Gov.UK, "The Report on the Iraq Inquiry," July 6, 2016, www.gov.uk/government/publications/the-report-of-the-iraq-inquiry.

8. Russell T. Davies, writer. *Doctor Who*. Season 1. "The Long Game." Brian Grant, director. Phil Collinson, producer. May 7, 2005. BBC One.

9. Jamie Mathieson, writer. *Doctor Who*. Season 10. "Oxygen." Charles Palmer, director. Nikki Wilson, producer. May 12, 2017. BBC One.

10. L. A. Orthia, "How Does Science Fiction Television Shape Fans' Relationships to Science? Results from a Survey of 575 'Doctor Who' Viewers," *Journal of Science Communication* 18(4) (2019): A08, https://doi.org/10.22323/2.18040208.

11. Aviva Philipp-Muller, Spike Lee, and Richard Petty, "Why Are People Antiscience, and What Can We Do about It?" *Proceedings of the National Academy of Sciences* 119 (2022), 10.1073/pnas.2120755119. 2022.

12. Doctor Who Worlds of Wonder, https://www.doctorwhoscience.com.

13. Steven Moffat, writer. *Doctor Who*. Season 5. "The Big Bang." Toby Haynes, director. Peter Bennett, producer. June 26, 2010. BBC One.

Index

ABC (Associated British Corporation), 4
Adric, 34, 87–88, 95
Amy Pond, 93, 102–6, 139–40
Andrew Cartmel, 56, 180, 192
anniversary, fiftieth, x, 11, 16, 80, 137, 140
Anthony Ainley, 32, 34, 57, 80, 87, 123–24, 138
army, 75, 91, 122, 130–31, 192
Ashildr, 185–87
Associated British Corporation. *See* ABC
Autons, 117–18, 122

baby, x, 103–4
Baker, Colin, 20, 34, 46, 54–55, 80, 89–90, 138, 155;
Baker, Tom, 37, 39, 43, 52–53, 61, 64, 75, 77–78, 85, 99, 123–24, 142, 158–59, 174, 183, 188, 202, 212
Barbara, 82, 87, 110, 166
Barrowman, John, 126, 148, 170, 174
Barton, 133–34
BBC, 45, 53–54, 57, 60, 63, 177, 208–10, 212–13
BBC America, 145, 168
BBC Culture, 201, 213
BBC IPLAYER, 179

BBC Media Centre, 201, 211
BBC News, 46, 63, 201, 203, 206–8, 211
BBC Online, 60, 62
BBC Wales, 61–62
BBC Worldwide, 60–61, 175, 205, 210
BBFC (British Board of Film Classification), 47
Bennett, Peter, 209–10, 212–14
Big Bang, 32, 103, 197, 214
Bill Potts, 132, 150, 188
Billie Piper, 29, 63, 91, 141, 163
Black Guardian, 39, 88
black hole, 71–72, 132, 151
Bradley, David, 100, 188
brain of Morbius, 43, 75–76, 154, 158, 201, 206, 209
Braybon, John, 4–5
Brigadier Sir Alistair Gordon Lethbridge-Stewart, 60, 84, 99
Britain, ix–x, 20, 32, 34, 82, 128, 148, 190–93
British Board of Film Classification. *See* BBFC
British Broadcasting, 54
British Broadcasting Corporation. *See* BBC
Broadcasting Standards Commission, 45
Bryant, 89–90; Nicola, 46, 53, 89, 167

Index

Butterworth, Peter, 33, 74
Byrne, Johnny, 209

Caecilius, 185
Campbell, Tom, 166
Canadian Broadcasting Company, 63
Capaldi, Peter, 25, 36, 65, 94, 100, 107, 116, 131, 150, 154, 175, 183–85, 193, 201, 208
Captain Catchlove, 116
Captain Jack Harkness, 126–28, 145, 148, 170
Captain Mike Yates, 98
Carole Ann Ford, 10, 32, 82, 110, 177
Cartmel, 56–57, 192
Chameleon Circuit, 33–34
Chancellor Goth, 77
Charlie Smith, 149
Cheetah people, 147
Chibnall, Chris, 26, 65–66, 134, 155, 157–59, 163, 168, 196, 201, 210, 213
children of earth, 175–76
Christmas story, 32, 92
Chronotis, 78–79
Clara Oswald, 32, 39, 94, 106, 131–32, 141, 163, 177, 183, 185–87
classic era, 35, 48, 62, 116, 196
Cloister Bells, 34, 72
Coleman, Jenna, 32, 39, 94, 106, 131, 141, 158, 163, 183, 185
Collinson, Phil, 62–63, 206, 208–10, 212–13
console room, 33, 35–36
controller of BBC, 4, 60–61
Cornell, Paul, 61, 180, 206
Cultural Forum, 202–3, 213
Cyber Masters, 80, 113, 134
Cybermen, xi, 46, 53, 80, 87, 91, 112–13, 131–34, 149, 151, 199–200, 207

Dalek Invasion, 82, 91, 141, 166
Daleks, 9–10, 45–47, 61–62, 91, 109–12, 130–32, 140–42, 165–67, 178–79, 183–84, 199–200, 212
Dark Water, 131, 154, 210

Darvill, Arthur, 103, 139, 170
David John McDonald, 24, 27
David Tennant, 23, 26, 202, 208
Davies, Russell T., 24, 27, 60–66, 80, 117, 147, 151, 174, 176–77, 180, 202, 206, 208, 210–11, 213
Davison, Peter, 20, 32, 46, 52, 73, 87–88, 99, 119, 147, 155, 179, 191, 200
Deadly Assassin, 44, 71, 77, 123, 200, 203, 207
Death Zone, 71–72
Derek Jacobi, 10, 126
destruction of Gallifrey, 39, 71
Doctor: new, 53, 55, 156, 167; next, 64–65, 155
Doctor regenerates, 85, 160
Doctor's identity, 57, 156
Doctor's lineage, 167–68
Doctor's regenerations, xii, 20, 24, 139
Doctor's Wife, 38, 154, 206
Donna, 92–93, 151, 184–85
Donna Noble, 92, 101, 147, 151, 184, 193
Dream Lord, 139–40

Eccleston, 62–64; Christopher, 23, 47, 62, 91, 117, 193
Eighth Doctor, 28, 125, 140
Eleventh Doctor, 24, 36, 38, 93, 102, 116, 139, 141–42, 154, 177, 183, 185
elixir, 75–77, 141, 154
Empty Child, 65, 148
Eric Roberts, 125
eye of harmony, 39, 71, 123, 125

fan fiction, 180
female Doctor, 154–57, 159–61, 169, 196, 211
Fifteenth Doctor, 27–28, 37, 164
Fifth Doctor, 28, 46, 73, 88, 99, 119, 147, 155, 179, 191
First Doctor, 10, 16, 28, 32, 39, 74, 82, 100, 110, 157, 188
flux, 158–59, 184, 202, 211
Fourteenth Doctors, 20, 37, 135

Fourth Doctor, 37, 39, 52, 75, 78, 85, 123–24, 183
Freema Agyeman, 91, 126, 163
Fugitive Doctor, 157, 163

Galactic Federation, 115, 191
galaxy, 70, 75, 110, 114–15, 195
Gallifrey, 39, 56, 62, 70–73, 77–78, 80, 85–86, 122–23, 125, 130, 141–42
Gallifreyans, 73, 86, 102, 131, 167
Genesis of the Daleks, 43, 110, 183, 200
Geoffrey Beevers, 123
God, 29, 42, 187
Gordon Tipple, 125
Grainer, 11
Grant, Richard E., 22, 61–62
Guardian, 65, 197, 202–4, 206–8

Harkness, 148–49, 175–76
Harmony, 39, 71, 123, 125
Harry Sullivan, 85
Hartnell, 9–10, 12; William, x, 32–33, 39, 72, 74, 82–83, 110, 179, 199
Heather, 150–51, 202
Heggessey, 60–61
Hinchcliffe, Phillip, 43–44, 54, 180, 209, 212–13
hospital, 88, 91, 125, 132
Hussein, 10–11, 202

Ian Chesterton, 7, 32, 82, 85, 87, 110, 166, 177, 202
Ice Warriors, 115–18
Independent Television. *See* ITV
Inspector Minerva, 169–70
Inspector Spacetime, 169–70
ITV (Independent Television), 56, 158, 162

Jacobs, Matthew, 210, 212
Jane, Sarah, 76, 85, 147, 177, 210
Jo Grant, 84, 117, 177
Jodie Whitaker, 26, 95, 160–61, 211

John, Caroline, 84, 117
John Nathan-Turner, 11, 19–21, 52, 89, 159, 167, 174, 192, 203, 207–10, 212–13
John Simms, 126–27

K-9, 174, 176–77
Kaleds, 43, 110
Karn, 75, 77, 140, 154
Kelly, Katherine, 177–78
Khan, Yasmin, 133, 163
Kovarian, 104–5

Lake Silencio, 103, 105–6
Lambert, 9–12
Leela, 85–86, 188
Lethbridge-Stewart, 98–101
Letts, Barry, 122, 179–80, 209
Lime Grove Studios, 10
Liz Shaw, 84, 117
London, ix–xi, 28, 33, 64, 90–91, 186, 192, 202, 206
Lucas, Matt, 132, 150, 170

Madame Vastra, 149
Maloney, David, 43–44, 202, 206, 212
Mandip Gill, 94, 133, 163
Mark Gatiss, 47, 61, 65, 100, 180
Martha Jones, 91–92, 126, 128, 163
Master's Tardis, 124
Matrix, 71–72, 77, 138–39
McCoy, Sylvester, 21, 55–57, 60, 80, 90, 99, 109, 125, 167, 180, 191–92
Mels, 80, 105
Missy, 131–33, 154
Moffat, Steven, 65–66, 80, 93, 107, 120, 137, 155, 157, 160, 206, 209–10, 212–14
Monk, 33, 74
monsters, 115, 119, 184, 187, 191
Morbius, 43, 75–77, 154, 158, 201, 206, 209

Nathan-Turner, 52–57
Nation, Terry, 9, 20, 111, 166, 212

National Geographic, 42, 202–3, 206, 209
Newman, 4, 6, 9–12, 159–60
Ninth Doctor, 29, 61–62, 91, 117, 193
Nyssa, 33, 87–88, 147–48

Omega, 56, 72–73, 78

painting, 141–42
Paradox Machine, 128
Parsons, Chris, 78
Paul, Denise, 210, 213
PBS (Public Broadcasting Service), 53, 167
Peladon, 115, 191
Peri, 46, 89–90, 167
Personality, 16–27
Pertwee, John, 98, 118
Pertwee, Jon, x, 70, 72, 84, 115, 117, 122, 190–91
Peter Capaldi, 25
Peter Cushing, 166
Peter Davison, 19, 35, 167, 210–11
Peter Pratt, 123
police box, 33–35, 37, 82, 165–66
Pompeii, 92, 184–85, 212
Pond, Melody, 102–6
Pope, 150
Powell, Jonathan, 55, 57, 160
President Borusa, 78
producer, 4, 11, 43, 52, 54, 56, 61, 65, 86, 89, 159–60, 206–14
Professor Docherty, 128
Professor Yana, 126
Pyroviles, 184

quantum fold chamber, 132
queen, 116, 187

Radio Times, 57, 63–65, 174, 202–4, 208, 212
Radiophonic Workshop, 11, 52
Rani, 79–80, 124
Rassilon, 56, 70–73, 78, 129–30, 138
Recurring Characters, 97–107

Red Dwarf, 171, 215
regenerates, 72, 86–87, 91, 104, 123, 126, 128–29, 133–34, 154, 157, 183–85, 196
regeneration process, 87, 103, 154
regenerations, 18–19, 25–27, 72, 84, 86–87, 98, 123, 141–42, 154, 157–58, 182–83, 196
renegade Time Lords, 73–75, 77–79, 132
Rhodians, 178
Ridley Scott, 167
Rippy, Matt, 148
rival Time Lord, 125
River Song, 40, 99–100, 104–7, 168, 183, 209
Roger Delgado, 117–18, 122–24
Romana, 61, 86–87
romantic interest, 90–91, 168
Rory, 103–4, 106, 140
Russell, William, 32, 63–64, 80, 82, 110, 177

Sacha Dhawan, 113, 133, 163
Salyavin, 78–79
Sarah Jane Adventures, 99, 147, 176
Sarah Jane Smith, 37, 75, 85, 98, 173–74, 176–77
Science History Institute, 118, 203, 209
Scotland, 27, 46, 194, 215
Sea Devils, 53, 118–19, 122, 191
Second Doctor, 74, 83, 98, 115
Seventh Doctor, 21, 28, 51, 60, 90, 99, 125, 180, 192
Shada, 61, 78–79
Shadow Kin, 177
SIDRAT (Space and Inter-time Dimensional Robot All-purpose Transporter), 75
SIDRAT machines, 75
Silurians, 53, 98–99, 118–19, 149, 190–91
Sinclair, Ryan, 133, 163
Sir Hugh Greene, 42, 206
Sir John Chilcot, 192

Sisterhood, 22, 76–77, 140
Sixth Doctor, 41, 46, 60, 80, 89, 138, 155
Sixtieth Anniversary Special, 73
Sladen, Elisabeth, 37, 85, 98, 147, 174, 176–77
Slater, Bill, 44
Smith, Matt, 36, 38, 65, 93, 99, 102, 116, 139, 141–42, 154, 177, 183, 185, 188, 197
Smith, Mickey, 91–92, 163
Solon, 76–77
Song, 45, 101–7, 187
sonic screwdriver, 16–17, 25, 28, 62, 86, 101–2, 107, 133
Sontarans, 77, 114–15
Space and Inter-time Dimensional Robot All-purpose Transporter. *See* SIDRAT
Spike Lee, 203, 214
spin-offs, 173, 175, 177, 179
Star Beast, 151, 211
star diamond, 130
Star Trek, 171, 195, 215
Star Wars, xii, 54, 177, 195, 215
Steed, John, 4
Stolen Earth, 29, 93, 206
Stormcage, 104–6
Stubbs, David, 44–45, 204, 206
students, 25, 73, 78, 82, 88, 149–50, 162, 169, 177–78
Susan, 7, 12, 32–33, 70, 82, 86–87, 110, 166
Sutton, Sarah, 33, 87

Talalay, Rachel, 209–13
Tamm, Mary, 86
Tardis, 11–12, 31–40, 74, 79, 82–83, 86–87, 91–95, 102–5, 125, 127, 132, 134, 150–51, 178, 180, 185
Tardis console, 35–36, 65, 79, 91, 105, 125, 132
Tardis console room, 35, 37
Tardis dematerializes, 120, 185
Tardis exterior, 34, 101

Tardis in disguise, 74, 79
Tardis keys, 65, 159
Tardises, 33, 38, 142
Tate, Catherine, 92, 101, 147, 151, 184, 193
Tegan Jovanka, 46, 53, 167
Tennant, David, 20, 24, 27, 37–38, 64–65, 70, 91, 112, 120, 126, 135, 142, 163, 184, 188, 193
Tenth Doctor, 23, 29, 62, 70, 91, 126, 142, 163, 170, 184, 193
Tenth Planet, 112, 199
Thatcher, Margaret, 191–92
Third Doctor, 70, 84, 98–99, 115, 117–18, 122–23, 190
Thomas Stewart Baker, 19, 128, 210
Thompson, Ethan, 202, 213
Three-Body Problem, 190
Time Agency, 127, 148
time lock, 130
Time Lord mythology, 72, 75, 79, 113, 127, 141, 178
Time Lord technology, 75, 104, 113, 128, 154
Time Lords, 37–39, 56, 69–80, 84, 86–87, 93–94, 102, 111, 127–30, 132, 134, 138–42, 154, 157–58, 184, 200
time machine, 5, 105, 169
Time Master, 170–71
Time Meddler, 33, 73–74
Time War, 22, 36, 47, 62, 71, 80, 111, 127, 130, 140–42, 200
Time Warrior, 85, 99, 115
Timeless Child, 134, 157
Toclafane, 127–28
Tom Baker, 18, 61, 64, 201
tomb, 71, 112, 199–200
Torchwood, 62, 66, 128, 148, 174–76, 212
Toymaker, 27, 135, 162
Traken, 87, 123–24, 209
trial, 55, 75, 89, 125, 138–39
Troughton, Patrick, x, 12, 53, 72, 74, 83–84, 98, 115
Turlough, 88–89, 119

Turn Left, 92, 193
Twelfth Doctor, 32, 36, 94, 100, 107, 116, 131, 181, 183–85, 193

Unearthly Child, 7, 10, 12, 82, 199
UNIT (United Nations Intelligence Taskforce), 46, 84–85, 93, 98–100, 128, 141
United Kingdom, ix–x, 4, 11, 21, 35, 43, 46, 111, 179, 191–93, 196, 215
universe, 22, 38–39, 70, 76, 126–28, 141, 157, 159–60, 163–64, 170, 184, 186
Utopia, 61, 126, 128, 210

Valeyard, 138–39
Valiant, 127–28
Vampire Slayer, 62, 178

War Chief, 74–75
War Doctor, 22, 38, 140–42, 157–58
War Lord, 74–75
Warriors of the Deep, 119, 191
weapons, 29, 73, 100, 104, 115, 117, 128, 133, 141, 188, 192

Webber, 5–8
webcast, 60–61, 147
Weeping Angels, 106, 119–20
Whitehouse, 42–45
Whittaker, Jodie, 37, 66, 94, 133, 154–55, 157–59, 161, 163–64, 188, 196, 201, 211
Wild Bill Hickok, 22
William Hartnell, 16, 87, 158
Williams, Graham, 44, 52
Williams, Rory, 52, 103–6, 139, 168, 202
Wilson, Donald, 4–6, 9, 11
Wilson, Harold, 42, 191
Wilson, Marcus, 206, 209–10, 213
Wilson, Nikki, 210, 212–14
World War, 118, 191–92
Worst Enemy, 137, 139, 141
Wright, Barbara, 7, 32, 82, 177

young girl, 103–4, 187
Yrcanos, 89–90

Zero Room, 32–33
Zoe, 83–84

About the Author

Graham Gibson is an author and playwright who has also written reviews and opinion pieces for various geek-culture outlets. He has a deep love for science fiction as a genre, spanning literature, television, movies, and games. He was brought up enjoying mainstream global sci-fi franchises such as *Star Trek* and *Star Wars*. However, being born in Scotland in the United Kingdom, he has a particular affection for homegrown sci-fi shows, such as *Blake's 7*, *Space 1999*, *The Tomorrow People*, *Sapphire & Steel*, *The Prisoner*, *Red Dwarf* and, of course, *Doctor Who*. He lives in Scotland with his wife and two sons.